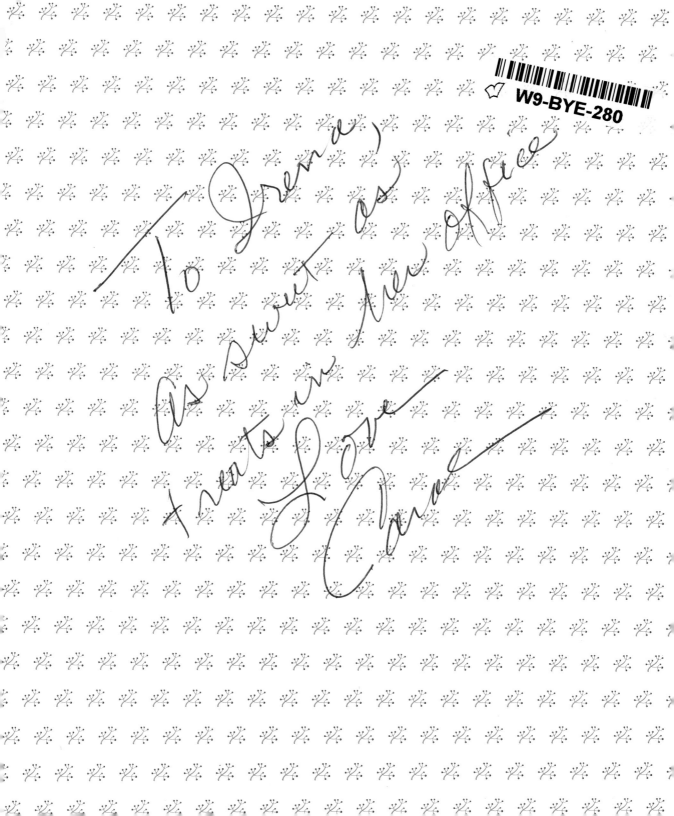

To Irena,

As sweet as
treats in new office

Love
Anne

Cooking with
LES DAMES D'ESCOFFIER

Foreword by
Alice Waters and
Jerry Anne Di Vecchio

Cooking with
LES DAMES D'ESCOFFIER

At Home with the Women Who Shape the Way We Eat and Drink

Edited by
Marcella Rosene *with* Pat Mozersky

Photography by
Tracey Maurer

SASQUATCH BOOKS
SEATTLE

"Marcella's Grilled Fish Steaks Sicilian Salmoriglio Syle" (p.118) is reprinted from *Essentials of Italian Cooking* by Marcella Hazan, © 1992 by Marcella Hazan. Used by permission of Alfred A. Knopf, a division of Random House, Inc.

"Prosciutto and Melon in Sambuca" (p.62) is reprinted from *The Zuni Café Cookbook* by Judy Rodgers, © 2002 by Judy Rodgers. Used by permission of W. W. Norton & Company, Inc.

"Fresh Blackberry Cobbler" (p.311) is reprinted from *The Taste of Country Cooking* by Edna Lewis, © 1976 by Edna Lewis. Used by permission of Alfred A. Knopf, a division of Random House, Inc.

"Bittersweet Chocolate Soufflés with Nibby Cream" (p.318) is excerpted from *Bittersweet* by Alice Medrich, © 2003 by Alice Medrich. Used by permission of Artisan, a division of Workman Publishing Co., Inc., New York. All rights reserved.

Printed in Canada
Published by Sasquatch Books
Distributed by PGW/Perseus
15 14 13 12 11 10 09 08   9 8 7 6 5 4 3 2

Cover photograph: © Stockbyte photography/veer.com
Cover design: Rosebud Eustace
Interior design and composition: Rosebud Eustace
Food photography: Tracey Maurer
Food stylist: Julie Hettiger

Library of Congress Cataloging-in-Publication Data
Cooking with Les Dames d'Escoffier : at home with the women who shape the way we eat and drink / edited by Marcella Rosene with Pat Mozersky ; foreword by Alice Waters and Jerry Anne Di Vecchio. -- 1st ed.
    p. cm.
  Includes index.
  ISBN-13: 978-1-57061-530-6
  ISBN-10: 1-57061-530-6
  1.   Cookery.   I. Rosene, Marcella, 1945- II. Mozersky, Pat. III. Les Dames d'Escoffier International.
  TX714.C654325 2008
  641.5--dc22

                  2008013760

Sasquatch Books
119 South Main Street, Suite 400
Seattle, WA 98104
(206) 467-4300
www.sasquatchbooks.com
custserv@sasquatchbooks.com

Dedicated to all women of vision, energy, and brilliance

Most especially to our founder, Carol Brock

*A portion of the proceeds from the sale of this cookbook fund
charitable and educational programs and activities of
Les Dames d'Escoffier International.*

CONTENTS

FOREWORD

The food we find at grocery stores, in the pantries of our friends, and on our own dinner tables is changing—slowly, but dramatically. As we learn the value of produce that is fresh, grown with care, and purchased directly from the producer, we're shopping more often at farmers' markets. As we learn that the way we eat determines our present and future well being, we're recognizing the sources of our food and seeking to improve them. As we re-learn the pleasures of eating good food with friends and family, we're re-forming communities around the table. Change, in this case, is good.

The distinguished professional women who make up Les Dames d'Escoffier deserve our thanks for being agents of this change. For over three decades, they have made it their personal duty to ensure that no one just "eats," but that we all eat well. Active and vocal as an organization, as individuals, and as friends, the Dames have promoted sustainable land use, clean water, local food production, humane animal husbandry, fair working conditions, strong food communities, and public education. Members of Les Dames d'Escoffier include farmers, founders of farmers' markets, winemakers, horticulturists, world-famous chefs and restaurateurs, educators, best-selling authors, caterers, manufacturers, scientists, marketers, writers, television and radio personalities, and many other experts devoted to good food, wine, and hospitality.

The recipes in this book reflect Les Dames' attention to quality. Cooking with good ingredients is easy, but it takes effort and more care to find the right products. A few key principles will guide you. When buying produce, select varieties grown for their flavor, harvested when perfectly ripe, and ready to be enjoyed at their peak—in other words, eat seasonally. The same applies to meat, eggs, dairy, and other animal products: the lives of the animals we eat should never be taken for granted. Seek out grass-fed beef and pastured or organically fed pork and poultry. Take care to buy your meat from producers who raise animals with care. Eat and serve a variety of foods, and consider our society's multicultural heritage and the food traditions of immigrant communities. Pay the true cost of your food. Think of your purchase as a donation that supports the environment and those who provide for us.

One mission of Les Dames d'Escoffier is to make connections through food. Local markets allow us to connect with the people who produce our food. School and home gardens connect children to the land that sustains us. Sharing food is the cornerstone of a closely knit, responsible society. Food can and must be an integral part of our lives at home, in schools, with friends, and through our communities.

With this book, we celebrate the delicious way to save the world—by cooking and eating. Enjoy these splendid recipes from Dames who have shared wonderful meals and want to share them with you. The instructions are all laid out for you; there's no expertise needed. All you need is to begin.

—San Francisco Grande Dames Alice Waters and Jerry Anne Di Vecchio

ACKNOWLEDGMENTS

A cookbook with nearly two hundred authors needs more than a publisher and an editor. It needs a political boss, a spiritual guide, and a kitchen crew. Pat Mozersky played all these roles and more: she edited my edits, tested my tests, reminded me over and over how to spell "foreword" and other mischievous words. A food columnist for the *San Antonio Express-News*, Pat was full-time liaison between LDEI, the publisher, and me. Her good judgment stamped nearly every page of this book.

Certainly, too, a book written by and about women can do with a good husband. Mine was, as always, extraordinary. Harvey encouraged, he understood, and he called himself "slop chef."

Of course, the sources of such a collaborative work as this are countless. LDEI founders like Carol Brock and Eda Saccone must be applauded for their vision. For vision, too, I thank the LDEI Executive Board. Testament to the best enabling intentions of our organization: from the very beginning, Seattle Dame Dorene Centioli-McTigue said to me, "You can do it. You should do it. Do it."

There were many "wise women" willing to help solicit, read, test, and candidly counsel. Alice Gautsch, CiCi Williamson, and Deborah Mintcheff top the list for zealously embracing this project. It goes on: Jerry Anne Di Vecchio, Toria Emas, Nancy Brussat Barocci, Susan Fuller Slack, Joyce Goldstein, Gloria Smiley, Peg Rahn, Patricia Ward, Connie Hay, Lois Tlusty—all were tireless at doing splendidly whatever was needed.

And there are more who helped time and again. Each name reminds me of a particularly probing e-mail or an especially encouraging phone call: Teresa Farney, Leslie Mackie, Marilyn Tausend, Susan Johnson, Holly Hadsell-El-Hajji, Carol Blomstrom, Colleen Isherwood, Barbara Pool Fenzl, Gina Batali, Jeanmarie Brownson, Katherine Newell Smith, Diane Tucker, Mary Bartz, Terry Thompson-Anderson, Ingrid Gangestad, Joanne Naganawa, Renie Steves, Cherine Fanning, Jane Morimoto, Sandy Hu, Jennifer Lidner McGlinn, Sarah Robinson Graham, Martha Marino, Lee Wooding, Lisa Ekus-Saffer, Karen Stiegler, Linda Pelaccio, Suzanne Brown, Kimberly Stewart, Corinne Trang, Elizabeth Schmitt, Nancy Merrill, Suzen O'Rourke, Jeanie Kozar, Julie Jones, Eileen Talanian,

Julie Kramis Hearne, Erin Collins, Lynn Fredericks, Dolores Cakebread, Barbara Fenzl, Joanna Pruess, Janeen Sarlin. Then there are the "baking impresarios"—Carol Prager and Beth Allen—and food safety advisor, Marion Nestle.

In addition to our Dames, I also had ten non-Dame personal friends (all fine home cooks) who tested recipes: Mary Neuschwanger, Janice Complita, Marilyn Webb, Mark and Lou Damborg, Susan McGill, Robina Allen, Heather Parker, Noelle Von Bargen, and Bette McIntyre.

We all have the indomitable and talented photographic team of Tracey Maurer, Julie Hettiger, and Carla Buerkle to thank. Supporting them were Di-Anna Arias, Rollie Blackwell, Mary Dunford, June Hayes (who also made sure I always made my *LDEI Quarterly* deadlines—even if she had to write the copy), Ann Thacker, Saundra Winokur, Cathryn Tarasovic, Bettie Lee Wilson (who taught me how to properly "boil" an egg), Jenny Mattingsley, and Molly McAdams. Outside the Dames' ranks were Lisa Dominguez, Alicia Mendez, and LDEI scholarship recipients Dolores Martinez and Joanna Burges. The San Antonio–based grocer H-E-B generously donated supplies for the photo shoot; baker Carlos Barrera at San Antonio restaurant Boudro's provided freshly baked breads; and the Austin, Texas, store Finch graciously loaned props. Then there was all the beverage copy, worked and reworked by Marianne Frantz, Barbara Glunz-Donovan, and Harriett Lembeck. Manning the data banks at headquarters was LDEI's Executive Director Greg Jewell, ever ready with carefully considered counsel. And then, of course, thank you to the several hundred Dames who dared to submit recipes.

At our publisher, Sasquatch Books, we must credit Gary Luke (inscrutable, sure-handed inventor of this improbable project) and his marketing, editorial, and design teams, including Sarah Hanson, Rachelle Longé, Kristi Hein, Beth Berkelhammer, and Rosebud Eustace (all nimble, fastidious, and charming in their professions).

One especially smart, genial Dame I met in the course of this project is Joan Reardon. In her book, *Oysters: A Culinary Celebration*, she opened with: "Come into my kitchen. I want my oysters to meet you." Now, I paraphrase: "Come into my kitchen. I want you to meet Les Dames."

—*Seattle Dame Marcella Rosene, Editor*

LES DAMES D'ESCOFFIER
INTERNATIONAL: WHO ARE WE?

We are 1,350 professional women leaders in food, beverage, and hospitality. We are chefs and restaurateurs, caterers, food stylists and photographers, authors, historians, food writers and editors, radio and television hosts, literary agents, public relations managers, educators, manufacturers and merchants, farmers and food scientists, vintners, mycologists—and more. We include legendary names like Julia Child and Alice Waters as well as many of today's newest culinary stars. We have twenty-six chapters across the United States and Canada, and we are growing.

Our story parallels the feminist movement that began in the 1960s. At that time the food, wine, and hospitality industries were no different from other fields. A woman's place was squarely in the home, and those who ventured out into the workplace were not recognized, not paid as well as men, not allowed the same opportunities. In fact, they were rather invisible. Atlanta Dame Nathalie Dupree—cookbook author, writer, and television luminary—recalls her mother's reaction when she announced she wanted to be a cook. "She reacted with dismay as great as if I had said I wanted to open a brothel. 'Ladies,' she said, 'don't cook.'"

In Boston in 1959, Eda Saccone was envious of her husband's yearly dinners at the Boston Chapter of Les Amis d'Escoffier, an all-male organization of eminent chefs. Nudging progress, Saccone planned a lavish dinner of her own. The dinner proved so extraordinary—"nothing short of sybaritic," recalls her daughter, Dame Lucille Giovino—that it led to the first-ever all-women's food society: Les Dames des Amis d'Escoffier. When the irrepressible Carol Brock, then Sunday food editor at the *New York Daily News*, learned about the Boston group, she envisioned an organization that would work to open doors to the professional world of food and beverage for women. Women leaders in these fields would unite to provide other women with education, mentoring, and networking opportunities as well as scholarship support. With the help of like-minded professional women, Brock received a charter from the

New York chapter of Les Amis d'Escoffier in 1973 to form the "ladies' chapter"—Les Dames d'Escoffier. In 1976, a landmark investiture and gala was held at the French Consulate. Les Dames welcomed fifty new members, including such culinary stars as Marcella Hazan, Paula Wolfert, and Barbara Kafka. From then on, chapters were added almost yearly: Washington, D.C.; Chicago; Dallas; Philadelphia; San Francisco; Seattle; and Saccone's Boston group, in 1991. The cities today number twenty-six and stretch from Honolulu to Los Angeles to Toronto to Miami. In 1986 the chapters formed an international umbrella organization, Les Dames d'Escoffier International (LDEI).

To date, LDEI and its chapters have raised nearly $4 million for scholarships and grants for mentoring women in the food and beverage industries. Indeed, a portion of the proceeds from this book will go to such efforts. In their communities, Dames provide education regarding food, fine beverages, and nutrition. Dames actively seek out young women interested in culinary arts, tracking them through their training programs and helping them plot careers. With the many philanthropic deeds of Auguste Escoffier as their inspiration, LDEI chapters play charitable roles in their local communities, whether it's feeding the hungry, educating at-risk young people, or providing aid in times of regional disasters. In San Antonio, Dame Jenny Mattingsley created a gardening and cooking program, working with at-risk teens who in turn began to provide lunches for the elderly at a facility across the street from their school. In the aftermath of Hurricane Katrina, Charleston Dame Nancie McDermott joined a group of volunteers to restore Willie Mae's Scotch House, a landmark neighborhood restaurant run by octogenarian Mrs. Willie Mae Seaton, "who," says McDermott, "has been cooking the world's best fried chicken and other feastable food there for decades."

Most recently, LDEI launched a chapter-wide initiative called Green Tables (see box, page 105) to further sustainable food practices, encourage farm-to-table movements, and fund and staff adjunct educational programs. The program is spearheaded by New York Dame Lynn Fredericks and guided by experts in the field including Grande Dame Alice Waters, of the legendary Chez Panisse restaurant and the much-publicized Edible Schoolyard program, and Dames Hilary Baum, Abby Mandel, and Ann-Harvey Yonkers. Waters describes their efforts: "The Green Tables initiative brings the resources of a wonderfully diverse group of talented women to teach adults and children about seasonal, local, and sustainable food."

In a conversation with Grande Dame and LDEI founder Carol Brock, Brock commented on the evolution of the group she started over a quarter of a century ago. "If any of us were asked today to name leading women in wine, food, and hospitality, there is no doubt that a wealth of names would come quickly to mind. Many of them are our members." She hastily added, "Unequivocally, Les Dames d'Escoffier is composed of the distinguished professional 'leaders among leaders' that the founders set out to identify thirty years ago. And never will we rest on our laurels!"

—*San Antonio Dame Pat Mozersky, LDEI Past President*

Les Grandes Dames

From the early days, we have recognized extraordinary and unusual contributors to the fields of food, beverage, and hospitality by naming them "Grandes Dames." The first, in 1977, was Grande Dame Julia Child. Now the list is long and includes such respected names in food as M. F. K. Fisher, Ella Brennan, Edna Lewis, Marion Cunningham, Anne Willan, Madeleine Kamman, Jerry Anne Di Vecchio, Abigail Kirsch, Rosemary Kowalski, Marcella Hazan, Alice Waters, and Carol Brock. LDEI also biannually recognizes women who excel in culinary writing with the prized M. F. K. Fisher award.

Many Paths to Successful Careers

"I get paid to eat and drink." It's a claim commonly made in jest, one that belies the challenges of women making successful careers in food, beverage, and hospitality. Some career paths are just what you'd expect: culinary school, years of apprenticing in other cooks' kitchens, then the pinnacle—celebrity chefdom, an arena traditionally (and even now) controlled by men. Dozens of Dames have taken that route, many quite famously. Far more women on our roster, however, have traveled less predictable career paths. Our ranks are filled with intriguing success stories involving everything from Ivy League schools to the American Diabetes Association to Four Seasons Hotels. Certainly, some Dames have been born to the business, inheriting family restaurants, wineries, hotels. Many have made their ethnic ancestry into career launch-pads. Language skills can help. Asked how one gets a start in food publishing, Corinne Trang, who describes her roots as "half French and half Chinese," says flatly: "The reason behind my personal focus on food cultures is that my family is Asian."

Similarly, Lourdes Castro is fluent in both English and Spanish, a skill that afforded her the opportunity early in her food career to serve as personal translator to famed Spanish chef Juan Mari Arzak. A like opportunity followed when she was asked to translate for the acclaimed Australian chef Tetsuya Wakuda during a stay in Madrid. "I learned from working with these two chefs the most important rule in the kitchen: restraint. Our job as cooks is to select the freshest ingredients and simply develop flavors and textures."

Serendipity plays a big part as well. Lila Gault, who runs her own New York public relations agency, admits she got her start "quite accidentally." She arrived in Seattle in the 1970s just as the Pacific Northwest was discovering itself as a culinary hot spot. Writing local food and wine features led to national assignments, including a decade as *Country Living* magazine's wine editor. She became the first marketing director for the Washington wine industry.

Lots of Dames have ended up in food as a result of career changes. Deborah Mintcheff taught elementary school for a decade, while cooking her way through Julia Child's *Mastering the Art of French Cooking*. Mintcheff worked for free on Saturdays at New York's Tavern on the Green. "I learned how to pipe like a pro, turn mushrooms, and make aspic. Then I hopscotched to a test kitchen where I learned from a talented and gentle boss. After styling dollops for Cool Whip ads, I moved on to making dog biscuits that sold for $32 a pound on New York's Upper East Side." Today, Mintcheff is a cookbook editor, known in the industry as a "tweaker par excellence."

Then there's niche-making. In 2005 Beatrice Ojakangas won the James Beard Hall of Fame award for her acknowledged expertise in Scandinavian cooking. Asked how one develops such a singular distinction, she replies, "A lot of little pieces of work add up and combine with a passion to pass on what one has learned." CiCi Williamson began as a home economist who, in the early days of microwave technology, spotted the little revolutionary ovens and launched a career as a food writer with a newspaper column called "Micro-Scope." Women in food often double-bill themselves. Business cards read "Food and Wine," "Food and Gardening," "Food and Travel." Early in her career Ingrid Gangestad, a registered dietitian who runs her own consulting firm, branched out into recipe development.

To everyone's surprise, finding a winning combination of specialties may *not* always include cooking. A few very successful Dames make absolutely no kitchen pretenses. Grande Dame Rosemary Kowalski freely admits, "I can't cook." Nonetheless, her peers applaud her unquestioned success in the food business. Her catering company, The RK Group, has offices in half a dozen cities, including its home base of San Antonio, Texas. As one admirer puts it, "Rosemary doesn't need to know how to cook. It's enough that she knows how to run a business."

As you read our recipes, our kitchen wisdom, and more about our professional lives, it is our hope that you will see that there are infinite ways to make careers from a love of the table. Les Dames d'Escoffier is reassuring proof.

AUGUSTE ESCOFFIER: WHO WAS HE?

Few people realize the role that Auguste Escoffier (1846–1935) played in shaping today's food and hospitality industries. His culinary career spanned more than seventy years, from the time he began working in 1859 as a chef's apprentice in the south of France until his death in 1935. Although trained in traditional nineteenth-century French haute cuisine, Escoffier witnessed the impact of modern technology and world politics on the twentieth-century palate.

Escoffier is perhaps best known as the manager and director of several luxury Belle Époque hotel restaurants in London, Paris, and other European cities. He flattered his wealthy and royal clientele by creating hundreds of dishes in their honor—often simply by modifying a sauce or garnish. Many of these dishes, including his famous pêche melba, were included in *Le Guide Culinaire*—a compilation of more than five thousand recipes first published by Escoffier in 1903 as a "useful tool" for professional hotel chefs. Now translated into many foreign languages, *Le Guide* continues to play a role in the training of young chefs throughout the world. Other publications by Escoffier focused on subjects such as menu planning, wine service, table décor, and proper table service.

Critics who consider Escoffier no longer relevant to today's culinary trends should consider some of his more "modern" accomplishments—simplifying rich sauces, encouraging farmers to supply markets with superior seasonal produce, designing safer and more efficient hotel kitchens, establishing funds for retired chefs at a time when social welfare was practically nonexistent, exploring the canning and preserving of foods for soldiers and the underprivileged, and donating surplus food to local charities.

Although men dominated professional cuisine during Escoffier's lifetime, women gradually began to play more visible roles. Escoffier's last book, *Ma Cuisine*, published in 1934, addressed a growing audience of family cooks—and inspired many women who pioneered the role of women in today's culinary professions. From chef to event planner, from food writer to marketing manager, we Dames are all inspired in some way by Auguste Escoffier.

—*Houston Dame Merrianne Timko, Culinary Historian*

INTRODUCTION

What do members of the world's largest invitational organization of women culinary and hospitality professionals cook for family and friends? What do they name as their favorite recipes? What do these women consider their most prized home-cooking tips? Their most useful beverage advice? Their favorite kitchen gadgets? What are the secrets to their career success, and what are their priorities in the wide world of food in which they work today? The answers to these questions have shaped the book you now hold in your hands.

Ask esteemed Italian food maven Marcella Hazan for her personal pick of her hundreds of published recipes, and she offers three. We selected one—a delicious grilled fish. Ask Gale Gand—called "one of the greatest living pastry chefs"—for a favorite dessert? She chooses two cookie recipes: lemon and chocolate. Culinary historian Joan Reardon recommends two previously unpublished recipes from Julia Child and M. F. K. Fisher. Alice Waters opts for a mushroom ragù. The list goes on and on. This is not just any anthology; this is a revelation of the kitchen and career ways of some most uncommon, strong-minded (though amiable) cooks: Les Dames d'Escoffier.

For starters, did you know that some people greatly prefer the asparagus stalk over its tip? PBS television personality Joanne Weir does. "Once the ends have been snapped, there's no need to waste stalks when they taste better than the tips," she insists. Chef Gail Nottberg shows us that turkey patties are delicious enhanced with dried dates. Food stylist Susan Fuller Slack proposes rose water and cornstarch for making a remarkable (and historic) cookie. Publicist Nancy Wong informs that wild rice in certain traditions is served "crunchy"—very deliciously crunchy. And when writer-cook Michele Scicolone says to strain the fat off a stew, she means *all* the fat—even that little bit clinging daintily to the vegetables.

For twelve months, we pored through some four hundred favorite recipes handpicked by these influential women. There were submissions from caterers and chefs, from authorities on native food ways, from event planners and winemakers, from lauded food scientists. The provenance of the recipes ranged from the most legitimate of culinary schools to informal family scrapbooks. Some came from lifetime *oeuvres*; some were composed especially for this book. We were looking for nothing less than "the best of the best," for a range of styles, a variety of ingredients, a mix of categories, a balance of regions and generations. The doyennes would be side by side with rising stars—the best young women chefs in cities like Dallas and San Francisco and Toronto. In the end, we chose in the only way cooks can: we cooked. Every recipe selected for this book was tested at least twice by someone other than its author. The recipe testers? Some twenty of the most qualified in the business, all Dames.

You'll hear the voices of many different Dames in this book: Lidia Bastianich saying "clear a hot spot, plop in the tomato paste"; Jane Mengenhauser admonishing that if you have too much filling, "just lick the bowl"; Judy Rodgers from the beloved San Francisco Zuni Café carving "elegant crescents" from a ripe cantaloupe. Some Dames, such as Marcella Hazan and Carole Bloom, are famous for their detailed, precise recipe writing (Bloom recently was called "a paean to precision"). Other Dames are like Dorie Greenspan, of whom *The New York Times* writes, "She tells you neither more nor less than you need to know." Still others fall into the Alice Waters camp: recipes are to be, at best, inspiring approximations.

So, with all this know-how, are the recipes hard to make? No. You won't be asked to painstakingly peel a single tomato or clarify butter or even make homemade stock unless you want to (and now and then, you should). We've made certain that even complicated-sounding recipes are presented as a practical series of steps. All are do-at-home fare: plain and fancy dishes, foods kids will love, classic dishes and somewhat zany dishes, ethnic dishes and regional American dishes, oodles of vegetarian options, even some heart-healthy foods—an amalgam that includes many very easy dishes.

Still, this is a book for those who care about food and its many nuances. Some things are not to be done by shortcuts: your black pepper, cardamom, and nutmeg need to be freshly ground; your lemons freshly squeezed; and your garlic freshly chopped. Do, at times, take the time to cook. Relish each step. Discover prime ingredients. Celebrate those who honor the earth and its natural abundance. Bring friends and family, even children, into the kitchen. And never take food for granted. The members of Les Dames d'Escoffier invite you home for dinner.

—Seattle Dame Marcella Rosene, Editor

ABOUT CERTAIN INGREDIENTS

Salt

In most cases, we call simply for "salt"—usually, but not always, we recommend a minimum amount. More or less salt is up to you. As a general rule, we prefer kosher salt to table salt. For "finishing" the flavor upon serving or for adding texture, we suggest more expensive sea salts in various grain sizes. Measurements will vary with the size of the salt grains. Larger grains do in fact salt less, simply because there are fewer of them in a given measure. For most dessert and baking recipes, use fine-grain salt.

Pepper

In most places where pepper is called for, we designate "freshly ground black pepper"—usually, but not always, we recommend a minimum number of grinds. We suggest that you use a grinder that allows you to adjust the grind from fine to very coarse, and that you choose high-quality peppercorns—all black or a mixture of black, white, pink, and green. Consider including a small amount of whole allspice in your pepper mix for a more complex pepper flavor.

Olive Oil

In most cases, we don't specify anything beyond "olive oil." For cooking, oil labeled "pure" or "extra-virgin" is usually fine. Keep in mind that olive oil is a "buyer beware" product for which the label can be meaningless. The decisive factors are taste and personal preference. When the oil is *not* used for cooking, but rather used in dressings or sauces, choose more expensive extra-virgin olive oils, usually labeled "cold pressed." These are considered "condiment quality" or "finishing" oils and range in taste from light and floral to bold and earthy. Think of olive oil as a flavoring, not just as a lubricant; as a freshly squeezed fruit juice rather than an industrial fat. It should have appreciable levels of pepperiness, bitterness, and fruitiness. It should not taste musty or rancid. Nor does it need to come in a fancy package. Selecting olive oil requires a combination of trusting your merchant, your own palate, and your good common sense.

Herbs

When a recipe requires parsley (Italian flat-leaf or curly-leaf), chives, cilantro, mint, lemongrass, or lime leaves, we intend for the cook to use *fresh* ingredients. When calling for basil, chervil, dill, oregano, rosemary, sage, savory, and thyme, we specify *fresh* or *dried*. For all other herbs, dried is fine; however, if you want to substitute fresh, the general rule is three parts fresh herbs to one part dried.

Flours

All but three of our recipes call for all-purpose flour. Two of those specify bleached flour; the other, cake flour.

ABOUT BEVERAGES

Among Les Dames d'Escoffier are some of today's most experienced authorities on beverages: winemakers, brewmasters, educators, sommeliers, importers, merchants. A team of these Dames has matched a beverage with each appetizer, first course, main course, and dessert included in this book. In addition, here they offer commentary on a range of beverage-related subjects.

Pairing Wine with Food

First and foremost, know that there are many ways to pair wine with food. Most agree with San Antonio Dame Bunny Becker of Becker Vineyards, who says, "The most basic way of pairing is to think of the heft or texture of the food and match with a wine of like heft and texture." New York Dame Harriet Lembeck, who is president of New York City's oldest wine school—The Wine and Spirits Program—and is widely considered the doyenne of wine teachers, adds, "Don't be afraid to try different pairings, and drink what you like!"

Beyond this, Cleveland Dame Marianne Frantz, who headed our beverage team, recommends a few guidelines that can ensure successful pairing:

* Foods high in salt should not be paired with high-tannin red wines such as Cabernet Sauvignon and Shiraz.

* Although the old adage "red wine with meats, white wine with fish" is somewhat outdated, care should be taken when pairing fish with red wine. Best bet: Pair fish with light-bodied reds that are low in tannins, such as Pinot Noir or Barbera.

* Fried foods are best paired with wines that are high in acidity: a crisp Sauvignon Blanc or a brut Champagne.

* Foods that are high in acidity, such as those dressed in vinaigrette, are best paired with wines that are also high in acidity.

* Dishes that are high in spice should be paired with lower-alcohol beverages, such as beer. When it comes to wine, that means selecting a wine from a cool growing region such as Germany, Austria, New York State, New Zealand, the Loire Valley, or Champagne. Cooler temperatures produce wines with less alcohol.

Pairing Sparkling Wines with Food

Chicago Dame Barbara Glunz-Donovan, proprietor of Chicago's oldest wine shop—The House of Glunz Wine Shop—writes, "Tradition deems Champagne the toast of celebration, but Champagne, or another fine sparkling wine, is always a delightful match at affairs from formal dining to casual picnic. It is classically paired with caviar—a match that makes the most of silky texture, length of flavor, and the aura of elegance—but there are other ideal pairings. The acidity of cool-climate sparklers cleanses the palate after fried foods and savory appetizers, while aromas from extended aging enhance smoked foods. There are styles perfect for sushi, light meats, gougères, toasted nuts, earthy mushrooms, creamy cheeses, fresh berries . . . the list goes on and on."

Pairing Beer with Food

Seattle Dame Rose Ann Finkel, co-owner of Pike Brewing Company and a pioneer in boutique brewing, has an obvious but well-grounded bias when she declares, "Beer goes with more dishes and styles of cooking than any other beverage. Basically, it goes with anything that bread goes with. The two have been dining staples for nine thousand years of recorded history." Finkel offers a few tips for pairing food with beer:

* Remember that barley is the principal taste characteristic in beer. It's an earthy, bread-like taste.

* Beer and cheese are meant for one another, like bread and butter. The dryness of beer is good with the richness of the butterfat.

* Beer makes a superb apéritif served with salty foods.

* Pale ales go particularly well with rich red meats and game.

* Stouts and porters are legendary with shellfish, particularly oysters on the half shell.

* Wheat beers (also called *weizen*, *weiss*, *wit*, and white beer) are good candidates to accompany salads and also to season classic vinaigrettes.

* Beer is lower in alcohol than other beverages. For cooking, it is often an excellent choice over wines and spirits.

Pairing Coffee—Yes, Coffee—with Food

Atlanta Dame Suzanne Brown, an international marketing consultant for the coffee and tea industries, points out that, generally speaking, lighter-roasted, single-origin coffees from Central and South America are the best choices for breakfast and brunch menus. Darker roasts, such as Italian, French, or espresso, and heavier-bodied coffees are preferred for rich desserts.

Proper Serving Temperatures for Wine

New York Dame Roberta Morrell, president of the wine and spirit merchant Morrell & Company, declares: "Americans drink red wine too warm and white wine too cold. 'Room temperature' for wine drinking was coined centuries ago and meant the temperature in a medieval castle. The optimum temperature for red wine is 62°F to 65°F; for white, 55°F. White wine that is too cold loses flavor." Dallas Dame Renie Steves cites the "twenty-twenty rule" as a general guide: "Take white wine out of the refrigerator 20 minutes before serving. Put red wine in the refrigerator 20 minutes before serving."

Breathing Time for Wine

Certified sommelier and co-owner of Restaurant Eugene (which won a Wine Spectator Award of Excellence), Atlanta Dame Gina Hopkins suggests that when handling an older bottle of wine, make sure you don't open it too soon prior to serving. There is a common misconception that older wines need a long time to breathe. In fact, older wines have done most of their work in the bottle, and if you open them far ahead of consumption, the lovely fruit that is left will likely dissipate. A good rule of thumb is the older the wine, the less time it needs to breathe. If you find that the one you've been waiting for is still tight and terribly tannic, swirl the wine vigorously in a large-bowl wine glass.

Decanting Wines: Why and How?

Chicago Dame Debbie Sharpe, restaurateur and wine merchant, writes: "Decant older red wines right before you are ready to serve them. The idea is to carefully pour the wine from the bottle into the decanter, separating the wine from any sediment that may have developed in the bottle as the wine aged. With younger wines, decant to allow the wine to aerate and flavors to 'open up.' Even some young white Burgundies, Chablis, and Savennières will benefit from decanting. Don't worry about sediment—just pour the wine into the decanter, swirl vigorously, and let sit for 15 to 20 minutes. The decanter need not be a "proper" one; a large, clean, glass measuring cup will do. Just avoid colored and ornate vessels; you want to see the color of the wine. As for cleaning decanters, avoid dish soap, which may leave a film. Best to clean by tossing a few tablespoons of salt and a handful of ice cubes into the decanter. Give a few good swirls to remove any tannins or coloring matter, drain, and rinse with clean, warm water."

The Cork

Atlanta Dame Gina Hopkins advises that if presented with the wine cork in a restaurant, look at it, feel it, just don't smell it. "Even if the cork appears moldy, it is not an indication that the wine is in poor condition. That can be determined only by smelling and tasting the wine itself," notes Hopkins.

"Popping" the Cork

According to Cleveland Dame Marianne Frantz, the point is to *avoid* the impolite "pop" of the cork. With a sparkling wine, make sure it is cold before angling the bottle away from your guests (and away from your face) and pulling the cork. Give the bottle a turn while holding the cork still. Keep turning; you should start to feel pressure from the cork as it works its way out of the neck of the bottle. Keep your thumb on top of the cork to prevent it from popping out. Although a loud pop may sound festive, it also releases thousands of little bubbles into the air instead of into your glass. A proper "pop" should really be just a soft sigh.

Choosing a Good Corkscrew

All of our wine experts agree: although there are many new corkscrew designs on the market, the best tool is still the traditional "waiter's [or server's] friend," which has a simple worm with at least five coils. With fewer you stand a good chance of not engaging the cork, especially as better wines often have longer corks.

Screw-Cap Wines

In Palm Springs, wine merchant Dame Zola Nichols says the issue of cork or screw cap remains an unresolved debate. But one point is certain: screw caps eliminate the risk of "corked" wines, a condition associated with faulty corks. "Consumers should recognize the signs of a corked wine [a musty, dank smell of wet cardboard]. Bad corks taint, to some degree, one in ten wines bottled with corks. For this reason, many highly respected wineries are now proudly using screw caps, particularly for wines that will most likely be drunk within two years, and they are becoming more acceptable," says Nichols.

Old World and New World Wines

New York Dame Harriet Lembeck explains that there used to be a clear line between Old World (European) wines and New World (everything that wasn't European) wines. For Old World wines, it was location and producer that mattered. No one cared much about the varietals, that Chablis was made from Chardonnay or Sancerre from Sauvignon Blanc. The wines were better served with food than alone as "sippers." New World wines, in contrast, were most often named for their varietal, and were made to be drunk young and to show a great deal of fruit, less complexity, and increasingly higher amounts of alcohol. These "modern" wines demonstrated clear market appeal.

Lately, the two styles are blurring. The Old World wine producers are adopting some of the New World's "accessibility" and the New World producers are aiming for more intriguing flavors similar to the Old World entries. Now we've added the notion of "flying winemakers" who make wine at harvest time in their own hemisphere, and then go to the opposite hemisphere, where the seasons are reversed, and make wine during their own downtime. With this, the cross-pollination of wine types is quite assured.

Decoding French Wines

For curious American wine lovers, here is a guide to some of the more common varietals and the location of their French counterparts from Washington, D.C., Dame and wine consultant Vickie Reh.

Chardonnay

* White Burgundy from the Côte d'Or, such as Puligny Montrachet, Chassagne Montrachet, and Meursault (rich, concentrated, complex, often aged in oak)

* White Burgundy from Chablis (often unoaked, with a steely and minerally profile)

* White Burgundy from the Mâconnais region, such as Pouilly Fuissé (the value winner, with bright, fresh, apple aromas)

Sauvignon Blanc

* Loire Valley—Sancerre, Pouilly Fumé, Touraine (high acid and minerally)
* Bordeaux—Graves (rounder, smoother, often blended with Semillon)

Cabernet Sauvignon or Merlot

* Left Bank Bordeaux blends (predominantly Cabernet Sauvignon blended with Merlot, Cabernet Franc, Malbec, and Petit Verdot)
* Right Bank Bordeaux blends (predominantly Merlot or Cabernet Franc blended with Cabernet Sauvignon, Malbec, and Petit Verdot)

Syrah

* Northern Rhône region
* Southern Rhône region, where it is blended with Grenache, Mouvèdre, Carignan, and other Rhône varietals

Watch for Wine Finds

Atlanta Dame Anita LaRaia, wine educator and importer, advises befriending your local independent wine merchant to steer you to interesting, moderately priced wines from small producers. Recent favorite "best food wines" include: unoaked Sauvignon Blanc from New Zealand ("terrific with goat cheese and vegetarian dishes"); light, dry French Pinot Blanc from Alsace; Spain's deep-flavored old vines Garnacha and rich Monastrell from Jumilla; Argentina's signature Malbec ("consistently good"); smooth Italian Sangiovese ("medium-bodied like Merlot"); California Cabernet Franc; and Sparkling Shiraz from Australia ("deep burgundy–colored sparkler to partner with pork tenderloin or chocolate—guaranteed to bring romance to the table").

For more information on beverages, see also: Pairing Wine and Cheese: Very Personal Picks *(page 43)*, Pantry Spirits *(page 103)*, Why Bother with Dessert Wines? *(page 280)*, An Introduction to Port *(page 283)*, Give the Gift of Port *(page 291)*

APPETIZERS

Snacks and Starters, Plain and Fancy   Here is how the Dames—including a food stylist, a journalist, a farmer, a restaurateur, a retailer, three caterers, two chefs, and some mighty fine home cooks in a dozen different cities—say, "Welcome, I'm glad you've come."

Here are meal starters, snacks, engaging little bites—in the food trade, sometimes called "standing apps." Paired with just the right beverage, they can make magic moments for a gathering. Some are casual; others, more tony. Each one of our appetizers has bright, fresh flavors. There may be something you've not tried before, like tiny okra cakes hot off the griddle or crusty sausage rolls steaming from the oven. There's cured salmon topped with a cucumber salsa so intriguing you're sure to be asked for the recipe; there are cocktail latkes and phyllo-wrapped wonders you can keep ready in your freezer. Each recipe is presented in convenient steps to make for the easiest entertaining.

Recipes

Black-Olive Tapenade with Tuna and Hard-Cooked Eggs
M. F. K. Fisher, *San Francisco Chapter*

Chicken Salad Bites
Georgeanne Brennan, *San Francisco Chapter*

Stuffed Calimyrna Figs
Georgeanne Brennan, *San Francisco Chapter*

Fresh Okra Cakes
Gloria Smiley, *Atlanta Chapter*

Walnut-Fennel Tarts
Lisa Dupar, *Seattle Chapter*

Phyllo Fontina Cheese Bites
Linda Hopkins, *Phoenix Chapter*

Home-Cured Salmon in Phyllo Cups with Cucumber-Sesame Salsa
Dolores Snyder, *Dallas Chapter*

Smoked Whitefish and Nori Pâté
Betty Fussell, *New York Chapter*

Abigail's Crusty Sausage Rolls
Abigail Kirsch, *New York Chapter*

Fresh Vietnamese Summer Rolls with Peanut Sauce
Linda Burner Augustine, *Seattle Chapter*

Golden Beet Slaw with Fresh Horseradish
Paulette Satur, *New York Chapter*

"Scalloped" Potatoes
Caren McSherry, *British Columbia, Canada, Chapter*

Cocktail Potato Latkes with Smoked-Salmon Tartare
Alison Barshak, *Philadelphia Chapter*

Rich Man Poor Man
Judy Zeidler, *Los Angeles Chapter*

Seasonal Mushroom Galette in a Cornmeal Crust
Jenny Mattingsley, *San Antonio Chapter*

See also: Best Grits *(page 129)*, Big Shrimp with Armenian "Pesto" *(page 130)*, Roasted-Corn Guacamole *(page 90)*

Notes

Use That Chicken Carcass

Finger Vegetables

Tips for Slicing and Grating

Working with Phyllo Dough

About Crème Fraîche

General Kitchen Tips

Dippers and Holders

Extra-Easy Starters

Caviar: New Possibilities

Fresh Fava Beans

Pairing Wine and Cheese: Very Personal Picks

BLACK-OLIVE TAPENADE WITH TUNA AND HARD-COOKED EGGS

Olive tapenade is today fairly common: on restaurant menus, in jars on specialty store shelves, in recipes in cooking magazines. Still, no one has described it more adroitly than Grande Dame M. F. K. Fisher, the foremost American writer on gastronomy in the 20th century, when she wrote back in the 1970s: "Tapenade is a funny paste to be eaten with bread and often hard-boiled eggs, and is based on the best possible black olives, although I now make it with what I can find in cans, already chopped and a poor imitation of what I can still taste happily on my mind's tongue."

This recipe is adapted from Fisher's *With Bold Knife and Fork*. These days most of us can obtain good-quality imported olives, even pitted ones. Choose an olive or a mix of olives that has not been flavored with other ingredients. Although Fisher specifies black olives, a green olive version is tempting. Fisher ground her ingredients with a mortar and pestle. We suggest a food processor, used with particular attention to the tapenade's texture. The use of tuna in Fisher's version is unusual, as are the peeled halves of hard-cooked eggs placed cut side down in the tapenade.

6 to 12 servings or 2 cups of tapenade

1 cup pitted and chopped black olives

One 12-ounce can white albacore tuna in olive oil

½ cup capers, drained

½ cup flat anchovy fillets, rinsed and drained

1 teaspoon dry mustard

Freshly ground black pepper

¼ cup high-quality extra-virgin olive oil plus additional for serving

2 tablespoons freshly squeezed lemon juice

2 tablespoons brandy

6 hard-cooked eggs, shelled and halved*

Prepare Ahead

The tapenade keeps refrigerated in an airtight container for at least a week.

Suggested Beverage

Sparkling wine or dry rosé. For a trendier twist, try vodka martinis with a splash of Bloody Mary mix.

Fresh basil leaves, cut in chiffonade (see box, page 59)

Slices of crusty bread

Place the olives, tuna with oil, capers, anchovies, mustard, and pepper to taste in the bowl of a food processor fitted with a steel blade. Pulse briefly to make a thick, rough paste.

With the motor running, slowly add the olive oil, then the lemon juice and brandy to taste. If the tapenade is not to be served within an hour or two, store covered in the refrigerator.

To serve, bring the tapenade and eggs to room temperature. If you want to serve with small plates and forks, spread the tapenade in a thick layer on each plate and top with a couple halved eggs (placed flat side down in the tapenade), basil, and a drizzle of olive oil. Serve with the bread. If you prefer to serve the tapenade as finger food, place a dollop of tapenade on the flat side of each egg and, immediately before serving, top with the basil and olive oil. Serve any remaining tapenade in a bowl and use as a spread on the bread.

The best way to hard-cook eggs is to put them in a pot with tap water to cover. Bring the water to a rolling boil. Cover the pot and remove it from the heat; let sit 20 minutes. Run cold water over the eggs until cool to the touch. Now they're ready to peel. Refrigerate until ready to use.

❋ CHICKEN SALAD BITES ❋

San Francisco Dame Georgeanne Brennan has been writing about food, agriculture, and life in Provence—where she has a second home—for over thirty years. Yet, when this author of numerous award-winning books chooses an appetizer for a political fundraiser, an Easter brunch, or her twin grandsons' birthday party, this straightforward recipe is often her pick. Whether you're looking for an appetizer or just a simply gratifying chicken salad, you'll want to try this recipe.

Brennan uses a favorite foccacia bread (2 sheets, 9 by 14 inches—just barely 1½ inches thick) that she likes to split in half, fill with the salad and fresh greens, then cut into bite-size sandwiches. However, should you not have access to such a bread, the salad scooped into individual petals of Belgian endive is just as winning.

Though the recipe makes enough appetizers for a large group, you can use the recipe to create appetizers for a small gathering, which will provide leftover salad for another meal. If you are short on time, use the meat from a carefully chosen store-roasted chicken rather than preparing one yourself.

50 appetizers or 5 cups of salad

1 whole chicken, about 3½ to 4 pounds

1 teaspoon kosher or coarse sea salt, divided, plus additional as needed

1 teaspoon freshly ground black pepper, divided, plus additional as needed

Half a dozen fresh thyme sprigs

2 cups finely chopped celery (about 3 stalks)

Heaping ½ cup finely chopped green onions, including half the green parts

½ cup plain nonfat or low-fat yogurt (Pavel's, Straus Family Creamery, or Fage brand preferred)

¼ cup mayonnaise

1 heaping tablespoon crème fraîche (see box, page 20)

2 sheets foccacia bread, each about 9 by 14 by 1½ inches, *or* 5 heads Belgian endive

1 head red leaf or butter lettuce, if using foccacia bread

1 cup young arugula leaves, if using foccacia bread (optional)

½ cup minced parsley or chives, if using Belgian endive

❉ Preheat the oven to 350°F. Rinse the chicken and pat dry, inside and out, with a paper towel. Rub the outside of the chicken with ½ teaspoon of the salt and ½ teaspoon of the pepper. Tuck the thyme sprigs into the cavity. Place the chicken in a roasting pan and roast until the thigh is easily pierced with a fork and the juices run clear, about 1½ hours (an instant-read thermometer inserted into the thickest part of the thigh will read 160°F to 165°F). Remove the chicken from the oven and let cool.

❉ When cool enough to handle, disjoint the chicken and discard the skin (see box below). Remove the meat from the bones and dice. Put the meat in a bowl with the celery and green onions. Fold in the yogurt, mayonnaise, crème fraîche, and remaining salt and pepper. Mix well. Add more salt and pepper to taste. At this point, the salad can be covered and refrigerated for up to 24 hours.

Use That Chicken Carcass

While today's busy schedules do not encourage making big pots of home-made stock, the carcass of a roasted chicken (store-bought or home-roasted), stripped of its meat, is far too promising to just toss in the garbage. Roughly break the carcass into half a dozen pieces and put it, along with the skin (if you desire) and any other remnants (including the juices that have accumulated in the roasting pan), in a large saucepan. If you've used a whole raw chicken, you probably also have a bag of chicken innards; remove them from the bag and add everything, except the liver, to the saucepan. Check your produce bin: if there's a bit of fresh parsley, a carrot, or a couple of stalks of celery, chop them into large pieces and add to the pan. Do the same with an onion. Cover with water and bring to a boil. Skim off any foam, then let the mixture simmer partially covered for as long as is convenient (at least an hour). Season the stock with salt and pepper to taste. Pour through a strainer into a clean container, pressing down on the bones and vegetables to extract the juices before discarding. Refrigerate the stock until the fat congeals on top. Strip off the fat and discard. You'll have 2 to 4 cups of good-quality stock for use in soups and sauces. Store, refrigerated, for up to a week, or freeze in 1-cup containers. So much flavor, so little effort—and it keeps your finger in the stockpot, so to speak.

✳ To assemble the "bites," if using foccacia bread, cut the sheets in half horizontally. Spread both sides with additional mayonnaise, if desired. Generously spread the chicken salad on the bottom halves and top with the upper halves. Cut into squares or triangles of desired size, anywhere from 1½ to 3 inches. Slip a bit of lettuce into each "bite" and add a leaf or two of arugula. Serve immediately, or cover and serve within the hour.

✳ If using the Belgian endive, cut the heads about 1 inch above the root end and separate each head into individual petals. Wash and dry the petals. Fill each petal with a heaping tablespoon of salad and arrange in an attractive pattern on a serving dish. Just before serving, sprinkle generously with parsley or chives.

Suggested Beverage

A Muscadet, a sparkling wine, or a crisp rosé. Muscadet is too often typecast as a seafood wine, but in fact, its dry, crisp acidity and notes of green apple make it perfect for this chicken salad.

✳ STUFFED CALIMYRNA FIGS ✳

Tying for Dame Georgeanne Brennan's pick as first-place appetizer is this one with roots in her beloved southern France.

24 appetizers

1 cup hard apple cider, brandy, or dry sherry

1 cup water

2 tablespoons sugar

12 dried Calimyrna or other dried figs, such as Mission, *or* 24 dried, pitted prunes

4 ounces cream cheese, at room temperature

2 ounces blue cheese, at room temperature

2 tablespoons cream (optional)

24 candied or plain walnut, pecan, or almond halves

Extra-virgin olive oil (optional)

Prepare Ahead

The figs can be prepared, covered, and refrigerated 24 hours ahead. Let them come to room temperature before serving.

**Suggested
Beverage**

If using an artisan-
made hard cider for
cooking the figs,
offer it, chilled, to
accompany them.
Otherwise, serve an
Amontillado sherry at
room temperature.
Either choice will
provide a crisp edge
to the full-bodied fruit.

In a medium saucepan over medium heat, bring the apple cider, water, and sugar to a boil. Reduce heat to low and add the figs. Simmer until the figs are plumped and soft, about 10 minutes. Remove the figs from the cider and pat dry. Discard the cider or reuse it to poach additional dried fruit (the cider mixture will become quite syrupy on second poaching). Trim off the tough fig tip ends, then cut the figs in half lengthwise. If using prunes, use them whole.

In a medium bowl, mash together the cream cheese and blue cheese until well combined. If the mixture seems stiff, add a small amount of cream. The mixture should be soft and spreadable, but not runny. Put a dab of the cheese mixture on the cut surface of each fig half, then gently press a nut half into the cheese. If using prunes, you'll see that there is a "dimple" in each one where the pit has been removed. Put the cheese mixture and a nut half into that "dimple." Arrange the figs on a serving platter or mound them in a bowl to serve. If they look a little dry, drizzle with your best extra-virgin olive oil.

❋ FRESH OKRA CAKES ❋

Prepare Ahead

The batter can be
prepared 24 hours
ahead of frying.

If you haven't already tasted okra, it's time. Make these Fresh Okra Cakes from Atlanta Dame Gloria Smiley at the height of okra season, late summer to early fall. Select smallish pods with no dark or shriveled spots. Smiley, a veteran food stylist who worked frequently with Julia Child, serves the cakes hot off the stove as a cocktail nibble or as a vegetable side dish alongside high-summer tomatoes and fresh corn. Or try this: serve hot with grilled pork chops saddled up against the Best Grits (page 129).

The trick to cooking okra, Southern Dames agree, is to cook it minimally, as in these fritter-like cakes. The result is a clean, green vegetal taste. Don't skimp on salting the cooked rice used to make the batter, and use the stronger seasoning option if the cakes will be served at room temperature rather than hot off the stove. Make no effort to keep the spoonfuls of batter in a uniform shape. Let them spread about, showing off the intriguing star shape of the sliced okra and its lacy interior.

Suggested Beverage

Sauvignon Blanc, or better yet, a Fino sherry, served chilled.

25 appetizer cakes or 10 side-dish cakes

- **½ pound fresh okra, tips and stems removed, cut into ¼-inch slices (about 2 cups)**
- **1 cup minced onion**
- **1 clove garlic, minced**
- **1 jalapeño or serrano chile pepper, seeded and minced**
- **½ cup cooked medium-grain rice, seasoned with 1 teaspoon salt** *or* **1 teaspoon of salt plus ¼ teaspoon cumin and ¼ cup chopped cilantro leaves**
- **3 tablespoons all-purpose flour**
- **2 large eggs, lightly beaten**
- **½ teaspoon Tabasco**
- **6 tablespoons vegetable oil**

※ Combine the okra, onion, garlic, jalapeño, rice, flour, eggs, and Tabasco in a large bowl.

※ Just before serving, preheat the oven to 200°F, and heat a 12-inch nonstick skillet over medium-high heat. Add the oil, and when it shimmers and sizzles when a bit of batter hits it, drop spoonfuls of the okra-rice mixture into the pan. Do not crowd the pan. You can make the cakes any size, from 1 tablespoon to ½ cup, depending on how you plan to serve them. Sauté for 2 minutes or until the cake is nicely browned. Turn and cook the other side for 2 minutes. Remove the cakes as they are done to absorbent paper towels and keep them warm in the preheated oven until all are cooked. The cakes are best served piping hot—consume them within 30 minutes of frying.

Finger Vegetables

The typical crudité platter is so often disappointing: withered, worn-out carrot and celery sticks and ungainly lumps of raw broccoli and cauliflower, all circling a bowl of some predictable dip. Vegetable crudités have taken a bad rap indeed. In fact, finger vegetables—with or without dipping sauces— remain a delicious, nutritious appetizer to be offered as an alternative to calorie-laden hors d'oeuvres. Make healthy eating attractive by incorporating some of the following ideas:

* Select slender young carrots. Cut them on an angle into thin slices (much easier than cutting "sticks"). Blanch very briefly until barely tender in boiling salted water, then rinse in very cold water to stop cooking—the blanching not only softens the carrots but it brightens the color and keeps them from looking dry on an appetizer plate. And never, ever use those whittled-down "baby carrots" sold in plastic bags, organic or not.

* Serve crisp, garden-fresh celery, cut similarly to the carrots. Select the tender but crunchy inner stalks. Serve them alongside vegetables other than the usual carrots: thinly sliced fennel bulbs and Belgian endive petals, all dressed lightly with freshly squeezed lemon juice to prevent browning.

* Choose very fresh broccoli and use the same brief blanching technique as for the carrots.

* Do the same with green and yellow beans; these are good choices when in season. Cut them in half on a sharp angle to use as dippers.

* Belgian endive petals (just cut from their heads) make good finger-food scoops. Fill them with dollops of Smoked-Salmon Tartare (page 35) or Cucumber-Sesame Salsa (page 19). See also Chicken Salad Bites (page 7).

* Cauliflower is wonderful raw or steamed. Consider cutting the flowerets into thick "chips." Do likewise with raw cucumber, zucchini, and jicama.

* Most of these vegetables (celery, carrots, cauliflower, fennel, zucchini) can be prepared bite-size à la grecque. Use the cooking solution from the Quail Escabeche (page 51). Add handfuls of shiny black and green olives for color and taste.

* Consider also spears or tips of asparagus (blanched according to instructions, page 73), sugar snap or snow peas, and edamame beans (in or out of their pods—available fresh or frozen in most markets).

* Tiny green onions at the peak of season make superb dippers—simply cleaned and trimmed, no cooking necessary—as do cherry tomatoes in their many shapes and colors.

* Cut brilliantly colored sweet bell peppers into random, bite-size shapes. They make nice containers for Black-Olive Tapenade (page 5). Hollowed-out squash cups are another option.

* And then there are "house fries": wedges of potato (Yukon golds or sweet potatoes are good choices) coated with olive oil, salt, pepper, and herbs, and roasted in a 400°F oven till crispy.

* As for the dips, everyone knows some easy ones, from chunky blue cheese dressings to sassy salsas. Among our favorites: In-Your-Face Dressing (page 68) and Armenian "Pesto" (page 132). And don't overlook a simple dip of a well-chosen olive oil and specialty sea salts—a bowl of each for dipping.

—*Monterey Dame Daryl Griffith, Director of Catering, The Pebble Beach Company*

❧ WALNUT-FENNEL TARTS ❧

Prepare Ahead

The dough can be prepared up to 2 days in advance, well wrapped and refrigerated. The tart shells can be baked off a day ahead and kept in an airtight tin. The filling can be made ahead, too. Assemble the tarts for final baking just before serving them hot from the oven. The recipe is easily halved for smaller parties.

As owner and chief creative officer of Lisa Dupar Catering, Seattle Dame Lisa Dupar has catered to the likes of Martha Stewart, Bill Cosby, and President Bill Clinton. Yet even after over twenty-five years in the business, she still considers it an important part of her "mission" to "find tasty little bites that hold up well during a cocktail party." These wee tarts—simple disks of nut-specked shortbread topped with caramelized vegetables, fruit, and cheese—are some of her most requested party nibbles.

30 tarts

Tart Shells

¼ cup walnut meats

½ cup (1 stick) unsalted butter, cold, cut into ½-inch pieces

1 cup plus 5 tablespoons all-purpose flour

⅔ teaspoon salt

¼ cup ice water (slightly more if needed to form dough), divided

Topping

1 large fennel bulb

1 tablespoon olive oil

1 medium onion, cut in ¼-inch dice (1½ cups)

1 medium tart apple (such as Granny Smith), peeled and cut into ¼-inch dice (¾ cup)

2 teaspoons finely chopped garlic

¾ cup dry white wine

3 tablespoons heavy cream

¼ teaspoon salt

Freshly ground black pepper

¾ cup grated Gruyère cheese, divided

¾ tablespoon fresh basil leaves, cut in chiffonade (see box, page 59)

✳ To make the tart shells, in the bowl of a food-processor fitted with a steel blade, place the walnut meats and roughly chop them, being careful not to turn them into meal. Remove the walnuts from the bowl and reserve. Add the butter, flour, and salt to the bowl. Pulse until the butter disappears into the flour, about 30 seconds. Add 3 tablespoons of the ice water and continue to pulse for a few more seconds. Then add 1 to 2 more tablespoons of water, pulsing very briefly until the dough begins to clump. Remove the dough to a piece of plastic wrap and pat it into a flat disk. Wrap well and refrigerate for 30 minutes or up to 2 days before using. (If you refrigerate the dough for more than 30 minutes, allow it to sit at room temperature for about 15 minutes or until it is pliable enough to roll.)

✳ Preheat the oven to 375°F. Roll out the dough on a lightly floured surface to about ¼ inch thick. Sprinkle the dough with the chopped walnuts. Using a rolling pin, roll the nuts into the dough, which will now be about ⅛ inch thick. Cut the dough into 2-inch rounds with a circle cutter. You should have at least 30 rounds (tart shells). (Any extras make great little crackers.) Place the shells 1 inch apart on a parchment-covered baking sheet and bake until pale and crisp, but not brown (the shells should still appear a bit "doughy" and can be handled without breaking), 5 to 7 minutes. Remove from the oven and transfer the shells to a wire rack to cool.

✳ To make the topping, trim the fennel bulb of fronds and any brown outside leaves. Core the fennel and cut it with the grain into thin slices. Heat the olive oil in a small sauté pan over medium-high heat. Add the onion and cook until golden brown and caramelized, about 20 minutes. Add the fennel, apple, and garlic; cook until tender, about 5 minutes. Add the wine and reduce by 90 percent or until the mixture is almost dry. Add the cream, salt, and pepper; stir, remove immediately from the heat, and cool to room temperature. Reserve 2 tablespoons of the cheese, and mix the rest into the topping mixture with the basil.

Suggested Beverage

A bourbon-based cocktail, or a dry Spanish Oloroso sherry (walnuts lend themselves to oak-aged beverages).

✳ To assemble and bake the tarts, preheat the oven to 375°F. Return the tart shells to the baking sheet. With a tablespoon, spoon the filling onto the center of each shell. Sprinkle the reserved cheese on top of each tart and bake until fully cooked and golden brown on top, about 8 minutes. Serve immediately.

✳ PHYLLO FONTINA CHEESE BITES ✳

Prepare Ahead

These appetizers can be assembled ahead, arranged on a baking sheet, and then placed in the freezer. Once frozen, remove them from the baking sheet, put in a sealable plastic bag, and freeze until ready to bake.

Need a little intriguing something to serve hot out of the oven? Perhaps a "house hors d'oeuvre" kept conveniently in the freezer for spur-of-the-moment entertaining? These one-bite phyllo rolls filled with cheese and fresh herbs are just what you're looking for. The recipe comes from Phoenix Dame Linda Hopkins, who runs Les Petites Gourmettes, a children's cooking school. She says that cooking with phyllo dough is simple enough for even children to do (see box, page 18).

30 appetizers

One 16-ounce package frozen phyllo sheets, thawed

½ cup (1 stick) unsalted butter, or more, as needed

1 cup (about ⅓ pound) grated fontina cheese (see box, opposite)

1 teaspoon minced fresh thyme leaves

1 teaspoon minced fresh parsley

1 teaspoon minced fresh rosemary leaves

½ teaspoon freshly ground black pepper

Heaping ⅓ cup finely minced shallots

✳ Cut a 5- by 8-inch paper template. Unfold the phyllo sheets and cover them with a piece of plastic wrap and a damp tea towel. If planning to bake immediately, preheat the oven to 350°F.

✳ Melt the butter in a small bowl in microwave. Put the cheese in a second bowl. Mix the thyme, parsley, rosemary, and pepper together in a third bowl. Put the shallots in a fourth bowl. When ready to work, place your template on the stack of phyllo sheets. With a sharp knife, cut them into 5- by 8-inch rectangles. You will need 30 rectangles; if necessary, cut more from the remaining dough. Return the unused portion of dough to the refrigerator or freezer for later use. Cover the cut rectangles with plastic wrap or parchment and the damp tea towel.

✳ Remove 3 cut rectangles to a clean work surface. Brush them lightly on one side with melted butter, then stack. On top of the stack, evenly sprinkle about 1½ tablespoons of the cheese, a light dusting of the herb mixture, and about 1½ teaspoons of the shallots. Roll from short side to short side to form a snug little tube 5 inches long. Brush lightly with butter. Repeat with the remaining ingredients to form 9 more tubes. With a sharp knife, cut each tube into 3 pieces. Lay them seam side down on a baking sheet about 1 inch apart. (At this point, they can be frozen per "Prepare Ahead.")

✳ When ready to serve, bake until golden, 8 to 10 minutes if thawed, 12 minutes if frozen. Serve immediately.

Suggested Beverage

Any brut sparkling wine or, to cut the buttery notes of the phyllo, a steely, high-acid Greek Assyrtico.

Tips for Slicing and Grating

Anything that tends to get "squishy" when sliced or grated is best placed in the freezer for up to two hours before slicing or grating. This includes soft cheeses, smoked salmon, bacon, pancetta, even meat and poultry that you want to slice thinly. If the cheese has an inedible coating, remove it before freezing. Lightly oiling the holes of the box grater (if used) is also helpful.

Working with Phyllo Dough

Most important, know that tissue-thin phyllo sheets (also known as filo and fillo), as delicate as they seem, are forgiving. A torn sheet can be buttered, patched with extra pastry pieces, then lightly buttered again. You won't notice the tears after baking. Phyllo sheets come in several sizes, all adaptable to most any recipe's requirements. You can create larger sheets by positioning two sheets next to each other, brushing with melted butter, and overlapping by half an inch. To defrost, place the unopened box of phyllo in the refrigerator overnight; remove 1 to 2 hours before use. The sheets should be soft and pliable. If brittle or sticking together, return them to the market.

Phyllo dries quickly when exposed to the air, becoming brittle and flaky. To prevent this, lay out the amount needed on a flat, dry surface. Cover with plastic wrap or parchment, then a clean, damp tea towel. Tightly wrap remaining pastry and refreeze or refrigerate. Use within 2 to 3 weeks; phyllo sheets will eventually become moldy.

Cut sheets to the size you need with a sharp paring knife or kitchen scissors. Sometimes it is helpful to cut a paper template the size required. If scrap pieces are large enough, they can be layered or rolled to make bite-size pastries. Cut leftover rolled pastry sheets into thin shreds, then toss with melted butter to just coat. Form into pastry nests or use to top a tart. Sprinkle with a blend of sugar and spice to taste. Discard smaller, scrappy pieces.

To butter phyllo, use a quality soft-bristle pastry brush and lightly dab each sheet with melted butter or olive oil, or a combination. Begin at the edges and work toward the center. You will need about 2 teaspoons of melted butter or oil per sheet. Dab butter over the shaped pastry to prevent drying. Clarified butter, with the milk solids removed, creates the crispiest pastries.

—*Charleston Dame Susan Fuller Slack*

HOME-CURED SALMON IN PHYLLO CUPS WITH CUCUMBER-SESAME SALSA

The big star of this recipe is the salsa that tops the cured salmon. You'll undoubtedly think of dozens of foods that the salsa (in much larger quantities) could complement—everything from good corn chips to grilled fish. Dallas Dame Dolores Snyder first conceived of it for her book, *Tea Time Entertaining*. The recipe took the appetizer prize in a national competition for professional chefs, winning Snyder twelve cases of phyllo. She laughs: the *grand*-prize winner received a new kitchen.

To save time, this appetizer can be made using store-bought lox and ready-made phyllo cups. The Fillo Factory (www.fillofactory.com) produces Mini Fillo Shells. Although good-looking and handy, they are nowhere near as tasty as Snyder's homemade ones. Try the original version before using the shortcut.

40 appetizers

Salmon

¼ cup rock salt

½ cup sugar

½ teaspoon freshly ground white pepper

One 12-ounce fresh salmon fillet, without skin

Phyllo Cups

6 frozen 14- by 18-inch phyllo sheets (or equivalent), thawed (see box, opposite)

½ cup (1 stick) unsalted butter or more as needed, melted

Cucumber-Sesame Salsa

½ cup English cucumber, peeled, seeded, and cut into ⅛-inch dice

Half of a jalapeño chile pepper, cored, seeded, and minced

1 teaspoon peeled and minced gingerroot

Prepare Ahead

Allow 6 hours for the salmon to cure. Once cured, the salmon easily keeps for 5 days. The phyllo cups can be made ahead and stored frozen; thaw a few hours in the refrigerator before using. The salsa can be made several hours before serving. And note: If you have extra salmon and salsa, the two served together without the phyllo cups make a lovely light lunch or first course.

1 teaspoon sugar

½ teaspoon sesame oil

Assembly

¼ cup sour cream or crème fraîche (see box below)

❋ To cure the salmon, combine the salt, sugar, and white pepper. Place the salmon on a sheet of plastic wrap large enough to wrap around it completely. Rub both sides of the salmon with the salt mixture, then fold and seal the plastic wrap around it. Place the salmon in a shallow dish and top it with a brick or other heavy object wrapped in foil. Refrigerate for 6 hours to cure. Remove the wrapping and wash and dry the salmon well. Cover it with fresh plastic wrap and refrigerate until ready to use.

❋ To make the phyllo cups, preheat the oven to 375°F. Unfold the phyllo sheets and place 1 sheet on a clean, dry surface. Brush lightly with melted butter. Top with the remaining pastry sheets, brushing each with butter. Using a 1⅞-inch fluted cutter, cut out enough rounds to line mini-muffin pans with the phyllo, buttered side down, and prick with a fork. Freeze for 10 minutes.

❋ Transfer the cups to the oven and bake for 5 minutes. Remove them from the oven and press out any bubbles with the bottom of a teaspoon. Return them to the oven and bake until golden, about 4 minutes. Turn

---

About Crème Fraîche

This slightly sour thickened cream has many uses: substitute it for sour cream in savory dishes and for whipped cream in desserts. If you cannot purchase ready-made crème fraîche (recommended brand: Bellwether Farms), make your own. Heat 2 cups of heavy cream with 2 teaspoons buttermilk in a small saucepan until lukewarm—not over 85°F. Remove from the heat. Transfer to a glass jar and cover with a towel. Let stand at room temperature (not under 60°F or over 85°F) until thickened, 1 to 3 days, then refrigerate. Crème fraîche will keep, refrigerated, for about 10 days.

---

the cups out to cool on wire rack. Repeat this process until you've made about 40 phyllo cups (keep phyllo sheets covered with plastic wrap or parchment and a damp tea towel while waiting for each batch to bake).

❀ To make the salsa, combine the cucumber, jalapeño, gingerroot, sugar, and oil in a bowl.

❀ To assemble, cut the salmon across the grain into paper-thin slices. Cut the slices into 40 bite-size pieces. Place a rounded teaspoonful of sour cream in each phyllo cup. Top with a piece of salmon and ¼ teaspoon of cucumber salsa, or reverse the order of salmon and salsa, ending with the salmon rolled into little rosettes. The assembled hors d'oeuvres can be held for 1 or 2 hours in a cool place before serving.

Suggested Beverage

A sparkling rosé, sake, off-dry Riesling, or New Zealand Sauvignon Blanc

SMOKED WHITEFISH
AND NORI PÂTÉ

Prepare Ahead

The pâté needs to be made at least 24 hours before serving. It will keep for several days. Remove from the refrigerator about 30 minutes prior to serving. If you are serving fewer than 6, divide the mixture into 2 smaller molds.

The New York Times food columnist, Dame Betty Fussell, has written a wide range of books. In one of her best-known, *I Hear America Cooking*, she pointed out that as a general rule, elements that grow together go together. This dressy pâté is proof. The combination of smoked fish and dried seaweed (*nori*) is a masterpiece of flavors and texture, easy to prepare and impressive when served with rice crackers as a starter.

12 servings

½ pound smoked whitefish

2 sheets toasted nori (each roughly 8 by 8 inches), divided

¾ cup (1½ sticks) unsalted butter, at room temperature, cut into tablespoon-size pieces

½ cup crème fraîche (see box, page 20)

1 tablespoon freshly squeezed lemon juice

½ teaspoon freshly ground black pepper plus additional as needed

1 cup Smoked-Salmon Tartare (page 35) *or* **1 ounce caviar of choice**

1 to 2 tablespoons very mild-flavored extra-virgin olive oil

Rice crackers

Carefully remove and discard all the skin and bones from the whitefish, and put the fish in the bowl of a food processor fitted with a steel blade. Reserve half a sheet of nori for topping the pâté. Tear the other sheets into pieces, add them to the processor bowl, and pulse until the ingredients are well mixed. Add the butter, crème fraîche, lemon juice, and pepper to the processor bowl. Purée the mixture until smooth and taste for seasoning. Add more lemon juice and pepper if desired. Scrape the purée into a metal or ceramic bowl at least 2 inches deep and large enough to hold the mixture. Cover the bowl with plastic wrap and refrigerate for at least 24 hours to allow the flavors to ripen.

❄ Unmold the pâté by placing the bowl in a pan of warm water for at least 5 minutes, or until you can easily run a knife around the outside edge of the pâté to loosen it. Place a serving plate upside down on top of the bowl, then invert. Remove the bowl, and with a spatula, smooth the top and sides of the pâté.

❄ Roll the reserved half sheet of nori into a tight scroll and cut with scissors into very thin strips. Scatter the strips, which will be in little curls, over and around the pâté.

❄ Return the pâté to the refrigerator. If storing for more than an hour, tent it lightly with plastic wrap, being careful not to disturb the nori strips. About 30 minutes before serving, remove the pâté from the refrigerator, top with the Smoked-Salmon Tartare, drizzle with the olive oil, and serve with the crackers.

Suggested Beverage

Champagne; also consider a high-acid still white wine such as a Spanish Albariño from Rias Biaxas or an Austrian Grüner Veltliner.

General Kitchen Tips

* Before you start to shop for ingredients or cook, take time to read the recipe from beginning to end.

* Before you start cooking, prepare (wash, cut, measure) all your ingredients.

* Always underset the timer by 5 to 10 minutes. You can always cook something a little longer; you can never cook it less.

* Keep your edge: knives should be honed and sharpened frequently.

* Don't be afraid to fail.

—*Cleveland Dame Bev Shaffer, Food Columnist,* Cleveland Plain Dealer

✸ ABIGAIL'S CRUSTY SAUSAGE ROLLS ✸

Prepare Ahead

The rolls can be made a day ahead of baking; refrigerate them, covered with plastic wrap. If you'd like, bake one and freeze the other to enjoy another time. Defrost in the refrigerator before baking.

For over thirty years, New York Grande Dame Abigail Kirsch has owned and operated the legendary catering firm that bears her name. Abigail Kirsch Culinary Productions today operates seven exclusive venues, including the New York Botanical Gardens, Pier 60 at Chelsea Piers, and the newest: Stage 6 at Steiner Studios at the Brooklyn Navy Yard. This recipe, adapted from her *Invitation to Dinner*, is one she frequently recommends for casual parties. Though Kirsch calls them "rolls," they are actually two loaves that make for handsome serving on a bread board. Using ready-made pizza dough and your best local pork sausage, this recipe is representative of Kirsch's approach to food: "My mantra since the day I poached my first salmon: startle your guests with exquisite presentation and uncomplicated, recognizable food."

2 rolls or 6 to 8 appetizer servings

1½ pounds ground pork sausage

2 cups (about ½ pound) coarsely grated mozzarella

1 cup (about 2 ounces) freshly grated Parmigiano-Reggiano

¼ cup finely chopped fresh basil *or* 1 tablespoon dried

3 large eggs, lightly beaten

¼ teaspoon ground cloves

¼ teaspoon ground allspice

¼ teaspoon ground sage

½ teaspoon salt

¼ teaspoon freshly ground black pepper

2 packages pizza dough (2 pounds total), thawed if frozen

¼ cup all-purpose flour

Prepared whole-grain mustard

✸ If baking immediately, preheat the oven to 375°F. Break up the sausage into small pieces and sauté it in a large skillet over medium-high heat until completely brown and cooked through. Using a slotted spoon, transfer the sausage to paper towels to drain.

✻ When drained and completely cooled, put the sausage in a bowl with the cheeses, basil, eggs, cloves, allspice, sage, salt, and pepper. Mix well.

✻ Place 1 pound of the pizza dough on a lightly floured board. A small amount of olive oil rubbed between your hands will assist you in handling the dough. Sprinkle the top of the dough lightly with flour and roll it out into a 10- by 12-inch rectangle, ½ inch thick. Once you begin to roll out the dough, you may find that it resists staying in a rectangular shape, and rather it contracts like a doughy rubber band. The idea is to get the dough to form an uneven rectangle as it is rolled and to remain in that shape. You might let it rest a bit as you roll it.

✻ Spread half the sausage filling (about 2½ cups) over the dough, allowing a 1½-inch border on all sides. Fold in the 1½-inch border of dough and press down. As you do this, nudge the dough into a rough rectangular shape with the edges enclosing the filling. Roll the rectangle jelly roll–style, beginning with a short side.

✻ Place the filled roll, seam side down, on a baking sheet. Make the second roll with the remaining ingredients and place it on the same baking sheet about 3 inches from the other roll. Bake the rolls until crusty and brown, 40 to 45 minutes. (Do not be concerned about any filling oozing out of the dough.) Cool the rolls on a wire rack. Serve warm on a clean bread board, allowing guests to cut their own slices and spread with the mustard.

Suggested Beverage

Earthy reds with a hint of spice and moderately high acidity—Chianti, Pinot Noir, Crianza Rioja, or Cru Beaujolais; for a white wine, an Alsatian Pinot Gris.

FRESH VIETNAMESE SUMMER ROLLS WITH PEANUT SAUCE

Prepare Ahead

The rolls can be assembled 3 hours ahead of serving. Any earlier, they become soggy. The peanut sauce can be prepared a day ahead.

A keen little "burst of salad" is the way Seattle Dame Linda Burner Augustine describes her Vietnamese-inspired rolls—an alternative to the more common fried spring rolls. For dipping, Augustine, a freelance food writer and cooking teacher, makes a peanut sauce with fresh lime and store-bought hoisin sauce—available, along with the rice wrappers (also called spring roll skins), in the Asian section of most supermarkets. Augustine, always the encouraging instructor, offers these tips: "Be patient with the process of softening and rolling the wrappers. It may take a few tries, but once you have the hang of it, it goes quickly." You can also substitute other fresh vegetables such as cucumbers, radishes, bean sprouts, and cabbage, as you desire.

Cellophane (bean thread or glass) noodles are thin, dry, wiry noodles that soften and become translucent when soaked. They can be tricky to cut into shorter pieces. If yours are particularly unruly, simply put them in a bowl, and with kitchen scissors, snip them a few times into more manageable lengths. The noodles are often sold in 2-ounce skeins, tied with strings or rubber bands. If soaked with the ties still intact, the slippery noodles can easily be cut into the desired lengths. Cut off and discard the ties after cutting the noodles.

24 appetizers

- **4 ounces dried cellophane (bean thread) or thin rice noodles**
- **2 tablespoons mirin (rice wine)**
- **Twelve 8-inch rice-paper wrappers**
- **3 cups very thinly sliced lettuce**
- **1 cup matchstick-cut peeled carrots, 2 inches long and ⅛ inch thick**
- **½ cup matchstick-cut green onions, 2 inches long and ⅛ inch thick, both green and white parts**
- **12 poached prawns, shelled (optional)**
- **1 cup cilantro leaves**

1 cup fresh basil leaves

Peanut Sauce (recipe follows)

Suggested Beverage

Chilled sake, New Zealand Sauvignon Blanc, dry Riesling, or red Beaujolais-Villages.

❋ Prepare the noodles according to package directions. Cut them into 3-inch lengths; put them in a small bowl and toss with the mirin. Dip a rice-paper wrapper in a bowl of warm water for 45 seconds; remove and place it on a paper towel to drain. Put the softened wrapper on a flat work surface; on the bottom third of the wrapper, layer about 3 tablespoons noodles, 3 tablespoons lettuce, 3 carrot sticks, 3 green-onion sticks, 1 prawn, and 1 heaping tablespoon each of the cilantro and basil leaves.

❋ Bring the bottom edge of the wrapper over the filling, fold in both ends, and roll into a tight log. Place on a serving plate and cover with a damp towel. Repeat process with the remaining wrappers. To serve, cut the rolls in half and serve with Peanut Sauce on the side for dipping.

Peanut Sauce

¾ cup

3 to 4 limes, zested for 1 teaspoon finely grated zest (see box, page 75) and squeezed for ¼ cup juice

¼ cup store-bought hoisin sauce

¼ cup water

2 tablespoons sugar

1 teaspoon finely chopped serrano chile pepper (optional)

¼ cup finely chopped roasted, unsalted peanuts

❋ Whisk together the lime zest and juice, hoisin sauce, water, sugar, and serrano pepper. Stir in the peanuts. Refrigerate until about an hour before serving.

GOLDEN BEET SLAW WITH
FRESH HORSERADISH

Prepare Ahead

The slaw can be made, up to the addition of the chives, parsley, and lemon juice, a day ahead of serving. Store in the refrigerator. Bring to room temperature to complete and serve.

Healthy, sophisticated, easy to prepare, and dazzling to serve, all freckled with bits of caper, caraway, and, yes, anchovy—this is it! The recipe comes from New York Dame Paulette Satur, who has a graduate degree in plant physiology. Today, she and her husband, Chef Eberhard Muller (who opened New York's many-starred Le Bernardin with Gilbert Le Coze and then was André Soltner's protégé at another New York dining mecca, Lutèce), operate a 140-acre farm on the North Fork of Long Island Sound, where they grow specialty produce for New York chefs. Satur's home cooking is a sort of contemporary "working farmhouse" style, taking advantage of the seasonal crops that grow right outside her kitchen door.

8 servings

- 1½ pounds golden, Chioggia (red-and-white striped), or red beets, less than 3 inches in diameter, unpeeled
- 2 tablespoons finely grated fresh horseradish or equal amount prepared horseradish
- ¾ cup finely diced red onion
- 1 tablespoon finely chopped capers
- 2 anchovy fillets, rinsed, patted dry, and finely chopped
- 1 tablespoon caraway seeds, lightly toasted (about 5 minutes in a 400°F oven)
- 1 tablespoon sherry vinegar
- 2 tablespoons olive oil
- ¼ teaspoon salt
- 5 grinds black pepper
- ½ tablespoon minced chives
- ½ tablespoon minced parsley

Freshly squeezed lemon juice

Good-quality corn chips or pita bread (cut in wedges and warmed)

Plain yogurt (Pavel's, Straus Family Creamery, or Fage brand preferred)

Suggested Beverage

A lower-tannin red Côtes du Rhône or Pinot Noir; for white wine, a Spanish Cava—all stand up to the horseradish.

✳ Preheat the oven to 400°F. Line a baking sheet with foil and put the beets on it. Roast for 1½ hours or until they are fork tender. Remove from the oven, and when they are cool enough to handle, peel them (if using red beets, wear rubber gloves to prevent stained hands). With the medium to large hole side of a box grater, grate beets into a shallow dish, such as a pie plate. Fold in the horseradish, onion, capers, anchovies, caraway seeds, vinegar, olive oil, salt, and pepper. Let sit for at least 30 minutes. Right before serving, top with the chives, parsley, and a few squirts of lemon juice. Taste for seasoning and adjust if desired. Accompany with corn chips or pita bread and yogurt.

Dippers and Holders

Turning high-quality breads into little bite-size carriers for any number of dips, spreads, and other savories is a good alternative to using store-bought crackers. All three of these breads are also good candidates for tucking alongside first-course dishes from soups to salads to composed plates. Seattle Dame Linda Burner Augustine shares her formulas.

PITA POINTS

With some dishes such as the Golden Beet Slaw (page 28), just warming pita breads and cutting them into triangles makes the perfect accompaniment. If you want crispy points that are more like well-seasoned chips, here's how.

40 points

> One 10-ounce package (5 rounds) pita bread
>
> 2 tablespoons olive oil
>
> 1½ teaspoons dried rosemary, oregano, thyme, or basil
>
>   *or* a combination
>
> 1 teaspoon coarse salt

* Preheat the oven to 425°F. Cut each pita bread into 8 wedges. Put them in a large bowl, drizzle with olive oil, and sprinkle with the herbs and salt. Toss to evenly distribute seasonings. Place the points in a single layer on a baking sheet; bake until golden brown, 8 to 10 minutes. Remove the baking sheet from the oven and with a large spatula, turn the pita points over. Return the sheet to the oven and bake until the pita points are crisp, about 8 minutes (be careful not to over-brown). Serve hot or at room temperature, or cool well and store in an airtight container for up to 2 weeks.

CROSTINI

The Italian name means "little toasts," just right for holding a spread, meat, or cheese. These are best consumed within a few hours of preparation—the fresher the better.

24 crostini

> **1 baguette, cut into 24 half-inch slices**
>
> **2 large cloves garlic, peeled and ends trimmed**
>
> **Olive oil**

* Preheat the broiler. Put the bread slices in a single layer on a baking sheet and toast about 4 inches from broiler until lightly browned, 1 to 2 minutes. Remove the baking sheet from the oven. Rub the toasted sides of the bread with the garlic; brush lightly with olive oil and turn the bread over. Repeat the toasting, garlic, and oil process. Be careful not to over-brown (you want quick results so the bread doesn't completely dry out). Serve hot or at room temperature, or cool well and store in an airtight container for a few days (the crostini will tolerate a 30-second reheating, if desired).

BRIOCHE POINTS

The eggy, buttery, yeasted bread called brioche makes marvelous toast points. The points will keep well in an airtight container for several days. Leftovers can be broken up to use as croutons in a soup or green salad.

100 points

> **1-pound loaf brioche, cut into ½-inch slices, crusts trimmed**

* Preheat the oven to 350°F. Cut the bread slices into randomly shaped triangle points. Place the points on a baking sheet and toast until lightly browned and just a bit crusty, about 8 minutes. Turn the points over and toast for 2 to 3 minutes. If not using immediately, the points can be served at room temperature or reheated for about 5 minutes in a 350°F oven.

❧ "SCALLOPED" POTATOES ❧

Prepare Ahead
Both the marinade and the potato rounds can be prepared several hours in advance.

This recipe's playful name refers to little bay scallops (see box, page 50) that here are boldly seasoned with an Asian marinade and served on slices of crispy potato, making for a dazzling starter. The dish comes from television and radio food personality, British Columbia Dame Caren McSherry, who enjoys putting an Asian spin on food, inspired by living on the west coast of Canada. McSherry, who began cooking family meals as a teenager, has been teaching cooking classes for over thirty years and has published numerous cookbooks. She now owns and operates Canada's Gourmet Warehouse—a 12,000-square-foot store that sells everything "gourmet" from truffle salt to turbot poachers.

36 appetizers

2 tablespoons roasted sesame oil

2 tablespoons peanut or grapeseed oil plus additional for brushing

2 cloves garlic, minced (about 1½ teaspoons)

1-inch piece gingerroot, peeled and finely minced (about 2 teaspoons)

1 tablespoon finely chopped Chinese fermented black beans

1 tablespoon rice vinegar

1 tablespoon store-bought hoisin sauce

3 large russet potatoes, well scrubbed, *or* 36 good-quality store-bought potato chips

36 fresh bay scallops *or* 36 small uncooked shrimp

Cilantro leaves

❋ Heat the oils in a small sauté pan over medium heat. Add the garlic, gingerroot, and beans. Sauté until the mixture becomes fragrant, about 3 minutes. Remove from the heat and stir in the rice vinegar and hoisin sauce; set aside to cool.

❋ Within a few hours of serving, preheat the oven to 400°F. Slice the potatoes about ⅛ inch thick (a mandoline will make this easy). With a

2-inch fluted, round cookie cutter, punch out 36 potato rounds. Brush both sides of the potato rounds with oil, place on a parchment-lined baking sheet, and bake until potatoes are golden brown and cooked through, 10 to 15 minutes. Transfer the potato rounds (or potato chips) to a serving platter.

✳ About 30 minutes before serving time, combine the scallops and the marinade; set aside in the refrigerator. When ready to serve, heat a large cast-iron fry pan or a grill pan over high heat. With a slotted spoon, remove the scallops from the marinade (allow a little bit of marinade to cling to the scallops) and add to the pan. Cook the scallops until just cooked through, 1 to 2 minutes (depending on size). Place a scallop on each potato slice and garnish with a cilantro leaf.

Suggested Beverage

Offer a less familiar French wine: a dry, aromatic Savennieres made from Chenin Blanc. The complex flavors and intense minerality of this wine make a fine pairing. Or, try a dry California Chenin Blanc or a Pinot Blanc—both will be more richly fruited than their Old-World counterpart but will make quite delicious aperitifs.

✳ COCKTAIL POTATO LATKES WITH SMOKED-SALMON TARTARE ✳

These are the very popular crispy, fried potato pancakes that Philadelphia Dame Alison Barshak serves at her newest restaurant, Alison at Blue Bell. The tiny latkes are topped with a not-to-be-missed combination: smoked salmon or sushi-grade raw tuna diced and flavored with truffle oil. We call for this topping combo with a number of other recipes and also suggest simply serving it with Brioche Points (see box, page 30) as an appetizer when there's no time for frying latkes.

Barshak achieved national acclaim when she was the debut chef at Philadelphia's Striped Bass Restaurant the year *Esquire* named it "best new restaurant in the country." Her star-studded career as a chef is particularly notable as she is almost entirely self-taught. Her only formal culinary training was a three-day seafood preparation course at the Culinary Institute of America, which she took prior to opening Striped Bass.

20 appetizers

Prepare Ahead

The latkes can be prepared ahead, frozen, thawed, and reheated to serve (3 to 5 minutes in a preheated 400°F oven). The tartare can be prepared and refrigerated ahead of serving. If using the tuna, do not prepare more than 3 hours in advance.

Latkes

  1 teaspoon vegetable oil plus additional for frying

  1 cup diced onion

  1 pound (2 to 3 small) russet potatoes, well scrubbed

  1 large egg, lightly beaten

  3 to 4 tablespoons all-purpose flour

  1 tablespoon salt plus additional as needed

  ¼ teaspoon freshly ground black pepper plus additional as needed

  2 tablespoons minced chives

  Smoked-Salmon Tartare (recipe follows)

Serving

  Crème fraîche (see box, page 20)—omit if using Tuna Tartare

  Chives, cut into matchstick-size pieces

  Fresh chervil sprigs

  Truffle oil or extra-virgin olive oil

❋ To make the latkes, heat the teaspoon of oil over medium heat in a small sauté pan. Add the onion and cook until soft, about 5 minutes. Set aside to cool. Using the large holes on a box grater, grate the potatoes into a bowl. Add the onion to the grated potatoes. Place the mixture in the bowl of a food processor fitted with a steel blade. Pulse the mixture briefly, three or four times, stopping to scrape down the sides of the bowl as needed. Pulse until it turns into a very rough paste. It should retain some bits of grated potato. Place the potato mixture in a sieve and set over a bowl to drain off excess liquid. Press to release as much liquid as possible. Discard the liquid and put the potato mixture in a bowl. Add the egg. Sprinkle in 3 tablespoons of the flour and mix together; add more if needed to make the batter hold together. Add the salt, pepper, and chives. Let the mixture rest for 5 minutes.

❋ If planning to serve the latkes immediately, preheat the oven to 200°F. Heat a 12-inch sauté pan over medium-high heat. Add about 2 tablespoons vegetable oil. When the oil shimmers, test a latke for taste and texture by dropping a level tablespoon of the latke mixture into the pan. Cook until brown, 2 to 3 minutes, then flip to cook the other side until brown. Remove from the pan and drain on paper towels. Taste and adjust the salt and flour if necessary. Continue to cook the latkes, discarding the oil after each batch and adding new oil, until all of the mixture is used. Keep the latkes warm in the oven for serving. If not serving immediately, cool the latkes in a single layer on a baking sheet. Place the baking sheet in the freezer. When the latkes are frozen, transfer them to a heavy-duty sealable plastic bag and return them to the freezer. When ready to serve, thaw and reheat per "Prepare Ahead" instructions.

Suggested Beverage

Brut Champagne or a Cru Chablis; if the truffle oil is used, an earthy Burgundian Pinot Noir.

❋ To serve, top each hot latke with a dollop of Smoked-Salmon Tartare and top with the garnishes. Serve immediately.

Smoked-Salmon (or Tuna) Tartare

2 cups

12 ounces cold-smoked salmon *or* sushi-grade raw tuna, cut into small dice (see box, page 17)

1 tablespoon minced shallots

1 tablespoon minced chives

2 tablespoons extra-virgin olive oil (the best available)

1 teaspoon black or white truffle oil

Salt and freshly ground black pepper

❋ Fold together the salmon, shallots, chives, and oils. Season with salt and pepper to taste.

Extra-Easy Starters

Sometimes just eliminating the work for one course can make the prospect of company for dinner more pleasant. The appetizer is a good place to take advantage of the myriad high-quality ready-to-eat foods. Some especially uncomplicated possibilities:

* A bowl of top-quality olives (always have a supply in the fridge), rinsed of brine, drizzled with a well-chosen extra-virgin olive oil, and topped with minced fresh herbs—or try minced candied ginger (easy to keep on hand).

* Cheeses, wonderful cheeses: every day there seem to be more available to us. Presenting one or two at room temperature (perhaps on a fresh fig or grape leaf) will free you up for what's to follow. Try serving a few cheeses with bread and a bowl of locally made honey. Or for the ultimate in rusticity, purchase a jagged chunk of Parmigiano-Reggiano and serve with a drizzle of the best balsamic vinegar you can find.

* Combine several kinds of raw nuts. Serve at room temperature, not cold. Better yet, warm briefly in a 350°F oven—but be careful not to burn them.

* In an ovenproof dish, bathe Medjool dates in a pool of extra-virgin olive oil and sprinkle lightly with sea salt and fresh thyme. Cover and warm briefly in a 350°F oven; serve immediately.

* And there's good bread with butter (especially one of the lovely artisan-made butters now in many markets). Try this: Put a couple of scoops of room-temperature, unsalted butter in a ramekin and drizzle with extra-virgin olive oil and a sprinkle of coarse sea salt. Look for truffled sea salt at your local food shop. It gets rave reviews when served with the butter and olive oil.

—Monterey Dame Mary Chamberlin, Caterer and Event Planner

❧ RICH MAN POOR MAN ❧

When you want an extraordinary starter, when you can get fresh, premium fava beans (usually springtime), and when you can enjoy the time-consuming task of preparing the fresh shell beans, this is your recipe. Los Angeles Dame Judy Zeidler says the dish she calls Rich Man Poor Man is a Tuscan specialty called *fagioli e caviali* (fava beans and caviar). As an alternative to the caviar version, Zeidler suggests tossing the beans with the best pecorino cheese you can obtain.

Zeidler—who with her husband owns and operates five west Los Angeles restaurants and has published several cookbooks, including *Home Cooking with a French Chef* (co-authored with Michel Richard) and *The Gourmet Jewish Cookbook*, serves this dish as a stand-up appetizer in espresso cups with tiny spoons. (The portions are small, measuring about ⅓ cup per person.) Not only is Rich Man Poor Man great conversation food, it illustrates how caviar (or a premium cheese) can add both texture and flavor—as well as extravagance—to a dish. Zeidler cooks the fava beans in water flavored with olive oil, garlic, and rosemary. The residue from this cooking water adds a subtle flavor to the beans when they are peeled.

Prepare Ahead

The beans can be prepared a day ahead of serving. Store refrigerated and then return to room temperature before topping with the caviar and serving.

6 to 8 servings

> **1½ pounds fresh fava beans in the pod**
>
> **¼ cup plus 3 tablespoons olive oil, divided**
>
> **3 cloves garlic, peeled and minced**
>
> **1 tablespoon fresh rosemary leaves or 1 teaspoon dried**
>
> **¼ teaspoon salt, or more, depending on the saltiness of the caviar**
>
> **Freshly ground black pepper**
>
> **3 ounces caviar (see box, page 38) *or* 1 cup finely chopped Pecorino Romano cheese**

❧ Peel the outer pods off the fava beans and discard (see box, opposite). Put 6 cups of water in a pot along with 3 tablespoons of the oil, garlic, and rosemary. Bring to a boil. Add the favas and as soon as the boil returns, cook for just 30 seconds. Immediately remove from the heat and drain under cold running water. Peel off the outer membrane of the favas by loosening with tip of thumbnail or knife and slipping it off. The bits of garlic and rosemary will cling to the peeled favas. Toss the favas with the remaining oil and season with the salt and pepper.

❋ Serve the favas at room temperature; distribute them among 6 to 8 espresso cups. Top with the caviar. (Use a nonmetallic spoon for scooping the caviar; inexpensive mother-of-pearl caviar spoons are a nice touch for eating the beans and caviar.) If using cheese in place of caviar, toss the beans with the cheese before spooning into the cups. Serve immediately.

Caviar: New Possibilities

Chicago Dame Carolyn Collins, who owns Collins Caviar Company and is credited with inventing "flavored" caviars, suggests the shiny black roe of American hackleback sturgeon (it offers the same sweet, nutty flavor of a good osetra for less cost) for Rich Man Poor Man. Another more affordable choice is the small bright yellow roe of the "American golden" whitefish. Collins encourages experimentation, but adds, "Avoid grocery store shelf-stable lumpfish. Among other disadvantages, it is dyed and the color runs. The most important rule: buy from a reputable vendor who can advise you on the choice of caviar, its freshness, and how it should be stored. There are reputable Internet vendors if you don't have a local caviar merchant you can trust."

Fresh Fava Beans

It may seem to be a daunting task: 1½ pounds of beans that require shelling not just once (of their pods), but then a second time after blanching (of their individual skins). How can this be reasonable in our increasingly busy lives?

It could be worse. Some chefs insist that the fava beans are best peeled of their individual skins *before* blanching—an even more difficult task, but one that better preserves the beans' exquisite pale-green color.

As one home cook who also has a full-time career outside the house puts it: "Some people knit. Some people shell fava beans." Indeed, at Grande Dame Alice Waters's famed Berkeley, California, restaurant Chez Panisse, where fava beans are ubiquitous on spring menus, the esteemed chef/owner says that shelling fava beans has become a seasonal ritual. "Big baskets of them are brought out to keep all hands busy during long meetings, menu discussions, and even job interviews." Make it a springtime tradition, and shelling fava beans transforms into a pleasant task.

Fava bean tips: Choose firm, bright-looking pods; avoid those with wrinkly skin or blackened ends. Early-season beans are best; late-season beans can be starchy and coarse tasting. When peeling, try to remove the tiny "germ" poking out from each bean; it can be bitter. And definitely do not overcook the fruits of your labor.

For basic cooking instructions and another fava bean recipe, see the Springtime Fresh Mozzarella Salad (page 72).

SEASONAL MUSHROOM GALETTE IN A CORNMEAL CRUST

Prepare Ahead

Since the galette is best hot out of the oven, prepare the dough up to a couple of days, or a month ahead and freeze. Prepare the filling up to a day ahead. Then a few hours before serving, assemble the galette and refrigerate until you want to bake it. Alternatively, bake the galette several hours ahead and serve at room temperature, or reheat at 400°F for about 10 minutes.

San Antonio Dame Jenny Mattingsley earned a philosophy degree but has never given up her professional kitchen life, which began with a part-time college job in a bakery. Today, she's reputed as one of San Antonio's most talented bakers. Here she goes savory with a galette featuring a buttery cornmeal crust.

If you are serving this dish as a first course, you may want to accompany it with a small mound of baby greens dressed in a vinaigrette, or simply drizzle each wedge with warmed crème fraîche (see box, page 20) or truffle oil, and shower with a light sprinkle of fresh thyme leaves.

One 9-inch galette for 8 appetizer servings or 6 first-course servings

Crust

   3 tablespoons sour cream

   ⅓ cup ice water

   1 cup all-purpose flour

   ¼ cup plus 1 tablespoon yellow cornmeal, divided

   1 teaspoon sugar

   ½ teaspoon salt

   7 tablespoons cold unsalted butter, cut into 6 to 8 pieces

Filling

   2 tablespoons olive oil

   1 tablespoon chopped shallots

   1 teaspoon finely chopped garlic

   1½ pounds wild mushrooms or a mix of wild and cultivated mushrooms, cleaned (with a brush or a damp cloth) and cut into ¼-inch slices

   ½ cup dry white wine, dry marsala, or dry sherry

   ½ teaspoon chopped fresh thyme leaves

1 tablespoon chopped parsley

½ teaspoon salt

5 grinds black pepper

❋ To make the crust, stir the sour cream and ice water together in a small bowl until thoroughly combined. Reserve. Put the flour, cornmeal, sugar, and salt in the bowl of a food processor fitted with a steel blade. Pulse to combine. Drop the butter into the bowl and pulse 8 to 10 times, or until the mixture resembles coarse bread crumbs. With the machine running, add the sour cream mixture through the feed tube and process just until the dough forms soft, moist curds. Remove dough from the processor and pat into a disk. Wrap in plastic wrap and chill for at least 2 hours or up to 2 days, or freeze for up to 1 month. When ready to assemble the tart, bring the dough to room temperature (if frozen, thaw it, wrapped, in the refrigerator). Place the dough on a piece of parchment paper sprinkled with about a tablespoon of cornmeal to prevent sticking. If the dough is still too moist, use a bit of flour patted on the surface. Roll into a roughly 11-inch round, cover with plastic wrap, and return the dough on the parchment paper to the refrigerator while you make the filling.

❋ To make the filling, in a large sauté pan heat the oil and cook the shallots and garlic over medium heat until wilted. Add the mushrooms and cook until they have given up their liquid and begin to shine, about 10 minutes. Add the wine, thyme, and parsley. Continue to cook and reduce until almost all of the liquid has evaporated, about 15 minutes. Season with salt and pepper. Set aside to cool.

❋ To assemble and bake the galette, position a rack in the lower third of the oven and preheat to 400°F. Place the rolled dough complete with its piece of parchment paper on a large baking sheet. Remove the plastic wrap. Place the mushroom filling in the center of the round of dough, leaving a 2- to 3-inch border. Fold the border up over the filling, allowing the dough to pleat as you lift it up and work your way around the galette (don't worry about the pleating being uneven). Bake until the galette is golden and crisp, 35 to 40 minutes. Transfer the baking sheet to a cooling rack and let the galette cool for 10 minutes. Then slip a wide spatula under the galette and slide it back onto the cooling rack. Serve cut in wedges, warm or at room temperature.

Pairing Wine and Cheese: Very Personal Picks

On December 9, 2007, *The New York Times* ran an intriguing article, called "White Noise," written by New York Dame Florence Fabricant. In it, Fabricant explored the long-held notion that red wine is best with cheese. While granting that robust reds can handle sturdy cheeses like cheddar and Parmigiano-Reggiano "with aplomb," Fabricant contended that when it comes to Brie, Époisses, Livarot, and most blues, there's no contest: the wine of choice should be white.

With distinguished cheeses increasingly available for home use, and with cheese and wine being frequently served as an appetizer rather than as a cheese course at the end of a meal, we asked a number of Dames to name wine and cheese pairings that live in their best culinary memories—ones they delight in re-creating over and over in their own homes. Here are a few of those—some in the red wine camp, others not.

Seattle Dame and cookbook author Julie Kramis Hearne contends Italian blue cheeses (predominantly cow's milk) have an irresistible affinity for well-chosen Barolos. She suggests accompanying the cheese with a bit of Italian honey—especially the rather distinctive chestnut honey.

Wine writer New York Dame Lila Gault suggests this current favorite new world–old world pairing: an Australian blue cheese (creamy and mildly pungent, called Roaring Forties) with a Cru Beaujolais, such as a Morgon or Juliénas, slightly aged, medium-bodied—a fruity red.

San Antonio Dame Bunny Becker of Becker Vineyards favors Champagne or a Riesling (slightly sweet) with soft, creamy cheeses such as Brillat Savarin. And she adds this pairing tip for the end of the meal: choose a cheese that will particularly complement whatever wine may remain after the main course. Becker is most likely to have a red Bordeaux or Burgundy lingering after the entrée and so would opt for an aged Gorgonzola or a spicy, strong cheddar for a "petite" cheese course.

Colorado Dame Carrie Stebbins, a wine and service specialist who teaches at Johnson & Wales University, favors a fruity New Zealand Sauvignon Blanc with young, creamy goat cheeses, and a crisp Chablis or Pouilly Fuissé with triple-cream cheeses. One rule she insists on: "Put away the oaky California Chardonnays when you bring out the cheese board." Yet, wine writer and Dallas Dame Renie Steves insists, "White cheddar and a big oaky Chardonnay are like Brahms—the heavy texture of the white cheddar matches the thick orchestration of the wine."

Some well-worn piece of eloquence advises, "In matters of taste, there can be no dispute"—this is certainly true of pairing wine and cheese and of all else related to food and beverage.

FIRST COURSES

Composed Plates and Salads   Serve a course before the entrée, and dinner becomes an occasion. The Dames encourage you to start your meal with new combinations. Your glory dish may be here. These recipes can also serve as the "small plates" so much in vogue. Any one or two of them could make a meal. Consider perfectly seared scallops drizzled with a browned-sugar sauce, quail prepared in an age-old tradition, turkey patties spiked with dates from desert climes, or a mix of grilled summer vegetables and shrimp. And yes, there are salads: for fall, winter, spring, and summer. You'll also be pleased to find a basic green salad with a particularly sassy dressing.

Recipes

Seared Scallops with Surprise Sauce
Dorie Greenspan, *New York Chapter*

Quail Escabeche
Mariquita Combes, *Houston Chapter*

Drunken Beans over Mexican White Cheese
Ida Rodriguez, *Los Angeles Chapter*

Grilled Gazpacho Salad with Shrimp
Elizabeth Karmel, *Chicago Chapter*

Little Molds of Roasted Peppers with Anchovy Sauce
Nancy Brussat Barocci, *Chicago Chapter*

Prosciutto and Melon in Sambuca
Judy Rodgers, *San Francisco Chapter*

Three-Sisters Salad
Carole Dulude, *British Columbia, Canada Chapter*

Oasis Salad
Gail Nottberg, *Palm Springs Chapter*

Basic Greens with an In-Your-Face Dressing
Terry Thompson-Anderson, *San Antonio Chapter*

Sweet Corn, Chanterelle, and Arugula Salad
Florence Fabricant, *New York Chapter*

Springtime Fresh Mozzarella Salad
Joanne Weir, *San Francisco Chapter*

Summer Salad of Watermelon, Feta Cheese, and Mint
Paula Lambert, *Dallas Chapter*

Winter Salad of Oranges and Pomegranate
Najmieh Batmanglij, *Washington, D.C., Chapter*

See also: Big Shrimp with Armenian "Pesto" *(page 130)*, Breakfast-for-Dinner Salad *(page 172)*, Mushroom Ragù *(page 195)*, Seasonal Mushroom Galette *(page 40)*, Souvenir Eggplant Gratin *(page 220)*

Notes

Know Your Scallops

Onions: Sliced or in Crescents?

Home-Kitchen Tools of Choice

Aleppo Pepper

Our Experts Talk About Grinding Spices at Home

How to Cut in Chiffonade

Begin a Meal with Cured Meats

Get Some Classic White Porcelains

The Uncomplicated Green Salad

Cutting Corn off the Cob

The Indispensable Microplane Grater and Zester

How to Section an Orange

How to Make Your Own Candied Orange Peel

SEARED SCALLOPS WITH
SURPRISE SAUCE

Do not miss this simple preparation for fresh scallops. It is easy. And it is impressive: something amazing occurs when you taste perfectly seared scallops drizzled with a caramel-orange sauce. Bump up the serving size of both the scallops and the accompanying vegetable, and the combination makes a fine entrée.

The recipe comes from New York Dame Dorie Greenspan, who, in her twenties, abandoned a doctoral program in gerontology in favor of food writing. Instead of writing her dissertation, she "baked, and baked, and baked." Finally she wrote a piece for *Food & Wine* magazine. "That clinched it. From then on, I was a food writer," recalls Greenspan.

4 to 6 servings

2 tablespoons sugar

Generous ⅓ cup freshly squeezed orange juice

½ cup dry white wine

1 pound (8 to 12) sea scallops, chilled

1 teaspoon salt

10 grinds white pepper

½ to 1 tablespoon olive oil

8 to 12 blanched asparagus tips (see instructions, page 73; use stalks for another meal) *or* about 8 ounces baby spinach, wilted just before serving (see box, page 227)

1 tablespoon cold unsalted butter, cut into 3 pieces

To make the sauce, sprinkle the sugar over the bottom of a small saucepan. Place the pan over medium-high heat and warm the sugar until it starts to melt and color. As soon as you see the sugar turn brown, start gently swirling the pan (you may need to briefly stir the sugar with a wooden spoon before it's liquid enough to swirl). When the sugar has turned a deep caramel color (put a drop of sugar on a white plate to

Prepare Ahead

You can make the sauce up to the addition of the butter 2 days ahead and store covered in the refrigerator. Prepare the accompanying asparagus or spinach ahead so that there will be no delay between cooking and serving the scallops.

test the color), after about 3 minutes, stand back and add the orange juice and white wine. It may bubble and splatter, so watch out. Turn the heat up to high, stir with a wooden spoon, and boil the sauce until it is reduced by half (you should have about ⅓ cup), about 10 minutes. Remove the pan from the heat and set it aside until serving time.

✳ To prepare the scallops, pat them dry between paper towels. Slice off the little muscle attached to the side of each scallop. Season them with the salt and white pepper. Have 4 warmed plates at the ready. Meanwhile, put the saucepan with the caramel sauce over very low heat so that it can warm while you cook the scallops.

✳ Put a large, heavy-bottomed skillet over high heat. When the pan is hot, pour in ½ tablespoon of the olive oil and swirl the pan to coat the bottom. Add the scallops and cook, without moving the scallops, for 2 minutes. Flip the scallops over, add a little more oil if needed, and

---

Know Your Scallops

Sea scallops are the largest of the commonly available scallops. They can range in diameter from quarter- to half-dollar-size, in thickness from half an inch to an inch, and in weight anywhere from half an ounce to several ounces. If your scallops are especially thick, you may want to slice them in half horizontally before cooking. Sea scallops are best cooked so that they are firm on the outside, but barely opaque in the center. Having the scallops cold to start will help you achieve this. *Bay* scallops, called for on page 32, are shaped like small corks, and because of their smaller size, require even more careful attention to prevent overcooking.

Both sea and bay scallops are expensive. If your market advertises them much under $10 a pound, you're probably getting what are referred to as "calico scallops," which are known for being rubbery when cooked. Fresh, in-season scallops are most desirable, but often you'll find them labeled "previously frozen." If so, request scallops that are still frozen, and then thaw in your own refrigerator as needed. Scallops are also often soaked in a phosphate solution, which results in their absorbing extra water and weight. Always ask for "dry" scallops. As with all seafood, buy only from a trusted fish monger.

cook until the scallops are firm on the outside and just barely opaque in the center, 1 to 2 minutes.

✳ Divide the scallops among the serving plates. On each plate, place 2 or 3 asparagus tips (these can be at room temperature) or a dollop of hot spinach alongside the scallops.

✳ Check that the caramel sauce is hot—give it more heat if necessary. When hot, remove the pan from the heat and add the butter, swirling the pan until the butter is melted and the sauce glistens. Season with salt and pepper to taste, then pour the sauce through a strainer into a pitcher. Drizzle some of the sauce over the scallops and pass the rest of the sauce at the table.

Suggested Beverage

A crisp California Sauvignon Blanc or a sparkling wine.

✳ QUAIL ESCABECHE ✳

In Houston, where Dame Mariquita Combes runs La Villette, one of the city's top catering companies, quail is commonly served. In other parts of the country, however, it is mostly restricted to fine-dining restaurants. Combes insists it's time home cooks everywhere add the tiny, tasty birds at least to their *company* cooking repertoires.

This recipe from her homeland, Argentina, is ideal for first-time quail cooks. We present it here as a first course, but the birds make monumental buffet fare on a large platter filled with their accompanying vegetables and the *escabeche* juices. Combes typically does a double batch, cooking twelve whole birds at a time.

If you purchase your quail partially boned, they will lie flat until you tie the legs together; then they will sit like little birds. The poached birds are pale in color. Do not skip the sprinkling of minced bright-green herbs over the top at serving.

6 servings

Prepare Ahead

This is a prepare-ahead dream. The traditional *escabeche* mixture is actually used to preserve quail in some cuisines. Definitely make the dish 1 to 3 days before serving, as the flavors improve with time.

6 whole quail

4 whole cloves garlic, peeled

1 large onion, cut into ¼-inch crescents (see box below)

4 medium carrots, peeled and cut on the diagonal into thin slices (about 1½ cups)

3 thin slices of lemon

1 cup olive oil

½ cup red wine vinegar

½ cup dry white wine

2 bay leaves*

½ teaspoon salt

½ teaspoon whole black peppercorns

¼ cup minced parsley, chives, or thyme leaves *or* a mixture of all three

✱ Wash the quail and tie the legs together with kitchen string. Place them in a Dutch oven or heavy-bottomed pot large enough to hold them in a single layer along with the vegetables. Add the garlic, onion, carrots, lemon, oil, vinegar, wine, bay leaves, salt, and peppercorns. Place over medium heat and bring to a boil. Cover and reduce heat to low. Let simmer until the quail are cooked and the vegetables are tender but not soft, 20 to 25 minutes. Remove from the heat, cool, refrigerate, and serve at least 1 day later, either at room temperature or reheated.

Onions: Sliced or in Crescents?

In some cases, cutting onions in a crescent shape is preferable to simple slices, which can result in ungainly rings of onion. For crescents, cut the onion in half from top to bottom. Lay the cut side flat on a cutting board and slice into the onion along the grain, depending on desired thickness. This cut produces wedges of onion that, when cut apart at the root end, have a crescent shape. When preparing onions for grilling, leave the wedges intact at the root end so that the pieces of onion will not fall through the grill. (Regular onion slices are usually cut *across* the grain of the whole onion. Or you can just cut the slices in halves for a half-moon cut.)

To serve, remove the bay leaves from the mixture. Place a quail in the middle of each individual serving dish. Remove the string from the legs. Distribute the vegetables about the birds and coat generously with the juices. Top with a light sprinkle of the minced herbs. Alternatively, serve the dish family style on a large platter. Warm bread is a nice accompaniment for sopping up the delicious juices.

Suggested Beverage

A lightly chilled young Spanish Tempranillo or dry Cava.

When you buy bay leaves, look for those labeled Turkish or Mediterranean, which impart a milder flavor. California bay leaves can overpower other flavors in a dish.

Home-Kitchen Tools of Choice

Most Dames agree: an accurate kitchen scale with a capacity of about 10 pounds is invaluable for home cooking; with it you can weigh both light and heavy ingredients, including everything from pasta to poultry to produce. A good-quality salad spinner aids immensely in drying greens so that water doesn't linger and dilute salad dressings. A pair of sturdy dishwasher-proof kitchen shears for hastily cutting everything from trussing twine to a chicken carcass is also on the "must" list. The other two kitchen tools are inexpensive items, likewise prized. Keep a number of flexible cutting boards (thin sheets of heavy-duty plastic) for all sorts of tasks, from handily transferring chopped vegetables into a cooking or storage vessel to manipulating dough. And when quarter inches matter, every cook needs a simple 12-inch plastic ruler, easy to clean and dedicated strictly to kitchen use.

DRUNKEN BEANS OVER MEXICAN WHITE CHEESE

Prepare Ahead

The dried beans can be cooked hours or days ahead up to the point of adding the tequila and cilantro. Reheat beans and add the remaining ingredients just before serving.

Begin a Southwest feast with these warm, tequila-spiked pinto beans served over little wedges of Mexican white cheese. Tortillas are recommended to soak up every last flavorful drop. The idea for this sassy starter comes from Los Angeles Dame Ida Rodriguez, corporate chef and head of the culinary team at Melissa's Produce Company. Though here the dish is a first course, it also makes a delicious side dish up against the Big Shrimp with Armenian "Pesto" (page 130) or a vegetarian entrée. Make the beans as fiery as you like; if you prefer them hotter, use even more serrano peppers; if you like them milder, use the jalapeños; to avoid chopping altogether, use the Aleppo pepper.

4 servings

8 ounces dried pinto beans

2 teaspoons salt

1 tablespoon olive oil

½ cup chopped onion

2 serrano or jalapeño chile peppers, chopped, *or* 1 heaping teaspoon or more Aleppo pepper (see box, opposite)

¼ cup good-quality tequila

⅓ cup plus a handful chopped cilantro leaves, divided

Eight ½-inch wedges of Mexican queso fresco (white cheese) or feta cheese

Sort through the beans, discarding any debris. Rinse the beans thoroughly and place in a pot large enough to hold them after they have cooked (they usually expand to two or three times their dried volume). Add water to cover the beans by about 3 inches. Cover and bring beans to a boil over low heat (this can easily take 20 minutes). Let the beans boil for 1 minute. Remove from the heat and let sit, covered, for 1 to 3 hours.

> ### Aleppo Pepper
> ──────────
>
> "I love Aleppo pepper because it has a smooth, warming heat that adds excitement to a dish but doesn't hit you in the face," says Washington, D.C., Dame Ann Wilder, founder of Wilder Spices, the much-touted premium herb and spice company. The scarlet-colored dried flakes come from a pepper that is grown in northern Syria, near the town of Aleppo. There is now such demand for it that the pepper that grows over the border in Turkey is also being sold as Aleppo pepper. "It is not the same," says herb and spice guru Chicago Dame Patricia Penzey Erd of The Spice House, a major Internet marketer of specialty herbs and spices. "When you shop for this really marvelous pepper, try to verify that it's truly Aleppo."
>
> Note: If you're lucky enough to obtain Aleppo pepper from specialty spice merchants such as Wilder Spices or The Spice House, it makes a lovely garnish sprinkled lightly to the side of a serving of something like the Drunken Beans over Mexican White Cheese. After making a brief visual statement, the few flakes will be absorbed into the dish.

✳ After presoaking, drain the beans, return them to the saucepan, and add water to cover by about 1 inch. Bring water to a boil. Return to a simmer and cook the beans until very tender; this can take as little as 30 minutes and as long as a few hours. Be sure the water covers the beans; add water as needed. Test for doneness by spooning a few beans into a small bowl; taste them as soon as they've cooled just a bit. The beans should be tender and show no trace of raw starch. Some beans will split open, which is fine. When the beans are done, remove the saucepan from the heat and stir in the salt. Carefully taste the liquid for seasoning. You may need more than 2 teaspoons of salt—beans can take a generous amount.

✳ Meanwhile, heat the oil in a small skillet over medium heat, add the onion and peppers, and cook until onions are tender. Add to the pot with the cooked beans. Continue simmering for 15 minutes to blend the flavors.

Suggested Beverage

A Provençal dry rosé or a good-quality Mexican beer served with lime.

✳ Just before serving, add the tequila and ⅓ cup of the cilantro to the hot beans. Place 2 wedges of cheese on each of 4 serving plates. Top the cheese with a couple of spoonfuls of beans and sprinkle with the remaining cilantro. Serve immediately, encouraging diners to mash the beans into the cheese as they eat.

Our Experts Talk About Grinding Spices at Home

The market for exotic herbs and spices has exploded in the last quarter century, and small specialty spice houses, like Dame Ann Wilder's Wilder Spices, have benefited. "In the fifties the average American had five or six spices in the cupboard; by 1990, twenty," says Wilder. Adds Dame Patricia Penzey Erd, co-owner of The Spice House, "What has changed over the last twenty-five years is our desire to make exotic dishes in our own kitchens. A single episode on the Food Network can cause a run of hundreds of pounds on a single esoteric spice. This is a good time to be a spice merchant."

Erd says that the most obvious spice to grind at home is pepper: "There is no substitute for freshly ground pepper out of a high-quality peppermill." She recommends Peugeot mills with their lifetime warranty. Although many consumers are tempted to similarly grind their own sea salt, Erd points out that salt, being a mineral, does not have an essential oil, so all that is accomplished in grinding is changing particle size. "Fancy sea salts are best just added as is with your fingertips."

Home grinding your own spices sounds like a wonderful idea, but it's difficult to get the same fine grind that's available from a commercial grinder. The best solution, according to Erd, is to find a good spice merchant who grinds in small, frequent batches (often to order), then buy small enough quantities that you can use them up within a year (the average shelf life for ground spices). A few spices, such as cardamom, are so volatile that only last-minute grinding is optimum (see box, page 261). Keep decorticated cardamom seeds on hand and grind just as needed. "You'll save money by not having to throw out stale spice," says Wilder. "Cardamom is famous for losing its flavor even a couple of weeks after grinding."

GRILLED GAZPACHO SALAD WITH SHRIMP

Chicago Dame Elizabeth Karmel is a nationally recognized expert on grilling and creator of Girls at the Grill, a company that encompasses her teaching, consulting, and writing, as well as her line of grilling and kitchen tools called Grill Friends.

This salad is adapted from her book *Taming the Flame: Secrets for Hot-and-Quick Grilling and Low-and-Slow BBQ*; it has become her own summertime staple, made when tomatoes are at their bursting best. Do not be discouraged by the recipe length. Proceeding one step at a time gives you a dazzling big bowl of juicy grilled vegetables, spiked with precisely the right amount of bread and shrimp. By leaving the root ends attached to the onion crescents, the pieces won't fall through the grill. If you decide to double the recipe, add a red bell pepper as the second to the yellow one for even more color and flavor.

Prepare Ahead

This dish is best if made a day ahead of serving.

8 servings

1 head (about 12 cloves) garlic, separated into cloves and peeled

4 tablespoons plus 1 teaspoon olive oil, divided

1 teaspoon kosher salt, divided, plus additional as needed

4 large, firm heirloom or Roma tomatoes, stemmed and cut in half lengthwise

1 yellow bell pepper, cored, seeded, and cut in half horizontally

1 small English cucumber, peeled and halved lengthwise

1 small sweet onion, such as Vidalia, peeled and cut into ½-inch crescents with root ends attached (see box, page 52)

1 bunch green onions, left whole except for root ends, any wilted parts removed

12 (16–20 count) fresh shrimp in the shell

One 1-inch slice (about 4 by 6 inches) rustic-style bread

2 tablespoons red wine vinegar

½ pint grape or cherry tomatoes, sliced in half lengthwise

3 tablespoons fresh basil leaves plus additional for garnish, cut in chiffonade (see box, opposite)

Tabasco

Freshly ground black pepper

Hollowed-out yellow or orange bell peppers *or* small *boules* of hollowed-out and lightly toasted sourdough bread as serving containers (optional)

Limes for squeezing

Prepare a charcoal fire or preheat a gas grill on high. Reserve 1 large clove of garlic and toss the rest in 1 teaspoon of the oil to coat. Place the cloves on 2 layers of heavy-duty foil and season with ½ teaspoon of the salt. Seal the foil packet and put it on the grill over indirect medium-high heat until the garlic is soft and golden, about 45 minutes. Remove from the grill and reduce heat to medium.

In 3 separate bowls, place the tomatoes, bell pepper, cucumber, onion, and green onions; the shrimp; and the bread. With 2 tablespoons of the olive oil, evenly coat the contents of each bowl with a thin layer. Season the vegetables with the remaining salt, tossing them gently. Place all the vegetables except the heirloom tomatoes directly on the cooking grate over medium heat. Grill until the vegetables are marked and crisp-tender, 10 to 15 minutes, turning once halfway through cooking. When they are done, transfer the vegetables from the grill to a bowl to collect the juices.

Next, clean the cooking grate if necessary with a brass-bristle brush, oil the grate, and place the heirloom tomatoes skin side down on the cooking grate. If there is enough room, place the shrimp and bread on the cooking grate as well. Grill about 5 minutes total, turning once halfway through (the shrimp are done when the shells are a rosy coral color; the bread should be lightly toasted with grill marks, but not burned). Remove the tomatoes from the grill and add to the bowl of vegetables. Place the shrimp and the grilled bread in 2 separate containers.

Immediately rub the grilled bread on both sides with the reserved garlic clove. Discard the garlic clove and reserve the bread.

❀ Coarsely chop the vegetables into 1-inch pieces and place in a large bowl. Add the roasted garlic. Whisk the remaining olive oil and vinegar together in a small bowl. Add this dressing and the cherry tomatoes to the vegetables and toss to combine. Sprinkle the basil over the dressed vegetables and toss to combine. Taste and adjust seasoning with Tabasco, salt, and pepper. The salad can be prepared a day ahead up to this point. Store it, the bread, and the shrimp covered and refrigerated.

❀ About 2 hours before serving, bring the salad to room temperature. Cut or tear the bread into bite-size croutons and toss with the vegetables (the bread will help absorb some of the juices from the vegetables and keep the salad from getting too soupy.) Finally, shortly before serving, peel and cut the shrimp in halves or thirds—you want them to be large chunks—and gently fold into the salad. Taste for seasoning and adjust as necessary; the salad should be highly seasoned. Serve at room temperature in hollowed-out peppers or sourdough *boules*. Alternatively, serve chilled in glass beakers, martini glasses, or simply on salad plates. Top each serving with a squeeze of lime juice and basil just before eating.

Suggested Beverage

An Australian Riesling or an Austrian Grüner Veltliner.

How to Cut in Chiffonade

Chiffonade means to cut leaves into thin strips. The cut can be applied to any fresh greens, from lettuce to kale to sage leaves, but it is most commonly called for when using fresh herb leaves. When cutting a chiffonade from a head of greens such as iceberg lettuce or cabbage, cut thin slices crosswise through the head. For leaves such as spinach or basil, make a stack of up to a dozen washed and dried leaves (largest on the bottom, smallest on top). Fold the stack in half along the center vein and cut crosswise every ⅛ to ¼ inch. You'll end up with a fluffy pile of green strips ready to add texture and color to any dish.

LITTLE MOLDS OF ROASTED PEPPERS WITH ANCHOVY SAUCE

Prepare Ahead

Prep the ingredients a day ahead. Assemble the 8 molds hours ahead. Bake immediately before serving.

Chicago Dame Nancy Brussat Barocci has booked a lot of time in Italy, researching products for her Convito Café & Market, which has won numerous awards, including the *Chicago Tribune*'s "Best Take-Out" and "Best Italian Wine Shop." This first-course dish combines two Italian classics: roasted red peppers and a raw vegetable dip called *bagna cauda* ("hot bath"). In addition to being a handsome first course, these little molds make an excellent side dish to grilled Italian sausages and Barocci's own Tuscan Beans and Potatoes (page 234).

8 servings

2 pounds red bell peppers

2 pounds yellow bell peppers

Eight ½-inch crosswise slices French baguette or Italian bread

¼ cup olive oil plus additional for serving, divided

One 14.5-ounce can Italian plum tomatoes, drained and roughly chopped

4 fresh basil leaves, coarsely chopped

½ teaspoon salt

Freshly ground black pepper

6 tablespoons unsalted butter

3 cloves garlic, finely minced

6 anchovy fillets, rinsed, patted dry, and finely chopped

2 tablespoons capers, drained and rinsed

1 tablespoon finely chopped parsley

Preheat the broiler. Place the peppers on a broiler pan. Broil the peppers 2 to 3 inches from the heat. Turn the peppers with tongs until they are completely blackened on all sides. Using tongs, transfer the peppers to a plastic bag and seal it well. Preheat the oven to 350°F for bread toasting. Let the peppers steam in the bag for approximately 20 minutes, then remove them and peel off the skin. Cut the peppers in half and remove the stems, seeds, and membranes. Cut lengthwise into strips ½ inch wide. Reserve.

Suggested Beverage

A Chianti or an Italian Prosecco.

❋ Arrange the baguette slices on a baking sheet. Toast the bread until the slices begin to turn light brown, about 5 minutes. Turn the slices over and briefly toast the other side, about 3 minutes. Remove from the oven and reserve.

❋ Heat 2 tablespoons of the oil in a small saucepan over medium-high heat. Add the tomatoes, basil, salt, and pepper. Simmer over medium-low heat for about 20 minutes. Put through a food mill or purée in a blender or food processor. Reserve.

❋ In a small saucepan over low heat, melt the butter with the remaining olive oil. Add the garlic and sauté for 1 minute. Remove the pan from the heat and add the anchovies. Stir well with a wooden spoon. Return the pan to low heat and continue cooking, stirring until the anchovies have dissolved into a paste, 1 to 2 minutes.

❋ To make the molds, preheat the oven to 350°F. Set out 8 small (6-ounce) ramekins. Place 1 toasted bread slice in the center of each. Spread 1 tablespoon of the tomato sauce on each of the slices. Cover with the pepper strips, alternating red and yellow, ending by wrapping the strips around the outside of the slice. Cover each with another tablespoon of the tomato sauce. Top this with 1 tablespoon of the anchovy mixture. Sprinkle each with capers. Bake until heated through, about 20 minutes. Remove from the oven and run the tip of a paring knife around the edge of each ramekin to loosen. Unmold the ramekins onto 8 plates. Top with the parsley, drizzle with a bit of olive oil, and serve immediately.

PROSCIUTTO AND MELON IN SAMBUCA

San Francisco Dame Judy Rodgers, the chef and co-owner of the city's legendary Zuni Café, does wonders with cured meats, as in this unusual twist included in her 2002 book, *The Zuni Café Cookbook*.

4 servings

1½ to 2 pounds ripe orange-fleshed melon, such as cantaloupe

A few pinches anise seeds

1 teaspoon Sambuca

4 to 6 ounces thinly sliced prosciutto di Parma

Halve and seed the melon. Cut into 1-inch wedges, then carve away rind deeply enough to remove any rindy-tasting, hard flesh, in a continuous, smooth stroke to produce elegant crescents. Place in a wide bowl.

Suggested Beverage

An Italian Prosecco or a young Valpolicella for a simple red.

Slightly crush the anise seeds and sprinkle over the melon. Drizzle a little Sambuca over all and fold gently to distribute without bruising the melon. Leave to macerate for about 10 minutes in a cool place or refrigerate.

To serve, turn the melon slices over on themselves, then slide onto plates or a platter. Cut the prosciutto into wide ribbons and drape them over the melon.

Begin a Meal with Cured Meats

Combining thinly sliced cured or smoked meats with a few choice ingredients is a classic way to begin a meal, especially when the entrée is poultry or seafood. Increasingly, there is a wide selection of high-quality cured meats at grocers and delis where you can purchase the meats thinly sliced to order. Be sure that the slices are separated by waxed paper so they do not all stick together and that they are well wrapped. Because the meats are ready to serve, they provide an easy first course option, best if served the same day as sliced. Store meats refrigerated, but bring to room temperature to serve. In addition to cured prosciutto, choose among such meats as *speck* (a lightly smoked and cured ham from Italy and Austria), *braesaola* (an air-dried beef fillet from Italy and Switzerland), *jamon serrano* (a Spanish dry-cured ham), and a whole array of salamis.

Here are some not-so-common combinations:

* Thinly sliced salami with slices of avocado, dressed with a vinaigrette

* Thinly sliced *jamon serrano* with slices of ripe persimmon and wedges of lemon

* Thinly sliced *speck* with paper-thin slices of English cucumber and a dab of horseradish

* Thinly sliced *braesaola* with paper-thin slices of cremini mushrooms, shaved Parmesan cheese, freshly ground black pepper—all drizzled with extra-virgin olive oil and lemon juice

* Or try Prosciutto-Wrapped Stuffed Pear Quarters from Seattle Dame Dorene Centioli-McTigue: Take a ripe pear, peeled, quartered, and cored. Dollop a tablespoon of mascarpone into each quarter and wrap with a thin slice of prosciutto. Cook in a preheated 450°F oven until the prosciutto is crisp. Drizzle with olive oil, top with freshly ground black pepper, and serve on little beds of arugula.

—Chicago Dame Nancy Brussat Barocci

❧ THREE-SISTERS SALAD ❧

Prepare Ahead

The bean and corn mixture can be made hours ahead. Add the mint close to serving time. The squash can be sautéed ahead as well and reheated right before plating.

British Columbia Dame Carole Dulude is an authority on the food of indigenous peoples. To her, our current efforts for sustainable agriculture are based on centuries-old practices. She points to this first-course salad as an example of food that is as healthy for the planet as it is for people. As she explains, "Centuries ago, agriculture provided 75 percent of the Iroquoian year-round diet, which consisted of three staple foods: corn, beans, and squash. They were known as *deohako* or 'life supporters'—the 'three sisters.'" If you don't want to take the time to prepare the squash, make a *two*-sisters salad with just the beans and corn mixed with the mint and seeds: an extremely tasty combination in itself (see box, page 236). The *three*-sisters version also makes an excellent vegetarian entrée or a vegetable side dish.

4 servings

- **⅔ cup shelled raw pumpkin seeds, salted or unsalted, divided**
- **1 pound butternut squash (ideally choose squash that will yield 2½- to 3-inch-diameter slices)**
- **1½ tablespoons sunflower, corn, or canola oil plus additional as needed**
- **½ teaspoon salt plus additional as needed**
- **4 ears fresh corn, shucked**
- **One 15-ounce can red kidney beans, rinsed and thoroughly drained**
- **Freshly ground black pepper**
- **½ cup mint leaves plus additional for garnish, cut in chiffonade (see box, page 59)**

❧ Preheat the oven to 350°F. Spread the pumpkin seeds on a baking sheet. Toast in the oven for 10 minutes. Transfer to a small bowl; reserve.

❧ Peel and cut the squash into 12 slices, ¼ inch thick. Remove any seeds and stringy fiber. Heat a small amount of the oil in a large sauté pan over medium-high heat. Sear the squash slices until they are a light golden color on both sides and fork tender, about 5 minutes on each side (regulating heat so they do not burn). As each slice is done cooking, remove to a baking sheet lined with paper towels. Repeat the sauté process (add oil as necessary) until all the slices are cooked. Remove the paper towels. Season the slices with the salt. Cover loosely with foil.

Suggested Beverage

A Macon-Villages Chardonnay or an Oregon Pinot Gris.

✳ With a sharp knife, cut the corn kernels off the cobs and into a large microwavable container (see box, page 71). Cover with a paper towel and microwave the corn at high power for 3 minutes. Remove from the microwave and fold in the beans and half of the pumpkin seeds. Alternatively, steam the corn in a covered sauté pan with 1 cup of water over medium heat for about 3 minutes; drain and proceed with recipe. Add 1½ tablespoons of the oil and toss to coat. Season with salt and pepper.

✳ When ready to serve, reheat the squash slices. Arrange the slices in a cloverleaf shape on 4 plates. Reheat the corn and bean mixture for 30 seconds on high in the microwave or on the stovetop until heated through. Remove from the microwave and fold in the mint. Mound the corn and bean mixture in the center of each cloverleaf. Sprinkle each with the remaining pumpkin seeds and mint. Serve immediately.

Get Some Classic White Porcelains

When asked about preferred ways of presenting food, Seattle Dame Gretchen Mathers, who made a career of marketing her own exuberant good taste, was adamant: "There's absolutely nothing better than plain white porcelain platters, bowls, plates, and baking dishes for displaying foods." When she first started her restaurant and catering company—Gretchen's Of Course—in the 1970s, such pieces were not yet easily available. "I was always on the lookout for sales. I'd haul the dishes back to Seattle from Bridge's in New York and Crate and Barrel in Chicago—there was only the one location in those days. You still can't beat them for timeless value. They make food look great. They rarely chip. They'll last a lifetime." Mathers, who pioneered high-style catering in Seattle whether designing parties or box lunches, added, "Those white dishes let my curried chicken salad and my mini-Reubens speak for themselves just like food should." *Gretchen, an icon in the realm of female hospitality entrepreneurs, passed away in August 2007.*

⁂ OASIS SALAD ⁂

Prepare Ahead

Patties can be formed
a day ahead. Fry them
early in the day and
reheat them briefly
in the oven right
before serving. Dress-
ing can be made
several days ahead.

Try these lively flavors for the start of a warm-weather meal. Or make entrée-size portions for a summer lunch. The lynchpin is the combination of ground turkey and chopped dates that Palm Springs caterer Dame Gail Nottberg originally conceived as a filling for empanadas for the 2007 Riverside County Fair and Date Festival. Here the filling is formed into little patties, sautéed, and served with ripe avocado and greens tossed with a lightly curried vinaigrette. Nottberg has been a chef at San Diego's legendary Hotel Del Coronado, as well as food-service manager at a small-town baseball stadium. Her empanadas can be made by cutting 3-inch rounds of puff pastry, filling them with a heaping teaspoon of the patty mixture, and sealing with an egg wash. Bake at 400°F until golden brown, about 20 minutes.

6 servings

Patties

   1 large egg

   1 large clove garlic, roasted and minced

   ⅔ teaspoon curry powder

   ⅓ teaspoon ground cinnamon

   ¼ teaspoon ground ginger

   ½ teaspoon salt

   10 grinds black pepper

   ⅓ pound ground turkey breast

   8 pitted dates, finely chopped

   ⅓ cup finely sliced green onions, both green and white parts

   Olive oil for frying

Curried Greens

   ⅓ cup vegetable oil

   2 tablespoons seasoned rice vinegar

⅛ teaspoon curry powder

1 small clove garlic, pressed through a garlic press or very finely minced

¼ teaspoon salt

4 grinds black pepper

4 cups mixed baby greens

Mashed Avocado

2 ripe avocados, pitted and peeled

Freshly squeezed lemon juice

※ To make the patties, whisk the egg together with the garlic, curry powder, cinnamon, ginger, salt, and pepper in a medium bowl. Add the turkey, dates, and green onions; mix to combine. Form into 6 patties, about 2 inches wide and 1 inch thick. Heat a small amount of olive oil in a large, nonstick sauté pan over medium-high heat. Add the patties and brown on both sides, regulating the heat so they do not burn. Remove the patties to an ovenproof dish. If not using right away, cool, cover, and refrigerate.

※ To make the dressing for the curried greens, whisk together the vegetable oil, vinegar, curry powder, garlic, salt, and pepper.

※ To serve, preheat the oven to 400°F. Ten minutes before serving, place the patties uncovered in the oven until they are sizzling hot, about 10 minutes. Meanwhile, toss the greens with a small amount (about 2 tablespoons) of the dressing. Mash the avocados with the lemon juice, salt, and pepper. Distribute the patties among 6 plates, along with the dressed greens and mashed avocado. Drizzle a bit of the extra dressing over the patties (remaining dressing can be used for other salads). Serve immediately.

Suggested Beverage

A sparkling wine or a dry Gewürztraminer or an Alsatian Pinot Blanc.

BASIC GREENS WITH AN IN-YOUR-FACE DRESSING

Prepare Ahead

Good news—the dressing keeps in the refrigerator for up to a week. In fact, it should be refrigerated for about 4 hours before using to allow time for the flavors to meld.

Sometimes greens, fresh from the garden or a farmers' market and scantily dressed with a favorite dressing, is the best of all ways to start a meal or follow a main course. Often that dressing is as simple as good oil and vinegar, deftly mixed and seasoned with sea salt and pepper. Occasionally, however, the dressing might make a bolder statement like this one, which San Antonio Dame Terry Thompson-Anderson calls her "house dressing."

Thompson-Anderson has worked as a professional chef and food writer for over twenty-five years. You'll find her "house dressing" so bold and good, you'll also want to use it as a sandwich spread, an appetizer dip, or a sauce for just about any meat or seafood you care to serve. This is a thick dressing; it takes only a small portion to dress a salad for four.

1½ cups dressing

- 2 cups lightly packed cilantro sprigs, both leaves and stems
- 1 cup Hellmann's or Best Foods prepared mayonnaise
- 4 large cloves garlic, coarsely chopped
- 1 or 2 limes, zested for ¾ teaspoon grated zest (see box, page 75) and squeezed for 1 tablespoon juice
- 1 large jalapeño chile pepper, seeds and veins removed, coarsely chopped
- 2 tablespoons white wine vinegar
- 1 teaspoon real maple syrup
- ¼ teaspoon salt
- 10 to 12 cups salad greens

✳ Combine the cilantro, mayonnaise, garlic, lime zest and juice, jalapeño, vinegar, maple syrup, and salt in the bowl of a food processor fitted with a steel blade. Process until smooth. Refrigerate, covered, for at least 4 hours. When ready to serve, toss just enough of the dressing (start with ¼ cup) with the greens to coat them lightly. Serve immediately.

Suggested Beverage

An Austrian Grüner Veltliner to match the "green" profile of the dressing.

The Uncomplicated Green Salad

When you want to dress fresh greens simply, the dressing used in the Breakfast-for-Dinner Salad (page 172) is both spirited and well balanced. The vinaigrette can easily be doubled and keeps well refrigerated for a week. Tip for the perfect green salad: do not overdress. For 6 cups of well-dried greens (a big salad for two), you'll probably need no more than 3 tablespoons of dressing. Use a large bowl, and with clean hands (better than any salad servers) gently but thoroughly toss the greens until they are evenly coated—no pool of dressing in the bottom of the bowl. The salad is now ready to serve.

SWEET CORN, CHANTERELLE, AND ARUGULA SALAD

Prepare Ahead

Prepare corn and chanterelles hours ahead. Reheat at the last minute to serve.

This salad from New York Dame Florence Fabricant is the essence of what is meant by cooking seasonally. *The New York Times* food columnist makes it only when the recipe's three main ingredients coincide in the market—usually late summer or early fall—and she adores the way sweet corn and fresh chanterelles complement each other against the pleasant bitterness of arugula. In fact, she advises, if you can find the even more peppery "wild" arugula (*Arugula selvatica*), with its spiky little leaves, by all means use it. That said, the salad is so appealing that once there's fresh peak-season corn in the market, you may want to compose the salad with more commonly available mushrooms, such as cremini or shiitake. The quality of the sherry vinegar will make a difference in this dish, so use the best you can find.

8 servings

6 ears corn, shucked

½ pound chanterelle mushrooms (small preferred)

8 tablespoons extra-virgin olive oil, divided

1½ cups thinly sliced red onion

Up to 4 tablespoons high-quality sherry vinegar, divided

Salt and freshly ground black pepper

6 cups (about 2 bunches) arugula, washed and dried, stems removed

1½ ounces Parmigiano-Reggiano cheese, in thin shavings (use a sharp potato peeler)

Cut the corn kernels off the cobs (see box, opposite) and set aside. Wipe any dirt from the chanterelles with a damp paper towel. Using a paring knife, trim a bit off the bottoms of the stems and scrape the outer skin from the stems, revealing the white underneath. Cut any large mushrooms into halves or quarters.

✳ Heat 6 tablespoons of the oil in a large, heavy skillet. Add the onion and sauté over medium heat until wilted. Stir in the mushrooms, increase heat to medium-high, and cook the mushrooms until softened and moist-looking. Stir in the corn and 2 tablespoons of the vinegar and simmer the mixture for just a minute or two. Taste and add up to another tablespoon of vinegar if you wish. Season to taste with salt and pepper. Remove from heat and reserve.

✳ To serve, toss the arugula in a large bowl with the remaining vinegar and oil to taste (use the vinegar—no more than 1 tablespoon—and oil sparingly to just barely coat the greens). Arrange on each of 8 plates. Briefly reheat the corn mixture and spoon over the arugula. Scatter cheese shavings over each portion. Serve immediately.

Suggested Beverage

A low- to no-oak Chardonnay.

Cutting Corn off the Cob

Certainly one of summer's luxuries is fresh corn kernels cut off the cob. The trick to shearing off the kernels is to place one end of the cob in a deep mixing bowl slightly taller than the ear and wide enough for you to reach around the ear with a very sharp paring knife to cut off the kernels. This way, you capture all the juices (milk) from the corn and prevent them from splattering about the kitchen. Once the corn kernels are off the cob, heat it briefly in a bit of olive oil or butter and season to taste with salt and pepper. Now it's ready to serve.

SPRINGTIME FRESH MOZZARELLA SALAD

Prepare Ahead

All the vegetables can be prepared hours ahead of serving. Cover with a couple of layers of damp paper towels and leave at room temperature. Cheese can be sliced an hour before serving and left at room temperature, covered with plastic wrap.

After a career as an art teacher, San Francisco Dame Joanne Weir studied with and received a Master Diploma from Grande Dame Madeleine Kamman. She then spent five years working in the kitchen with Grande Dame Alice Waters at Chez Panisse in Berkeley before going off on her own—writing award-winning cookbooks, spending seven months each year teaching cooking overseas and the rest of her time at her San Francisco cooking school, which is also the site of her PBS television series, *Joanne Weir's Cooking Class*. Weir is known for her creative spins on classic dishes, like this springtime version of the much-loved summer salad of tomatoes and fresh basil layered with mozzarella cheese. Here fresh spring produce is scattered about a bed of fresh mozzarella and drizzled with extra-virgin olive oil. (This is an ideal time to show off a condiment-quality extra-virgin olive oil. Choose one with a delicate flavor that won't overwhelm the vegetables and cheese.) An even more glorious variation substitutes the very creamy fresh *burrata* cheese for some or all of the mozzarella.

You can serve the combination on individual salad plates, but the presentation of green spring bounty on a large white platter is also very appealing. Everyone loves spooning up their own serving when the dish looks this beautiful.

6 servings

1½ pounds fresh fava beans in the pod

2 teaspoons salt plus additional as needed

½ pound asparagus, ends snapped, stalks cut diagonally into 2-inch lengths

½ pound fresh English peas, shelled (about 1 cup)

12 ounces mozzarella di bufala, fresh-milk mozzarella, or fresh *burrata*, *or* a combination of both fresh mozzarella and burrata

1 tablespoon chopped mint leaves

2 teaspoons chopped fresh savory (optional)

2 teaspoons chopped fresh oregano

¼ cup extra-virgin olive oil

Freshly ground black pepper

2 cups mâche or other young, tender greens such as frisée *or* mixed baby greens

Suggested Beverage
High-acid Champagne, Sauvignon Blanc, or Pinot Grigio to tame the asparagus.

❉ Peel the outer pod off the fava beans and discard (see box, page 39). Bring a pot of water to a boil, add the fava beans, and boil just 30 seconds once the water returns to the boil. Drain and cool the beans immediately under very cold running water. Peel the beans, discarding their skins. You should have about 1¾ cups.

❉ Bring 2 cups water to a boil in a saucepan. Add the salt and asparagus and boil until the asparagus is bright green and almost tender, 3 to 5 minutes. Remove with a slotted spoon and cool under very cold running water. Add the asparagus to the fava beans. Add the peas to the boiling water and simmer just 30 seconds. Drain, cool under cold water, and add to the asparagus and fava beans.

❉ Cut the cheese into thin slices and place on a platter or distribute among 6 individual plates. Sprinkle the vegetables, mint, savory, and oregano around the cheese. Drizzle with the oil and season with salt and pepper. Sprinkle the mâche on top. Serve immediately.

SUMMER SALAD OF WATERMELON, FETA CHEESE, AND MINT

Prepare Ahead

Prepare all the ingredients and assemble all but the toppings a few hours ahead of serving.

Dallas Dame Paula Lambert helped launch a revolution: the rise over the last quarter of a century of the artisanal cheese-making business in the United States. In the early 1980s, when she returned home after spending several years in Italy, what she missed most was fresh mozzarella cheese. So the indomitable Lambert opened a small cheese factory in Dallas and became a cheese maker. At first, the company made about a hundred pounds of fresh mozzarella a week, selling most of its production to local restaurants and individuals who showed up at the factory door. Today her Mozzarella Company makes nearly five thousand pounds of specialty cheeses a week and sells them coast to coast and internationally. Lambert has published two cookbooks, *The Cheese Lover's Cookbook and Guide* and *Cheese, Glorious Cheese*. Here Lambert shares a dish just right for warm-weather dining.

6 servings

4 cups watermelon, cut off the rind and into 1-inch pieces, seeded

4 green onions, cut crosswise into very thin slices, both green and white parts

2 tablespoons minced chives

½ teaspoon grated lemon zest (see box, opposite)

8 large mint leaves, cut in chiffonade (see box, page 59), divided

2 tablespoons extra-virgin olive oil plus additional for serving

1 tablespoon freshly squeezed lemon juice

Salt and freshly ground black pepper

1 cup (4 ounces) feta cheese, crumbled, divided

In a large bowl, combine the watermelon, green onions, chives, lemon zest, and half of the mint leaves. Pour the oil and lemon juice over and toss well. Season with salt and pepper, and toss again. Distribute ¾ cup of the cheese over the salad. Toss very gently to distribute. Refrigerate until serving time. To serve, portion among 6 plates and top with the remaining cheese and mint. Drizzle very lightly with oil and serve immediately.

Suggested Beverage

A sparkling Moscato d'Asti or a slightly chilled Beaujolais.

The Indispensable Microplane Grater and Zester

Modeled after a carpenter's rasp, the Microplane zester and grater with its razor-sharp edges (formed by photo-etching) effortlessly produces very fine zest with no pith (the bitter white layer under the zest). It's become the preferred tool over the traditional zester, which produces a much coarser zest. Use the microplane also for grating fresh nutmeg, ginger, chocolate, coconut, garlic cloves, and hard cheeses.

WINTER SALAD OF ORANGES AND POMEGRANATE

Prepare Ahead

Combine fruit and refrigerate for no less than 30 minutes or up to several hours ahead of serving.

The foods of the Silk Road—the ancient network of trade routes that stretched from China to the Mediterranean with Persia at its center, looking both east and west—are the specialty of Washington, D.C., Dame Najmieh Batmanglij. With five published cookbooks to her credit, she has become acclaimed not only for her ethnic menus but also for, as *The New York Times* put it, writing cookbooks that read "like a good novel."

This recipe, adapted from her most recent book, *Silk Road Cooking: A Vegetarian Journey*, takes advantage of peak winter oranges and pomegranate seeds (the jewels of tasty flesh that encapsulate the seeds are called *arils*) by pairing their sweet and tart tastes with a slightly pungent cheese. The dish can be served as a light dessert as well as a first course. Orange blossom water (sometimes called "orange flower water") can be found at specialty food stores and Middle Eastern grocers. The "water" is the liquid distilled during the extraction of essential oil from orange blossoms and is a principal flavoring extract in the Middle East.

4 servings

How to Section an Orange

Pastry chef and Honolulu Dame Elisabeth Iwata offers this efficient method of cutting individual sections of oranges (also called "supremes") with no trace of the bitter white pith. Using a very sharp chef's knife, trim off the ends of the orange. (A flexible cutting board is ideal; by gathering up the ends of the board, you can easily collect any juices and pour them into a bowl.) Stand the orange on one end and cut off the skin and membrane in vertical sections, following the curve of the orange. This exposes the meat of the orange. Next, hold the orange in one hand over a small bowl and, again using a very sharp knife (a smaller one than used for peeling), slice the membrane away from the sides of each orange segment. Catch the juice in the bowl (it will likely be used in any recipe calling for the segments) and lay the segments aside in a separate bowl as you remove them from the membrane.

---

1 cup (about 1 large pomegranate) pomegranate seeds *or* 1 cup pitted and sliced Medjool dates

6 large oranges, peeled and cut into sections, membrane removed (see box, opposite)

¼ cup finely chopped candied orange peel (store-bought or home-made—see box below), if using pomegranate seeds *or* 1 teaspoon finely chopped orange zest (no pith), if using dates

½ cup freshly squeezed orange juice

1 tablespoon freshly squeezed lime juice

1 teaspoon orange blossom water

8 ounces sheep's milk cheese, such as Pecorino Romano, *or* aged goat cheese, cut into shavings with a potato peeler

⅓ cup chopped pistachios

Pistachio oil or light-bodied extra-virgin olive oil

Suggested Beverage

A Brachetto d'Acqui from Piedmont if using the pomegranate; if using the Medjool dates, a more earthy Italian Sangiovese or a Spanish Tempranillo.

❈ In a bowl, combine the pomegranate seeds, orange segments, candied orange peel, orange juice, lime juice, and orange blossom water. Cover and chill in the refrigerator for at least 30 minutes. To serve, distribute the fruit mixture among 4 plates. Alongside the fruit, place a portion of cheese and top with the chopped pistachios and a light drizzle of oil. Serve immediately.

How to Make Your Own Candied Orange Peel

Combine 1 cup of ½-inch-wide strips of orange peel (trimmed of all white pith) with 1 cup of water and 1 cup of sugar. Bring to a boil in a small saucepan. Reduce heat to medium and simmer uncovered for 20 minutes or until the water has evaporated. Watch carefully and remove the pan from the heat the minute the liquid is gone. Spread on parchment paper to dry. Transfer to an airtight container and store in the refrigerator for up to 3 months.

SOUPS

For a First Course or for a Meal   Here are soups that tell stories—of faraway lands, of the Western frontier, of backyard gardens, and of summers by the shore. There are everyday soups for family gatherings (encouraging a child's involvement), and there are special soups for celebratory occasions; soups that capture bumper crops at harvest time, others that invite us to sample disparaged vegetables like parsnips or less familiar ones like chayote squash. You'll find an urging toward family dining, too: children tend to be better nourished when they eat with their parents and siblings. Our organization is named for Auguste Escoffier, king of chefs and chef to kings. Surely he would share our preoccupation with mealtimes well spent together at the table.

Recipes

Greek Yellow Split-Pea Soup with Red Onion and Lemon
Joyce Goldstein, San Francisco Chapter

Cream of Chayote Soup
Barbara Pool Fenzl, Phoenix Chapter

Vidalia Onion Soup with Bacon Flans
Virginia Willis, Atlanta Chapter

Fresh Tomato Soup with Roasted-Corn Guacamole
Lourdes Castro, Miami Chapter

Chilled Cucumber-Buttermilk Soup
Katherine Newell Smith, Washington, D.C., Chapter

Winter Minestrone with Butternut Squash and Kale
Abby Mandel, Chicago Chapter

Creamy Roasted Parsnip Soup with Chèvre and Walnut Crostini
Kathy Casey, Seattle Chapter

Bowl of the Wife of Kit Carson
Holly Arnold Kinney, Colorado Chapter

Sweet Pepper, Tomato, and Leek Soup
Roberta Duyff, Kansas City Chapter

Piedmontese Wedding Soup
Jerry Anne Di Vecchio, San Francisco Chapter

Cotuit Bay Oyster Bisque
Joan Reardon, Chicago Chapter

Notes

About Sweet Onions, and How to Clean Leeks

Parmigiano-Reggiano Rinds

Making Low-Fat Soups

Blender, Food Processor, or Immersion Blender?

Pantry Spirits

Green Tables

The Family Table

GREEK YELLOW SPLIT-PEA SOUP WITH RED ONION AND LEMON

San Francisco Dame Joyce Goldstein first tasted the dish that inspired this soup in a small taverna on the Greek island of Santorini. Her Greek hosts called it a purée of fava beans. It was spread on individual plates, topped with a small pool of extra-virgin olive oil, minced red onion, and freshly ground black pepper. It was served with wedges of fresh lemon and hot bread. As purées are often a hard sell, she turned the dish into a soup, drizzled with the same olive oil and several garnishes. While shopping for the beans on the Island, she discovered that the dish could be made with common yellow split peas.

This seemingly simple, yet memorable soup is typical of the kind of Mediterranean fare that has marked Goldstein's prolific career in food, including the writing of many award-winning cookbooks. For twelve years she was chef and owner of the groundbreaking San Francisco restaurant Square One, where she earned the James Beard Award for Best Chef in California.

Prepare Ahead

The soup can be prepared several days before serving. It will thicken as it stands, so be prepared to thin it with additional hot broth (probably quite a lot) at serving time.

12 cups

2 teaspoons ground cumin*

6 tablespoons extra-virgin olive oil, divided

2 cups coarsely diced onion

One 16-ounce bag (2¼ cups) yellow split peas, sorted for debris
  and rinsed

6 cups chicken or vegetable broth (more as needed)

1 to 2 lemons, zested for 1 teaspoon grated zest (see box, page 75)
  and squeezed for 2 tablespoons juice

¾ teaspoon salt plus additional as needed

2 teaspoons freshly ground black pepper plus additional as needed

3 tablespoons finely chopped red onion

⁂ Start by toasting the cumin to give it a richer, rounder flavor. Place a small skillet over moderate heat and when hot, add the cumin. Stir about a minute or until the spice gives off a roasty aroma. Immediately remove from heat and reserve.

⁂ Warm 3 tablespoons of the oil in a large, heavy saucepan over medium heat. Add the onion and cook until tender and translucent, about 8 minutes. Add the cumin and stir for a few minutes. Add the split peas and broth and simmer, stirring occasionally, until the peas are falling apart, about an hour. Purée the pea mixture in a blender or food processor, or use an immersion blender (see box, page 101). Thin it with water or broth if it is too thick. Season with the lemon zest and juice, salt, and pepper.

⁂ To serve, ladle into bowls. Top with the red onion, pepper, and oil.

Better yet, toast 1 tablespoon of whole cumin seeds as described, then grind finely in a spice grinder.

⁂ CREAM OF CHAYOTE SOUP ⁂

Prepare Ahead

The soup can be prepared a couple of days ahead of serving and reheated. The recipe is easily doubled and the soup freezes well.

Phoenix Dame Barbara Pool Fenzl is an expert on the cuisine of the Southwest. She's hosted the PBS series *Savor the Southwest* and published three cookbooks on Southwestern cooking. So when she was collaborating on a dinner with her mentor, Grande Dame Julia Child, in 1997, and Julia wanted to know about the "vegetable pear" she was getting ready to prepare, Fenzl was ready with an answer: it's a chayote squash, commonly used in Mexican, Southwest, and Southern dishes. It's available throughout North America, mostly in winter; its skin must be removed because it causes indigestion; and it has a delicate flavor that showcases the ingredients with which it is combined. Fenzl then proceeded to turn out a sautéed chayote dish (from her first cookbook,

Southwest the Beautiful) that Child, then 83, rated "one of the best dishes of the evening."

Here Fenzl combines the chayote with a bit of chile heat, the tangy green flavor of cilantro, and the richness of a touch of heavy cream. Make this soup with vegetable broth, and it's quintessential vegetarian fare. Serve the soup with cornmeal muffins.

Suggested Beverage

A crisp Pinot Blanc or spicy Pinot Gris.

7 cups

1 tablespoon unsalted butter

½ cup diced onion

1 tablespoon finely chopped garlic

1 serrano chile pepper, seeded and finely chopped

1½ pounds chayote, peeled, cored, and cut into ½-inch dice

1 teaspoon salt plus additional as needed

10 grinds black pepper plus additional as needed

2 cups vegetable or chicken broth (more to thin if desired)

½ cup chopped cilantro leaves, divided

1 cup heavy cream, divided

❋ Heat the butter in a medium saucepan over medium heat; add the onion, garlic, and serrano pepper. Cook until softened, about 5 minutes. Add the chayote, salt, and pepper, and continue to cook, stirring, another 2 to 3 minutes. Add the broth and bring to a boil. Lower heat, cover, and cook until the squash is tender, about 20 minutes. Cool slightly and put the mixture into the bowl of a food processor fitted with a steel blade. Do not overfill. If necessary, purée the mixture in two batches, adding ¼ cup of the cilantro and processing until the mixture is smooth. Return the mixture to the saucepan and add ½ cup of the cream. Reheat the soup to a simmer and check for seasoning and thickness. If desired, add salt or pepper, or thin the soup with broth.

❋ To serve, ladle the soup into bowls. Drizzle the remaining cream over the top and sprinkle with the remaining cilantro. Serve immediately.

VIDALIA ONION SOUP
WITH BACON FLANS

Prepare Ahead

The soup can be made several days before serving, refrigerated, and reheated. Flans can be made hours ahead of serving. Refrigerate them to store and bring them back to room temperature before serving. Be certain that the soup is very hot when it is poured over the flans.

Here's a surprise of an onion soup. It's reminiscent of the classic French recipe, but this fragrant soup is poured over and around individual bacon-flavored flans. You might also use either the soup or the flans (accompanied by lightly dressed fresh greens) on their own as a first course.

The recipe comes from a Dame who knows a lot about the theatrics of meal preparation: Atlanta Dame Virginia Willis (see box, page 125). She makes the flans in clear glass half-pint or pint mason jars or recycled French yogurt jars, then pours the soup on top, to reveal the unusual layering. Alternatively, use individual 6-ounce porcelain ramekins and unmold the flans into wide soup bowls before pouring the hot soup over them.

8 cups

¼ cup (½ stick) unsalted butter

2 pounds Vidalia or other sweet onions, cut into ¼-inch crescents or half moons (see box, page 52)

2 leeks, cut into half-moon slices and washed well (see box, page 88)

1 shallot, finely chopped

1 teaspoon salt

½ teaspoon freshly ground black pepper

1 teaspoon sugar

1 tablespoon all-purpose flour

½ cup dry sherry

6 cups homemade beef stock or canned low-sodium beef broth

1 tablespoon chopped fresh thyme leaves plus additional for garnish

Bacon Flans (recipe follows)

To make the soup, melt the butter in a large, heavy pot over medium-low heat. Add the onions, leeks, shallot, salt, and pepper. Sprinkle with

Fresh Okra Cakes

page 10

Walnut-Fennel Tarts

page 14

Grilled Gazpacho Salad with Shrimp

page 57

Three-Sisters Salad

page 64

Cream of Chayote Soup

page 84

Winter Minestrone with Butternut Squash and Kale

page 92

Japanese Black Sea Bass with Julienned Carrots, Fennel, and Sweet Peppers

page 120

Italian-Style Braised Short Ribs with Rosemary Polenta

page 145

the sugar and cook, stirring just as needed to keep the vegetables from sticking, until they are soft, golden brown, and beginning to caramelize, 30 to 45 minutes.

✷ Sprinkle the flour over the vegetables and stir to coat. Add the sherry, stock, and thyme. Bring to a boil; reduce heat to a simmer and cook, partially covered, for about 30 minutes. Taste for seasoning and adjust as needed.

✷ When ready to serve, heat the soup to near boiling. Ladle the soup over the Bacon Flans, garnish with thyme leaves, and serve immediately.

Bacon Flans

8 flans

6 slices bacon, cut into ¼-inch pieces

¾ cup chopped shallots

3 large eggs, lightly beaten

1½ cups whole milk

½ teaspoon salt

¼ teaspoon freshly ground black pepper

Butter to coat eight 6-ounce 3½- by 1½-inch ramekins

✷ Heat the oven to 350°F. Heat a medium skillet over medium heat. Add the bacon and cook until crisp, 5 to 7 minutes. Remove the bacon with a slotted spoon to a plate lined with paper towels. Remove all but 1 tablespoon of the bacon fat from the skillet. Save the excess fat for another use or discard. Add the shallots to the reserved bacon fat and reduce heat to medium-low. Cook the shallots until translucent, about 3 minutes. Cool the bacon and shallots for about 15 minutes. Put the eggs in the jar of a blender or in the bowl of a food processor. Process the eggs briefly, then add the milk, bacon, and shallots. Purée until almost smooth (there will be bits of bacon remaining). Season the mixture with the salt and pepper.

Suggested Beverage

An earthy French Pinot Noir or Cru Beaujolais (a Parisian tradition).

If using ramekins, lightly butter them. (If using jars, you don't need to butter them since you will not be unmolding the flans.) Divide the flan mixture evenly among the ramekins so the mixture is about ½-inch deep. Cover each with tin foil and place in a shallow baking pan (you may need to use 2 pans to hold all the ramekins—see box, page 314). Place the pan on the oven rack. Pour hot water into the pan until it comes halfway up the sides of the ramekins. Close the oven door and cook until the flans are just set but still jiggly and slightly soft in the center, about 30 minutes. With tongs, remove the ramekins from the baking pan and place them on a rack to cool. Unmold the flans by loosening their edges with the blade of a thin metal spatula and inverting each of them directly into the center of each of 8 wide, shallow soup bowls. If not serving immediately, invert them into a container that will hold them in a single layer. Cover and refrigerate. If using the jars and not serving immediately, store the jars, covered, in the refrigerator. Bring the flans to room temperature before serving and make sure the soup is very hot before pouring it over the flans.

About Sweet Onions, and How to Clean Leeks

Southern Dames swear by their Vidalia and Texas 1015 onions; West Coast Dames rave about their Walla Walla and Maui onions. Whatever seasonal sweet onions are available to you, use them for the Vidalia Onion Soup with Bacon Flans. When it comes to the leeks, however, heed Virginia Willis's unyielding advice: "Leeks grow in sandy soil and can be very dirty. Chewing on a mouthful of gritty leeks is the gastronomic equivalent of fingernails on a chalkboard. Using a chef's knife, remove the hairy root bottoms and tough dark-green tops. Slice the leeks in half and then cut crosswise into half moons. Separate the half rings with your fingers and place the leeks in a sink full of cold water. Swish the leeks around and let the dirt fall to the bottom of the sink. Using your hands or a fine mesh sieve, scoop the leeks from the water. Drain, clean, and refill the sink. Repeat the procedure until the leeks are perfectly clean and no sand or dirt are present."

FRESH TOMATO SOUP WITH ROASTED-CORN GUACAMOLE

Miami Dame Lourdes Castro has always been an academic who loves to cook. With a master's degree in food and nutrition from Columbia University, she has taught in the Department of Food Studies and Nutrition at New York University and at Johnson & Wales University. This recipe is one of her warm-weather entertaining choices. She likes to make it with summer tomatoes—"particularly the overripe ones, since the tomatoes are puréed and texture doesn't matter." Any tomato variety is fine, as long as they are "top of the season."

6 cups

2 pounds tomatoes, stemmed and cut into quarters

¼ cup extra-virgin olive oil plus additional for garnish

1 tablespoon red wine vinegar

½ teaspoon salt

10 grinds black pepper

Roasted-Corn Guacamole (recipe follows)

½ cup cilantro leaves

❊ Place the tomatoes in the bowl of a food processor fitted with a steel blade. Process to a smooth purée. Drizzle the oil through the feed tube and process until the mixture is well emulsified. Add the vinegar and purée for a few seconds. Transfer the mixture to a bowl and season with the salt and pepper. Refrigerate the soup until it is chilled.

❊ To serve, check the soup for salt and correct if needed. Ladle into soup bowls. Add a mound of corn guacamole (warm or at room temperature) in the center of each bowl of soup, top with a few cilantro leaves, and drizzle with oil. Serve immediately.

Prepare Ahead

The soup can be made a day ahead. Allow at least enough time for it to chill before serving. Although the guacamole can be served at room temperature, it is a nice touch to have it warm on top of the cold soup; in that case, you can roast the corn kernels ahead, then reheat before combining with the guacamole ingredients right before serving.

Suggested Beverage

A dry Spanish Grenache-based rosé or a crisp Alsatian Riesling.

Roasted-Corn Guacamole

2½ cups

- 1½ cups fresh (see box, page 71) or frozen corn kernels
- 1 tablespoon extra-virgin olive oil
- ¼ teaspoon salt plus additional as needed
- Freshly ground black pepper
- 1 tablespoon finely chopped red onion
- 1½ tablespoons finely chopped cilantro leaves
- 1 tablespoon freshly squeezed lime juice
- 1 teaspoon cored, seeded, and very finely chopped jalapeño chile pepper (optional)
- 1 large, ripe avocado, coarsely chopped

❧ Preheat the oven to 400°F. Spread the corn on a baking sheet lined with foil, drizzle with the oil, and season with salt and pepper. Roast until golden brown, approximately 15 minutes. Remove from the oven and reserve on the baking sheet.

❧ Shortly before serving, in a medium bowl, combine the onion, cilantro, lime juice, and jalapeño. Gently fold in the avocado and reserved corn. (If you want to serve the guacamole warm, return the corn to a 400°F oven just long enough to reheat before combining with the guacamole mixture.) Season with salt and pepper to taste and serve.

CHILLED CUCUMBER-
BUTTERMILK SOUP

Dame Katherine Newell Smith of Washington, D.C., heads her own marketing and public relations firm, and has handled corporate communications for companies as diverse as Balducci's and Chipotle Mexican Grill. When she entertains at home, she looks for ease as well as high taste in her recipes. She likes this chilled soup especially for its versatility. It makes a fine warm-weather luncheon soup (even a picnic soup served from a thermos) or a dressy first-course dinner soup. Sometimes she garnishes the soup with handfuls of small salad shrimp. When time allows, she fries up half-dollar-size crab cakes, crowning the cold soup with the hot crusty delicacy.

6 cups

1 quart buttermilk

2 teaspoons ground cumin

Heaping tablespoon prepared Dijon mustard

1 large English cucumber, peeled, seeded, and cut into ¼-inch dice

½ large red bell pepper, cored, seeded, and cut into ¼-inch dice

2 tablespoons fresh dill, chopped

½ teaspoon salt

Big pinch of cayenne pepper

1 cup cooked small shrimp

Sprigs of fresh dill

Pour the buttermilk into a large bowl. Add the cumin and mustard. (For enhanced flavor, toast whole cumin in a dry skillet over medium heat just until fragrant, about 2 minutes; be careful not to burn. Remove from the heat and proceed with the recipe.) Whisk until the ingredients are well combined. Add the cucumber, bell pepper, dill, salt, and cayenne pepper. Taste for seasoning and adjust if necessary. Refrigerate until ready to serve. Garnish with the shrimp and dill sprigs.

Prepare Ahead

The soup should chill at least 1 hour before serving and can be prepared up to 3 days ahead. Add your choice of garnish right before serving.

Suggested Beverage

Something to match the topping of choice—with shrimp, Sauvignon Blanc; with crab, an unoaked Chardonnay.

WINTER MINESTRONE WITH BUTTERNUT SQUASH AND KALE

Prepare Ahead

The soup can be made up to 3 days ahead of serving. It also freezes well.

This eye-popping combination of vegetables demands some prep time. But beyond that, it's easy to make, produces a large batch, and freezes well. Topped generously with freshly grated Parmigiano-Reggiano cheese and served with warm bread, the soup makes a family meal that encourages kids to eat their vegetables. The soup also is easily varied. Try puréeing part of the batch and seasoning with toasted cumin, then garnish with dollops of good yogurt (see box, page 99).

The recipe, which puts seasonal produce to work, comes, not surprisingly, from farmers' market advocate and Chicago Dame Abby Mandel. The cookbook author and syndicated food columnist has been instrumental in launching LDEI's Green Tables initiative (see box, page 105).

16 cups

3 tablespoons olive oil

1 large sweet onion, chopped (about 2 cups)

1 medium banana pepper, cored, seeded, and sliced (about ¼ cup)

1 bunch (about 1 pound) cavalo nero kale or chard, stem ends trimmed, cut into slices

1 tablespoon minced garlic

One 15.5-ounce can cannellini beans, rinsed and drained

One 14.5-ounce can diced tomatoes with their juice

Four 14.5-ounce cans low-salt chicken broth

2 rinds of Parmigiano-Reggiano cheese, each about ½ by 6 inches (see box, opposite)

2 medium carrots, peeled and thinly sliced (about 1 cup)

1 small red bell pepper, cored, seeded, and cut into ½-inch dice (about 1 cup)

2 zucchini, cut into ½-inch dice (about 2 cups)

1 small butternut squash, peeled and cut into ½-inch dice (about 2 cups)

2 teaspoons kosher or coarse sea salt

Freshly ground black pepper

¼ cup chopped fresh, seasonal herbs such as sage, thyme, or Italian parsley

Parmigiano-Reggiano cheese for grating

Suggested Beverage

A young Sangiovese or Barbera; for white, Vernaccia.

❉ Heat the oil in a large soup pot over medium-high heat. When hot, add the onion, banana pepper, kale, and garlic. Cook, stirring often, until the vegetables are wilted, about 10 minutes. Add the beans, tomatoes and their juice, broth, cheese rinds, carrots, and red pepper. Simmer, covered, for 20 minutes, stirring occasionally. Add the zucchini and butternut squash; cook, covered, until the squash is just tender, 5 to 7 minutes. Add the salt and pepper to taste. Add water or stock if the soup is too thick. To serve, remove the cheese rinds and top with a grating of cheese. Pass additional cheese separately.

Parmigiano-Reggiano Rinds

Mandel suggests that when you use this top-quality grating cheese, be sure to save the rinds. Store them in a sealed plastic bag in the freezer. Wipe the outside of the rinds clean with hot water and add them to soups such as her Winter Minestrone while cooking. "This soup is never as good without the flavor of the simmering rinds," says Mandel.

CREAMY ROASTED PARSNIP ❧ SOUP WITH CHÈVRE AND ❧ WALNUT CROSTINI

Prepare Ahead

The soup can be prepared up to 3 days ahead, refrigerated, and then gently reheated to serve. You can also toast the croutons up to 3 days ahead. Be sure to let them cool thoroughly, then keep in a tightly closed container. If needed, recrisp them in the oven before spreading with the goat cheese.

If we are to cook seasonally and use the crops of local farmers, we need to reconsider often-overlooked varieties of produce like the parsnip. Here Seattle Dame Kathy Casey turns the frequently neglected vegetable into a rich and elegant soup, as easy to adore as it is to prepare.

As an executive chef for Sheraton Hotels in the 1980s, Casey was a poster girl for women chefs. She went on to start her own companies—Kathy Casey Food Studios, which provides food, beverage, and concept consulting to the industry, and Dish D'Lish gourmet cafés and specialty foods. She is also a television personality and cookbook author. Casey remains committed to the many little details that distinguish good cooking, as in this recipe when she stresses, "Be sure to cook the parsnips till they're completely tender and 'roasty' looking."

6 cups

Six ¼-inch baguette slices

1 tablespoon olive oil plus additional for brushing

1½ pounds parsnips, peeled and cut into ½-inch slices (about 4 cups)

2 tablespoons salted butter

1 stalk celery, chopped (about ½ cup)

¼ cup thinly sliced shallots

3 cloves garlic, finely minced

½ cup dry white wine

4 cups chicken broth

1 cup heavy cream

½ teaspoon salt

⅛ teaspoon cayenne pepper

3 ounces chèvre (fresh goat cheese)

3 tablespoons chopped walnuts, lightly toasted, divided

Minced chives and/or celery leaves

Suggested
Beverage

A Pinot Gris or
Viognier; for red, a
Côtes du Rhône.

✳ To make the crostini, preheat the oven to 425°F. Lay the bread on a baking sheet, brush slices lightly on both sides with oil, and toast until just lightly golden, about 5 minutes. Remove and let cool, leaving oven on for the next step.

✳ Toss the parsnips and the oil together in a bowl to coat evenly. Spread out on a baking sheet (you can reuse the one used for the bread) and roast in the oven until golden brown and very tender, about 40 minutes.

✳ Heat the butter in a large pot over medium-high heat. Sauté the celery and shallots until very tender, about 3 minutes; do not brown. Add the garlic and cook, stirring, for about 30 seconds more. Add the wine and bring to a boil. Add the broth, cream, and roasted parsnips and bring to a simmer. Reduce heat to medium-low to maintain a slow simmer. Cook for about 5 minutes, then add the salt and cayenne. In small batches, purée the mixture in a blender—be careful, it's hot! Alternatively, use an immersion blender (see box, page 101) or a food processor (the purée will not be as smooth). Return the soup to the pot and adjust the seasoning if needed. Cool and refrigerate for up to 3 days before serving.

✳ To finish the crostini and serve the soup, preheat the oven to 375°F. Spread the cheese on the crostini, then top each one with ½ tablespoon of the walnuts. Press in slightly and bake until the cheese is warmed, about 4 minutes.

✳ Meanwhile, heat the soup, stirring often, over medium heat until hot, making sure it does not stick on the bottom. Serve the soup topped with chives and the warm goat-cheese crostini on the side.

❧ BOWL OF THE WIFE OF KIT CARSON ❧

Prepare Ahead

The soup can be prepared days ahead of serving up to the addition of the avocado, cheese, and other garnishes. The recipe is easily doubled.

Colorado Dame Holly Arnold Kinney grew up in the restaurant trade. Her father, Sam Arnold, built the famous Fort Restaurant in southwest Denver, and the family lived over the restaurant. Today, Kinney owns and operates the Fort, as well as its mail order business and her own public relations firm, Arnold Media Services. This soup became a signature item for the restaurant back in the 1960s. At that time, Kit Carson's granddaughter was working in the Fort's gift shop and said it reminded her of the soup her grandmother used to make for her famous grandfather. Hence, the recipe's somewhat unusual name. If you'd like a spicier dish, top with pico de gallo.

8 cups

One 1-pound whole boneless, skinless chicken breast

4 cups chicken broth

Pinch dried oregano, preferably Mexican leaf oregano

1 cup cooked rice

1 cup cooked garbanzo beans, preferably from dried (if using canned, drain and rinse well)

½ to 1 canned chipotle chile pepper packed in adobo sauce, minced

1 ripe avocado, peeled, pitted, and sliced lengthwise

4 to 6 ounces Monterey Jack or Havarti cheese, cut into ½-inch cubes

Sour cream, crème fraîche (see box, page 20), or Mexican crema

Chopped cilantro leaves

Pico de Gallo (optional; recipe follows)

8 wedges fresh lime

❧ Place the chicken breast in a medium pot; pour on the broth. Bring to a boil, then turn off the heat, cover, and poach gently for 12 minutes. Remove the chicken from the pot and cut it into strips 1½ inches long. Return the chicken strips to the broth and add the oregano, rice, beans, and chipotle. Taste for seasoning. The chipotle flavor will intensify as the soup sits. However, if you'd like more chipotle flavor, stir in a bit of the adobo sauce.

To serve, divide the avocado and cheese among 4 deep soup bowls. Quickly reheat the soup to a boil, then ladle it into the bowls. Garnish with sour cream, cilantro, and Pico de Gallo. Pass the lime wedges to squeeze into the soup as it's eaten.

Pico de Gallo

2½ cups

2 cups chopped fresh tomato

½ cup chopped sweet onion or green onions

3 tablespoons freshly squeezed lime juice

2 tablespoons chopped fresh jalapeño or serrano chile pepper

2 tablespoons chopped cilantro leaves

½ teaspoon salt

½ teaspoon freshly ground black pepper

Combine the tomato, onion, lime juice, jalapeño, cilantro, salt, and pepper. The mixture keeps well for a few days. After spooning a bit on the top of each bowl of soup, you can pass the rest around the table with a bowl of corn chips. Leftovers make a tasty topping for endless dishes from omelets to steamed rice.

Suggested Beverage

An Australian Chardonnay or Shiraz, or a light Mexican beer with lime wedges.

Soups 97

SWEET PEPPER, TOMATO, AND LEEK SOUP

Prepare Ahead

The soup can be made 1 or 2 days ahead of serving and carefully reheated, or in summer, serve it cold (and season it accordingly—see box, page 132).

Today the food processor is so ubiquitous, we forget that it was a revolutionary kitchen tool when it first arrived in home kitchens thirty years ago. One of the best uses for the processor is to purée limitless combinations of cooked vegetables into rich, flavorful soups. This recipe is a quintessential example. It comes from Kansas City Dame Roberta Duyff, a registered dietitian based in St. Louis and a nationally recognized authority on nutrition. She wanted a heart-healthy, nutritious, casual meal of a soup, delicious enough to dress up as a first course for guests. She boldly combines fresh leeks, tomatoes, bell peppers, and gingerroot with a minimum of fat to create a soup that tastes as rich as many a cream soup.

Using a food processor (or immersion blender—see box, page 101), it's a quick soup to make, especially appealing when all the vegetables are fresh from local gardens. During the winter, you might enrich the flavor by pre-roasting the peppers—the charred skins will add depth.

4 cups

1 tablespoon olive or vegetable oil

1 cup thinly sliced leeks, both white and light green parts (see box, page 88)

1 clove garlic, minced

2 pounds (about 8) plum tomatoes, quartered

2 large red bell peppers, cored, seeded, cut into strips

¼ cup freshly squeezed lemon juice

1 teaspoon grated gingerroot (see box, page 171)

1 teaspoon salt

⅛ teaspoon freshly ground black pepper

About ½ cup plain nonfat yogurt (see box, opposite) to thin soup (you may also use buttermilk *or* chicken or vegetable broth)

Fresh thyme leaves or minced chives

Heat the oil in a medium-size saucepan over medium heat; add the leeks and garlic. Cook and stir until the leeks are tender, about 5 minutes. Add the tomatoes, bell peppers, lemon juice, gingerroot, salt, and pepper. Cover and simmer over medium-low heat until the peppers are tender, about 30 minutes. Stir occasionally and regulate heat so the mixture does not stick. Remove from heat; cool slightly.

In the bowl of a food processor fitted with a steel blade, purée the vegetable mixture in batches until smooth. Thin to desired consistency with the yogurt (Duyff uses as little as 2 tablespoons). Serve hot or cold, garnished with thyme.

Suggested Beverage

An Argentine Torrontes (an unusual white with a profile between Sauvignon Blanc and Gewürztraminer).

Making Low-Fat Soups

There are surefire ways to make rich-tasting vegetable soups using a minimum of fat. Adding yogurt is one. In recent years, a bevy of low- and nonfat yogurts have come on the market that taste nothing like the watery, acidic products that American cooks used to know as yogurt. Look for brands such as Pavel's, Straus Family Creamery, and Fage.

And then there's buttermilk—it's arguably the most misperceived ingredient in the kitchen. Originally it was the liquid left over from making butter. These days, most buttermilk is made by adding "friendly" bacteria to nonfat or low-fat milk, and at most, it contains 1 percent fat, despite its thick texture. All this makes buttermilk an enticing way to make puréed vegetables seem rich and creamy without adding significant amounts of fat.

PIEDMONTESE WEDDING SOUP

Prepare Ahead

Make the butter-
cheese mixture up to
1 day ahead and
chill. Cook pasta in
broth as much as
2 hours ahead.

San Francisco Grande Dame Jerry Anne Di Vecchio was a writer and food editor at *Sunset Magazine* for forty-three years. A Dame since 1989, Di Vecchio was elected a Grande Dame in 2001. She recalls a time when, as the divorced working mother of a young daughter, she would take her toddler to a posh Italian restaurant near her home. They would go early so they could have the restaurant to themselves, and the chef repeatedly kept the youngster contented with the most exquisite of soups. The child's delight prompted the chef to offer the recipe to Di Vecchio, and to this day it is the soup she serves for special occasions. As indulgent as it appears, it is easy to prepare and worth every calorie. In fact, Di Vecchio predicts home cooks will experience the same ecstasy first demonstrated by her daughter upon eating the soup: "Eyes will roll heavenward." Be sure to use a stock that is full bodied but not excessively salty. And when serving, you can pass additional truffle paste or oil around in case someone wants an extra dose. Undoubtedly, they will.

9 cups

½ cup (1 stick) unsalted butter, cut into about 8 pieces

1¼ cups freshly grated Parmigiano-Reggiano cheese

5 large egg yolks

1 cup heavy cream

6 cups richly flavored chicken, veal, or beef broth, fat skimmed off

½ cup dried tiny star-shaped pasta or dried *acini di pepe* (pastina)

1 tablespoon white truffle paste or oil plus additional (optional)

Freshly grated nutmeg

❋ Combine the butter, cheese, and egg yolks in the bowl of a food processor fitted with a steel blade. Process until blended. With the motor running, pour in the cream through the feed tube and continue to process until blended. Scrape the mixture into a large bowl. If making ahead, let stand at room temperature for up to 1 hour or refrigerate.

Suggested Beverage

An Italian Arneis, a Dolcetto, or a Barbera—all from Piedmont.

✻ In a large saucepan, bring the broth to a boil and add the pasta. Boil until the pasta is tender to bite—about 4 minutes for stars, about 9 minutes for acini de pepe. If making ahead, set the pan off the heat and, with a small strainer, scoop out the pasta with just enough of the broth to keep it from sticking together; reserve.

✻ To finish the soup, bring the butter-cheese mixture to room temperature. Reheat the broth to boiling. Whisk in the truffle paste, then whisk the broth into the butter-cheese mixture until blended. If you've removed the pasta, stir it back into the broth. Return the broth to the pan and stir, being very careful that the soup heats without boiling. Serve immediately in your best soup bowls, dusting each serving lightly with nutmeg, and pass around additional truffle paste or oil.

Blender, Food Processor, or Immersion Blender?

Kansas City Dames Kathy Moore and Roxanne Wyss run a consulting firm called Electrified Cooks that specializes in testing small appliances. They point out that in many cases (even making a chocolate emulsion for truffles), the blender and the food processor are interchangable. Where the blender must give way is when it comes to kneading dough; the processor, when it comes to crushing ice and making frozen drinks. Dame Lee Wooding, who spent six years as Test Kitchen Manager at Cuisinart, is a big fan of a professional kitchen favorite: the immersion blender. "It eliminates the need to dirty another vessel. You can purée right on the stove. Nothing can beat it for making cream soups, purées, and sauces. Plus, they can be used for making smoothies and shakes."

❧ COTUIT BAY OYSTER BISQUE ❧

Prepare Ahead

The soup can be made ahead and gently, very gently reheated. It also freezes well, which recommends it for making in advance of a festive dinner.

Chicago Dame Joan Reardon writes about this festive soup, "Although oyster stew is one of the 'plain Janes' of oyster cookery, Oyster Bisque is worthy of a Champagne toast, and it introduces a holiday dinner with style." Reardon originally made the soup with her local Cotuit Bay freshly shucked oysters. However, the velvety soup is just as easily made with shucked oysters purchased from reputable markets.

Reardon credits oysters—or at least a decade living part-time in the oyster community of Cotuit Bay on Cape Cod—for her career change from professor of English literature to cookbook author and culinary historian. Her first book—*Oysters: A Culinary Celebration*—reflects that experience. Combining her academic background with her love of food, she has gone on to publish a number of award-winning books, including *M. F. K. Fisher, Julia Child, and Alice Waters: Celebrating the Pleasures of the Table*. In 2005, Reardon received the coveted IACP Award for Culinary Literary Writing for her biography of M. F. K. Fisher.

This bisque lends itself to a range of garnishes. Chives or dill add their reliable touch; however, if freshly shucked oysters are available, do garnish each bowl with a raw one—and if you're looking for a slightly less conventional treatment, pass around a bowl of Torn and Fried Croutons (page 174) for spooning into the bisque.

8 cups

1½ pints shucked oysters and their liquor

1 pint fish stock or clam juice plus additional as needed

1½ cups dry white wine (see box, opposite)

2 celery stalks, coarsely chopped (about 1 cup)

2 carrots, peeled and coarsely chopped (about 1 cup)

2 shallots, coarsely chopped (about ¼ cup)

2 lemon slices

1 tablespoon coarsely chopped parsley

12 peppercorns

Sprig of fresh thyme

Pinch of mace or nutmeg

5 tablespoons unsalted butter

5 tablespoons all-purpose flour

2 large egg yolks

3 cups heavy cream, divided

1 teaspoon dry sherry

½ teaspoon salt

¼ teaspoon cayenne pepper

Minced chives or dill *or* freshly shucked raw oysters *or*
Torn and Fried Croutons (page 174)

❋ In a large saucepan, combine the oysters and liquor, stock, wine, celery, carrots, shallots, lemon, parsley, peppercorns, thyme, and mace. Bring to a boil, reduce heat, and simmer, uncovered, for 45 minutes.

❋ Strain through a fine sieve or cheesecloth-lined strainer. Discard the solids and measure 5 cups of the liquid into another saucepan. If there is less than 5 cups, add more stock or clam juice to make up the difference. Bring to a simmer.

Pantry Spirits

Chicago Dame Barbara Glunz-Donovan, proprietor of Chicago's oldest wine shop, The House of Glunz, recommends keeping certain spirits on hand for cooking. Fino sherry, she says, is a subtle deglazer and perky addition to many soups. Dry white vermouth can replace dry white wine, especially if the recipe is heavy on herbs. Rainwater or other dry Madeira, which keeps virtually forever, enriches earthy dishes, especially those with mushrooms. Keep half-bottles of pear and raspberry eau-de-vie on hand to use in fruit dishes and dessert sauces. A Spanish brandy or a "modest" Cognac will find endless uses in the kitchen. Be mindful that with all these spirits, a little goes a very long way. Buy quality "within reason." All these products can be recorked after opening—the T-top cork (embedded in the cap) on a bottle confirms this. Some of them may lose their freshness for drinking but will keep their flavor for cooking. And never buy anything labeled "cooking wine."

Suggested Beverage

A Chablis (unoaked Chardonnay), a Muscadet (a Loire Valley seaside white), or, of course, a dry bubbly—the three major whites that classically pair with oysters.

※ Melt the butter in a large, heavy-bottomed saucepan. Stir in the flour and cook until pale yellow. Slowly whisk in the hot liquid and bring to a boil, stirring constantly. Reduce heat and cook for a minimum of 5 minutes.

※ In a medium bowl, whisk the egg yolks and ½ cup of the cream. Slowly stir in ½ cup of the thickened liquid, a spoonful at a time. Continuing to stir, slowly add about 1 cup more of the liquid. Pour the mixture into the saucepan of liquid and, stirring carefully, bring to a boil. Remove from the heat. The bisque can be refrigerated or frozen.

※ To serve, reheat the bisque and stir in the remaining cream, sherry, salt, and cayenne pepper to taste. Serve in soup bowls, garnished with your choice of topping.

Those of us who work with food suffer from an image of being involved in an elite, frivolous pastime that has little relation to anything important or meaningful. But in fact we are in a position to cause people to make important connections between what they are eating and a host of crucial environmental, social, and health issues.

—Grande Dame Alice Waters

Green Tables

In 2005, Les Dames d'Escoffier International actively embraced the idea that collectively, through the leadership of our chapters, we could really improve how and what people eat. In 2006, LDEI launched Green Tables: The LDEI Civic Agriculture & Garden Initiative. Green Tables is designed to help consumers better understand the link between farms and their own family tables. Since its beginning, Green Tables has involved nearly every chapter in fundraising and educational activities on a multitude of fronts. The Hawaii chapter produced *The Hawaii Farmers' Market Cookbook: Fresh Island Products from A to Z* to encourage Hawaiian consumer use of locally grown produce. In Cleveland, Dames created and continue to support the Tremont Urban Learning Garden where inner city youth grow food for a community pantry and for local chefs. In Seattle, our chapter raised $50,000 to help build a greenhouse to be used in the teaching of sustainable foods in a community college culinary arts department. In addition to consumer education efforts, chapters such as Dallas and Atlanta have worked to improve distribution systems for local farmers by linking them with chefs and other food industry leaders. And in Miami, our chapter has sponsored several farming initiatives, including a day care center for children of migrant farm workers and scholarships for women to study agriculture. The list of achievements continues as we strive to provide visionary leadership, one morsel at a time.

—New York Dame Lynn Fredericks

The Family Table

One of the objectives of Les Dames d'Escoffier's Green Tables initiative is to educate the next generation about food and its critical role in nurturing family relationships. The Dames are adamant about the importance of what Seattle Dame Diana Dillard, a professor of culinary arts and mother of two young daughters, calls "bonus time at the table engaged in positive conversation." Another Seattle Dame, Martha Marino, a nutritionist with the Washington State Dairy Council, says her children, now grown, tell their friends that they grew up "old-fashioned style" because every night they set the table and lit a candle for dinnertime.

Some Dames have taken the family dining imperative to the next step to make it a family *cooking* imperative. New York Dame Lynn Fredericks, president of FamilyCook Productions, went from a food and wine journalism career to being an advocate for "bringing children into the mealtime process." Her firm now works on numerous state and federal programs that include nutrition counseling and a training curriculum stressing the importance of family cooking and eating. Fredericks's career change began one evening when, in desperation, she handed her 2-year-old son a bunch of fresh basil and said, "Stephan, I have a job for you." To her delight, he loved plucking basil leaves. "Don't shoo your kids out of the kitchen," advises Fredericks, who adds: "The first mantra of family cooking is 'don't worry about the mess.'"

The following recipe is well within the abilities of children ages 4 and up. Fredericks estimates prep time at 10 minutes, cooking time at 20 minutes. The recipe's format is typical of Fredericks's book, *Cooking Time Is Family Time*.

TUSCAN BEAN SOUP

13 cups

    1 medium onion

    2 cloves garlic

    2 tablespoons olive oil

    ½ bunch kale

    ½ bunch broccoli rabe

Two 15-ounce cans cannellini beans

One 28-ounce can whole tomatoes with their juice

4 cups chicken broth

3 sprigs fresh thyme

Kosher salt and freshly ground black pepper

One 1-pound loaf crusty Italian bread

1. CHILD After parent or instructor CUTS it with a chef's knife, DICE the onion using a table or plastic knife.

2. ADULT SMASH the garlic with the flat side of the chef's knife.

3. ADULT HEAT the oil in a large pot over medium heat. ADD the chopped onion and COOK, stirring occasionally, over low heat until translucent, about 10 minutes.

4. CHILD Help CHOP the garlic and add to the onion. Help stir, using oven mitts to protect hands from heat.

5. CHILD While the onions are cooking, help TEAR up the kale and broccoli rabe (discarding tough stalks/stems).

6. ADULT ADD the greens to the pot, increase heat to medium, and stir the greens until they wilt.

7. CHILD Help OPEN the cans of beans and tomatoes with a can opener. (Adult should remove and discard the sharp lid.)

8. CHILD With clean hands, SQUEEZE the tomatoes into the pot.

9. ADULT DRAIN and RINSE the beans in a colander. Add to the pot.

10. CHILD Help STIR while adult adds the chicken broth (child always uses oven mitts to protect hands while stirring).

11. CHILD PLUCK the thyme leaves from the stems. Add to the pot.

12. ADULT Season with salt and pepper and cook for another 10 minutes.

13. ADULT SERVE with the loaf of bread.

MAIN COURSES

For Every Day and Every Occasion   We open with a lobster recipe from Grande Dame Julia Child, and appropriately so—she inspired so many of us to cook. The recipes in this section span our culinary evolution. They come as much from street foods as from fancy French cuisine. Our chefs agree: fine dining has taken on a new attitude. A favorite "company" dish is a take on the Philly cheese steak, first created to entertain then-president Bill Clinton; Sunday supper can be as stylish as Saturday dinner at eight; women no longer shun the backyard barbecue. We celebrate our regional and ethnic roots: New World and Old World both—deep South, Northwest, Italian, Armenian, Czech-Polish, Shanghai Chinese.

The last several decades in food have been quite a journey. Les Dames d'Escoffier has helped lead the way from Julia's "miraculous" Lobster Newburg to Alice's Edible Schoolyard, from emulating men's eating clubs to advocating family meals, farmers' markets, and safe fisheries. As we say, it's all "one morsel at a time."

Recipes

SEAFOOD

Julia's Favorite Lobster Dish
Julia Child, *Boston Chapter*

Marcella's Grilled Fish Steaks Sicilian Salmoriglio Style
Marcella Hazan, *New York Chapter*

Japanese Black Sea Bass with Julienned Carrots, Fennel, and Sweet Peppers
Marlene Parrish, *Washington, D.C., Chapter*

Roasted Black Cod with Horseradish Coulis and Farmers' Carrots
Susan Feniger, *Los Angeles Chapter*

Salmon Fillets Baked in Grape-Leaf Wraps
Braiden Rex-Johnson, *Seattle Chapter*

Best Grits with Greens and Shrimp
Nathalie Dupree, *Charleston Chapter*

Big Shrimp with Armenian "Pesto"
Zov Karamardian, *Los Angeles Chapter*

See also: Seared Scallops with Surprise Sauce *(page 49)*

BEEF

Tuxedo Philly Cheese Steak
Lynn Buono, *Philadelphia Chapter*

Asian Steak Nora with Shaved Fennel Salad
Nora Pouillon, *Washington, D.C., Chapter*

Swedish Meatballs with Eastern-European Sauerkraut
Toria Emas, *Chicago Chapter*
Dawn Orsak, *Austin Chapter*

Wine-Dark Beef Stew with Horseradish Potato Purée
Rozanne Gold, *New York Chapter*

Italian-Style Braised Short Ribs with Rosemary Polenta
Michele Scicolone, *New York Chapter*

POULTRY

Chicken Thai Basil
Nongkran Daks, *Washington, D.C., Chapter*

Annabell's Oven Chicken and Squash Casserole
Sarah Robinson Graham, *Charleston Chapter*

Notes

A Memory of Julia

A Favorite Hazan Kitchen Tip

About Seafood Safety

Food Television: A Grand Illusion with an Army of Cooks

On Temperature and Food Safety

Room-Temperature Foods

Storing Gingerroot

In Praise of Stale Bread

In Praise of the Lowly Lentil

Fool-Proof Degreasing

Making Food Attractive

Sharing Family Recipes

How to Marinate in a Bag

Notes

How to Choose an Artichoke

The Useful Toothed Grapefruit Spoon

Poaching Eggs in Advance

Small Farm Eggs 101

Braising: Some Standard and Unexpected Tips

An Easy Way to Peel Fresh Tomatoes: Grate Them

If You Can't Find Fideos

Lids: Heat Management

Stir-Frying

Improving Your Farmers' Market

Recipes

Filipino Chicken Adobo over Fresh Greens
Sharon Kobayashi, *Honolulu Chapter*

Brie and Basil Stuffed Turkey Breast
Karen Adler and Judith Fertig, *Kansas City Chapter*

Duck Breast with Sautéed Potatoes
Ariane Daguin, *New York Chapter*

See also: Chicken Salad Bites *(page 6)*

PORK

Pork Loin with Winter Citrus Gravy
Lucy Wing, *New York Chapter*

Shanghai Noodles with Shredded Pork and Cabbage
Joyce Jue, *San Francisco Chapter*

Pork Rib Guazzetto
Lidia Bastianich, *New York Chapter*

Batali Family Stuffed Artichokes
Gina Batali, *Seattle Chapter*

Breakfast-for-Dinner Salad
Mary Sue Milliken, *Los Angeles Chapter*

OTHER MEATS

Veal and Wild Mushroom Ragout
Janis McLean, *Washington, D.C., Chapter*

Lemon, Mustard, and Mint Butterflied Leg of Lamb
Sue Sims, *Dallas Chapter*

A Favorite Moussaka
Pat Mozersky, *San Antonio Chapter*

PASTA

Catalan Pasta with Garlic Sauce
Marilyn Tausend, *Seattle Chapter*

Hali'imaile General Store Chicken Fettuccine Casserole
Beverly Gannon, *Hawaii Chapter*

See also: Shanghai Noodles with Shredded Pork and Cabbage *(page 163)*

Recipes

VEGETARIAN DISHES

Mushroom Ragù for Noodles
Alice Waters, *San Francisco Chapter*

Texas Chiles Rellenos
Blanca Aldaco, *San Antonio Chapter*

Tofu with Spicy Stir-Fry and Asian Greens
Corinne Trang, *New York Chapter*

Vegetarian Cassoulet
Diane Tucker, *Austin Chapter*

Late Summer Harvest Stew
Ann-Harvey Yonkers, *Washington, D.C., Chapter*

See also: Fresh Fennel Ratatouille *(page 229)*, Souvenir Eggplant Gratin *(page 220)*, Three-Sisters Salad *(page 64)*

Seafood

❧ JULIA'S FAVORITE LOBSTER DISH ❧

Culinary historian Dame Joan Reardon is one of the late Grande Dame Julia Child's biographers. Doing research in the collection of Child's papers at the Schlesinger Library, Reardon discovered this previously unpublished recipe. It comes from Child's early years of testing recipes for *Mastering the Art of French Cooking*. She wrote on September 2, 1954, to her French collaborator, Simone Beck (known as Simca) that in Maine, "We have lobsters here à go go, and I imagine this is one of the prime places in the world besides Norway, Brittany, and Nova Scotia where one has them at their very best. We have a float sitting about 20 meters from our shore, and a box sunk in it where we keep our lobsters."

She went on to explain how they removed the lobsters just before cooking them, and that she had prepared Lobster Américaine, Thermidor, and Newburg. There was much more to cooking lobster than she thought, she told Simca, and Julia described how she broiled and boiled them and experimented with using the coral, tomalley, and white coagulated stuff that clung to the shell. "I have about come to the conclusion that broiling is only for eating the lobster in the shell, no sauce or anything, and that such great care must be taken that the meat does not dry out . . . I do not think that broiling should be used for Thermidor. In fact I don't find Thermidor particularly interesting, as it is not much more than a velouté. I like Cardinal or à la crème. But I find Newburg the most interesting of all, in that it brings into question the use of coral, rosiness, and flavor."

Despite her preference for the dish, a recipe for Lobster Newburg never appeared in any of her books. Here it is in Child's original and inimitable words. (As the recipe was never finished for publication, we have placed additional and updated cooking instructions in brackets.)

The dish is extraordinarily rich. Small portions with the simplest accompaniment, such as blanched asparagus tips (see instructions, page 73), will make an impressive meal. Precede it with an easy starter (see box, page 36) and a first course of one of our seasonal salads, such as Sweet Corn, Chanterelle, and Arugula Salad (page 70). Dessert can be light: perhaps just fruit and cheese (see box, page 332).

4 to 6 servings

1 to 2 lobsters, to yield about 1½ cups cooked lobster meat (see instructions below)

¼ cup (½ stick) butter, cut into 4 pieces

½ cup Madeira

1 cup heavy cream

3 egg yolks

Salt

Freshly ground black pepper

❋ Boil or steam the lobsters and let cool. [Undercook the lobster, as it will continue cooking in the sauce. Four minutes in boiling water after it returns to the boil should be sufficient.] Remove all the meat from the tail, claws, knuckles, legs, and chest. Reserve meat in one bowl. [Set aside any coral (roe) and the greenish tomalley (liver).] Discard stomach, sack, and intestinal vein.

❋ Place all coral, tomalley, and white coagulated stuff that clings to the shell [scrape off the shell then dispose of the shell] in an enameled large saucepan with butter and simmer for 8 minutes. It turns from greenish to a rosy brownish color. [Strain through a sieve, discarding solids, and return liquid to the saucepan.] Then add meat and simmer for 5 minutes [3 minutes] covered; turn meat and simmer 5 minutes [3 minutes] more [covered]. Meat will have turned a pretty rosy color, like a miracle.

✳ Add Madeira and simmer 10 to 15 minutes [4 minutes should be sufficient] more. [While lobster cooks in Madeira] beat cream and egg yolks in a bowl. Remove lobster from heat and pour in the yolk/cream mixture gradually. Then set over the heat and shake the pan until the sauce thickens, but do not boil. Add salt and pepper (to taste).

✳ Serve in patty shells or on rice [alongside a simple green vegetable such as blanched asparagus tips].

Suggested Beverage

An unoaked Chardonnay from western Australia or an Oregon Pinot Gris (both of similar body to the lobster) or a Blanc de Blancs sparkling wine.

A Memory of Julia

In 1978, Philadelphia Dame Aliza Green was a young sous chef at Philadelphia's Barclay Hotel. The fact that there was a woman chef working at the hotel was enough to make Julia Child, who was dining at the hotel, leave the table and ask to be escorted deep into the hotel's back kitchens to see this woman at work. "We just had a few precious minutes together there in the steam and commotion of the kitchen, but her trip to my workplace was such a validation for me," remembers Green, who went on to be a pioneering woman chef at several top Philadelphia restaurants and to author a number of cookbooks.

MARCELLA'S GRILLED FISH STEAKS SICILIAN SALMORIGLIO STYLE

Prepare Ahead
Hazan writes, "Fresh-
ness is essential
to the fragrance of
salmoriglio sauce. Do
not prepare it long
in advance. It is so
simple and quick to
do that you can make
it while the grill is
warming up."

When we asked Grande Dame Marcella Hazan to choose among her thousands of recipes, she selected four personal favorites: Sautéed Rapini with Chickpeas from *Marcella Says*, and the Chicken with Two Lemons, Tomato Sauce with Butter and Onion, and Swordfish Salmoriglio from *Essentials of Classic Italian Cooking*. Our pick is the swordfish recipe, for three reasons: its essence is the notion that thinly sliced fish cooks differently (exquisitely so) from thickly sliced fish; Hazan's way of seasoning is so quintessentially Mediterranean; and the recipe draws attention to the fact that these days, we perhaps should *not* be eating swordfish (see box, page 122). Happily, Hazan pointed out in her originally published recipe that although swordfish would be the "fish of choice" in Sicily, "other steak fish such as tuna, halibut, mako shark, or tilefish are acceptable alternatives." Add salmon to that list, and heed Hazan's explanation: "The Sicilian practice of using rather thin slices is ideal because it makes it possible to keep the fish on the grill such a brief time that it doesn't have a chance to dry out." Salt this dish to your preference; Hazan herself likes the heavier salting. The fish can be "aromatized" in other ways as well, such as with thyme, or spiced up with the addition of crushed red pepper.

To accompany this most basic fish dish, choose a Mediterranean-inspired side dish: Fresh Fennel Ratatouille (page 229) or Tuscan Beans and Potatoes (page 234). If the season is right and the event warrants it, serve an appetizer of Rich Man Poor Man (page 37); otherwise serve a bit of cured meat and cheese (see box, page 63). Follow with a first course of Little Molds of Roasted Peppers with Anchovy Sauce (page 60). End with a dessert also of Italian origin: Chocolate Hazelnut Tart (page 277).

4 to 6 servings

1½ to 3 teaspoons kosher or coarse sea salt

2 tablespoons freshly squeezed lemon juice

2 to 3 teaspoons chopped fresh oregano leaves *or* 1 teaspoon dried

¼ cup extra-virgin olive oil

Freshly ground black pepper

2 pounds ½-inch-thick fresh fish steaks

Suggested Beverage

Stay Italian—a quality Vermentino from Sardinia or Pinot Grigio from Friuli-Venezia Giulia.

❋ If using charcoal, light it in time for it to form white ash before cooking. If using a gas or electric grill, preheat at least 15 minutes before you are ready to cook. (Oil the grill as needed.)

❋ Put the salt in a small bowl. Add the lemon juice and beat with a fork until the salt has dissolved. Add the oregano, mixing it in with the fork. Trickle in the oil, drop by drop, beating it in with the fork to blend with the lemon juice. Add several grinds of pepper, stirring to distribute evenly.

❋ When the grill is ready, place the fish close to the source of heat so that it cooks quickly. Grill the fish for no more than 2 minutes on one side, then turn it and grill the other side for no more than 2 minutes. It does not need to become brown on the surface.

❋ Transfer the fish to a large, warm serving platter. Prick each steak with a fork in several places to let the sauce penetrate deeper. Use a spoon to beat and at the same time to pour the *salmoriglio* mixture of oil and lemon juice over the fish, spreading it evenly. Serve at once, spooning some sauce from the platter over each individual portion.

A Favorite Hazan Kitchen Tip

This tip comes in an e-mail written with the Hazan trademark charm by her husband Victor: "If you can use helpful tips, Marcella greatly reduces the use of clumsy pot holders by wedging corks under the handles of her pot lids." Imagine never having to scramble for a pot holder when juggling pots around the stove. If only all handles were the right size and shape (and many are) to accommodate a bit of cork (wine corks work for many), cooking would be so much easier.

JAPANESE BLACK SEA BASS WITH ❉ JULIENNED CARROTS, FENNEL, ❉ AND SWEET PEPPERS

Prepare Ahead

The fish needs to marinate at least 2 hours (or even overnight) before cooking. Prepare the vegetable topping before cooking the fish, and the last-minute assembly is easy.

Washington, D.C., Dame Marlene Parrish, a food and travel writer for the *Pittsburgh Post-Gazette* and Scripps Howard News Service, adapted this recipe (a variation on the popular Japanese preparation *kasu* cod) from a dish she was served at the Pattigeorge Restaurant in Long Boat Key, Florida.

The fish and vegetables need nothing more to make an entrée unless you'd like to add steamed rice. Following Dame Joyce Jue's observation that conforming to Asian menus can be unnecessarily difficult for Western cooks, a simple appetizer of olives and nuts or bread and butter is a good start, followed by a soup like Sweet Pepper, Tomato, and Leek (page 98). Fruit with Fresh Ginger Cream (page 335) makes an appropriate wrap to the meal.

4 servings

6 tablespoons white miso (fermented soybean paste)

⅓ cup sugar

¼ cup plus 3 tablespoons mirin (Japanese sweet rice wine), divided

¼ cup plus 2 tablespoons sake, divided

Four 6-ounce black sea bass, black cod fillets (also known as sablefish), or grouper, each cut ¾ to 1 inch thick

1 cup water

Julienned Carrots, Fennel, and Sweet Peppers (recipe follows)

❉ In a small bowl, whisk the miso, sugar, ¼ cup of the mirin, and ¼ cup of the sake until smooth. Transfer the mixture to a resealable quart plastic bag (see box, page 160). Add the fish fillets, turning them to coat. Seal the bag and refrigerate for 2 to 4 hours or even overnight.

❉ Bring the fish and marinade to room temperature. Preheat the broiler.

✳ Remove the fish fillets from the marinade. Place them, along with any marinade that clings to them, in a 9-inch pie pan or other small baking pan with sides. Do not crowd the pan. Discard remaining marinade.

✳ In a microwavable container, stir together the water, remaining mirin, and remaining sake. Heat in the microwave for 1 minute. Pour enough of the liquid into the pan to come about a third of the way up the side of the fillets, about ¼ inch. (This steams the fish a bit while allowing the top to caramelize under the broiler.)

✳ Put the pan under the broiler and broil until the fish is just opaque in the center, 5 to 6 minutes. For the most succulent results, the fish should be barely done in the center.

✳ Serve the fish in wide, shallow bowls. Spoon some of the cooking liquid, about ¼ cup per serving, into each dish. Top with the Julienned Carrots, Fennel, and Sweet Peppers.

Julienned Carrots, Fennel, and Sweet Peppers

You'll want to adopt this eye-popping vegetable topping as a side to many other dishes, from grilled pork to beef to chicken to other seafood. Choose fennel bulbs that are firm, plump, and heavy for their size.

3 cups

1 medium carrot

1 small fennel bulb

1 small red or green bell pepper

1 tablespoon peanut oil

½ teaspoon toasted sesame oil

✳ Peel the carrot and cut it into thin strips. Trim the fennel bulb of fronds and any brown outside leaves, then core and cut into thin strips. Core and seed the bell pepper and cut into thin strips. Place the oils in a large skillet. Add the vegetables and cook over low heat until just softened, not browned.

About Seafood Safety

Are you confused about fish safety? You're not alone. With all the conflicting information grabbing headlines these days, it's not easy to make educated decisions when buying fish. We know that fish is a high-quality protein and is low in saturated fat. We hear that the oils in fish (omega-3 fatty acids) are good for us—essential for brain development and beneficial for our hearts. But we're warned about the dire effects on our bodies of the methylmercury, PCBs, and other environmental pollutants found in some fish. It's prudent for those with a compromised immune system, young children, and pregnant women (and those who might become pregnant)—all of whom can be at additional risk from both pollutants and seafood-borne illnesses—to proceed with caution. Most of us are not part of this high-risk population.

So what's a consumer to do? As scientific research yields more information, the truth may one day be clear, but in the meantime those with concerns can read the various advisories, educate themselves about the latest scientific findings, and make their own decisions. The following may be useful in assessing risks and benefits for you and your family:

* The Food and Drug Administration's advisory at www.cfsan.fda .gov/~dms/admeh.

* The Institute of Medicine's landmark report on the risks and benefits of eating fish. Read their report by searching for "Institute of Medicine fish advisory."

* You may be interested in reading about the growing evidence of selenium's protective effects pertaining to mercury toxicity: go to www.realmercury facts.org. You can also contact scientist J. John Kaneko to review his research on selenium and mercury at johnkaneko@pacmarinc.com.

* Also visit the Monterey Bay Advisory Seafood Watch Web site for current consumer guidelines regarding safety and sustainability.

* And for a thoroughly researched discussion of this and other health issues, read Dame Marion Nestle's acclaimed book *What to Eat*.

—*San Antonio Dame Pat Mozersky*

ROASTED BLACK COD WITH ⚹ HORSERADISH COULIS AND ⚹ FARMERS' CARROTS

Los Angeles Dame Susan Feniger—who with her business partner Dame Mary Sue Milliken operates Border Grill and Ciudad restaurants, writes cookbooks, and starred in *Too Hot Tamales* for the Food Network—is a stickler for sustainable seafood. Her restaurants make frequent use of the advisories from the Monterey Bay Aquarium Seafood Watch program (see box, opposite). Seafood Watch usually rates black cod, also known as sablefish, as a Best or Good choice.

A starter to the cod might be as simple as cheese and olives. For a first course, a seasonal soup; for dessert, the Passion Fruit–Macadamia Nut Tart (page 284).

6 servings

Six 6-ounce black cod fillets

2 teaspoons salt

10 grinds black pepper

¼ cup (½ stick) unsalted butter, cut into 4 pieces

Farmers' Carrots (recipe follows)

Horseradish Coulis (recipe follows)

3 limes, peeled and diced

Daikon sprouts

Freshly grated horseradish

⚹ Preheat the oven to 450°F. Season the fish all over with the salt and pepper. Melt the butter in a large, ovenproof skillet over high heat. Sauté the fish for 1 minute. Turn over, transfer to the oven, and bake for 3 to 5 minutes—do not cover.

⚹ To serve, arrange the fish on individual plates with the Farmers' Carrots. Spoon over the warm Horseradish Coulis and top with the limes, daikon sprouts, and fresh horseradish. Serve immediately.

Prepare Ahead

Horseradish Coulis can be prepared ahead of time and reheated by bringing to a simmer and reserving in a warm place until use. Black cod fillets can be pan-seared on both sides ahead of time and then reheated in the oven just before serving.

Suggested Beverage

High-quality chilled sake, served in white wine glasses; or, an off-dry Alsatian Riesling or Pinot Gris.

Farmers' Carrots

These carrots cook with no more liquid than what comes from the wilting of the lettuce leaf. The result is a fork-tender vegetable with unadulterated carrot flavor. Nantes is a good carrot variety to use.

1 pound carrots, peeled and cut into ½-inch chunks

1 teaspoon salt

10 grinds black pepper

A pinch of sugar

1 large romaine lettuce leaf

1 tablespoon unsalted butter

½ teaspoon freshly squeezed lemon juice

❀ Combine the carrots, salt, pepper, and sugar in a small, heavy saucepan and cover with the lettuce leaf. Cover the saucepan and cook carrots over very low heat until tender, 15 to 20 minutes. Occasionally check that the saucepan is not cooking dry. If necessary, add just a small amount of water to complete cooking. Discard the lettuce leaf. Stir in the butter and lemon juice and serve.

Horseradish Coulis

5 tablespoons cold unsalted butter, divided

4 shallots, thinly sliced (about 2 cups)

4 cultivated brown mushrooms, thinly sliced

1 teaspoon salt

¼ teaspoon freshly ground black pepper

1½ cups dry white wine

1½ cups fish stock or bottled clam juice

1½ cups heavy cream

Juice of 1 lime

4 dashes Tabasco

6 tablespoons freshly grated horseradish

✻ Melt 2 tablespoons of the butter in a medium saucepan over low heat. Add the shallots, mushrooms, salt, and pepper; cook until the mushrooms are soft. Turn heat to high, add the wine, and reduce by half. Add the fish stock and reduce again by half.

✻ Return the pan to high heat, add the cream, and reduce by half, being careful not to over-reduce. (If the sauce should break at this point, you can bring it back together with a quick turn in the blender.) Stir in the lime juice, Tabasco, and horseradish. Cut the remaining butter into small pieces and whisk into the sauce until smooth. Reserve in a warm place or refrigerate and gently reheat to serve.

Food Television:
A Grand Illusion with an Army of Cooks

Dames Susan Feniger and Mary Sue Milliken (*Too Hot Tamales* from the Food Network) are just two of the many Dames who have had star billing on television, starting most famously with Grande Dame Julia Child. Other Dames, like Virginia Willis, have made behind-the-scenes their career path. Willis has produced more than a thousand television cooking shows in her fifteen years in the business. She served as kitchen director for the Emmy-winning *Martha Stewart Living* television show and executive producer for *Epicurious* on The Discovery Channel. And she tells many tales of the rigors of polishing her trade—like the time that she was sure that a failed ginger flan had ruined her culinary career. "I've endured what seems like a thousand life lessons similar to that of the failed flan." She started as an unpaid apprentice with a Southern cooking expert, Charleston Dame Nathalie Dupree. Her career has included cooking for U.S. presidents and Michelin-starred chefs, and she even made Lapin Moutarde á la Normande with Julia Child. She studied cookbook writing with culinary expert Grande Dame Anne Willan and served as an editor for *The All New Joy of Cooking*. When it comes to food television, she says "It is often a grand illusion, yet beyond the camera there is always an army of cooks getting the job done." Willis recently added "cookbook author" to her resume with the publication of her book, *Bon Appétit, Y'all: Recipes and Stories from Three Generations of Southern Cooking*.

SALMON FILLETS BAKED IN GRAPE-LEAF WRAPS

Prepare Ahead

The packets can be prepared up to the point of cooking early in the day and refrigerated. Bring to room temperature for about an hour, then bake immediately before serving.

Food, wine, and travel writer Seattle Dame Braiden Rex-Johnson is best known for her cookbooks featuring the Pacific Northwest and Seattle's Pike Place Market, from which she lives a "tomato toss away." In this recipe, she uses grape leaves to protect the delicate flesh of salmon fillets as they bake. The leaves add an earthy look, as well as a pleasantly salty flavor and a bit of suspense as guests unwrap their entrée and discover a rich paste of fresh basil and sun-dried tomatoes topping the salmon inside the packets. They can choose to eat the grape leaves or not.

Dotting each fillet with butter before topping with the paste mixture and wrapping in the leaves makes them richer and more succulent. Note: The recipe uses about half of a jar of preserved grape leaves. Those not used can be rewound and repacked into the jar with their brine; add water if necessary to cover the leaves.

Serve the salmon with Marion Cunningham's Simple Side of Orzo (page 238) and, in summer, a bit of sliced fresh tomatoes dressed with olive oil, salt, and pepper. Start the meal with Walnut-Fennel Tarts (page 14) and end with Berry Puff Torte in summer (page 315) and Bittersweet Chocolate Soufflés with Nibby Cream in winter (page 318).

4 servings

Olive oil

3 ounces (about ½ cup) sun-dried tomatoes packed in oil

½ cup firmly packed fresh basil leaves (about 4 to 5 sprigs of fresh basil, stemmed)

4 cloves garlic, coarsely chopped

4 teaspoons capers, drained and rinsed

24 preserved grape leaves (about half a 16-ounce jar)

Four 6-ounce salmon fillets, ½ to ¾ inch thick, skinned and boned, rinsed, and patted dry

Salt and freshly ground black pepper

8 teaspoons unsalted butter, cold (optional)

❁ Preheat the oven to 400°F. Lightly brush a rimmed baking sheet with olive oil. Drain the sun-dried tomatoes and reserve 1 tablespoon of the oil. (Some oil will continue to cling to the tomatoes; this is okay. If draining the tomatoes does not yield 1 tablespoon of oil, add olive oil to make up the difference.) Coarsely chop the tomatoes and add with the reserved oil to the bowl of a food processor fitted with a steel blade. Add the basil, garlic, and capers, and process until the ingredients are finely chopped and form a thick paste. Scrape down the sides of bowl two or three times as needed to blend the mixture completely. Scoop the tomato-basil paste into a small bowl and set aside.

❁ Lay out 6 of the grape leaves on a large cutting board so they form a patch approximately 10 by 10 inches. The dull side of the leaf (the side with the protruding veins) should face up so the shiny outside of the leaf faces out when fillets are wrapped. The grape leaf patch should be large enough to accommodate a salmon fillet, with enough overlapping to wrap the salmon completely.

❁ Place a salmon fillet in the center of the grape leaves. Lightly sprinkle the fillet with salt and pepper (about ¼ teaspoon salt and 4 grinds of black pepper per fillet). For each fillet, cut 2 teaspoons of cold butter into 4 pieces and dot evenly over the fillet. With a spatula, spread one quarter of the tomato-basil paste over the top of the fish. Fold the grape leaves, first from the top and bottom, then from the right and left sides toward the center, overlapping. Place the salmon packet on the baking sheet seam side down. Repeat this process with the remaining grape leaves and fillets.

❁ Cook the packets for 8 to 12 minutes, depending on the degree of doneness desired. To test for doneness, cut into the center of a packet with the tip of a small, sharp knife and pull the salmon apart gently. If it is still slightly translucent in the center, it is cooked medium rare. If it

Suggested Beverage

A California rosé or a Greek Moscho-filero (the brine from the grape leaves and capers suggests avoiding the more typical light red pairing).

is opaque in the center, it is well done. Be very careful not to overcook, as the salmon will continue to cook after you remove it from the oven.

✄ Place the packets on dinner plates and serve immediately, allowing guests to open their own packets. Or you can open the packets part way so that just a bit of the steamy fish peeks through.

On Temperature and Food Safety

No matter what you do, food will never be 100 percent safe, but it makes sense to keep problems to a minimum. I like foods cooked, not least because one terrific benefit of cooking—beyond releasing flavors (and some nutrients), of course—is that it kills harmful bacteria. Bacteria are everywhere on foods, a situation that is distasteful but not necessarily harmful. It's only the bad bacteria that really matter. But you have to kill the benign to get at the bad ones. There are two rules about killing bacteria with cooking: (1) the hotter the temperature, the more bacteria are killed, and (2) the longer foods are kept at higher-than-normal temperatures, the more bacteria are killed. The standard advice to cook meats to 165°F is designed to be absolutely certain that all bacteria are killed. Most will be killed at slightly lower temperatures, and many will be killed at even lower temperatures. If you cook foods long enough, even at somewhat lower temperatures, the foods will be sterile—until they cool down and become recontaminated. So how safe you want food to be is yours to decide. You have to figure out how much of a risk you are willing to take if you want to cook foods at lower temperatures to preserve flavor and texture.

—*New York Dame Marion Nestle*

Probably no food writer working today is more respected for her advice on nutrition and food safety than Nestle. Her most recent tome, the six-hundred-page What to Eat, *was called "the perfect guidebook" to American food and nutrition by* USA Today.

BEST GRITS WITH GREENS AND SHRIMP

Charleston Dame Nathalie Dupree is an undisputed expert on Southern cooking. She is the author of many cookbooks and has won two coveted James Beard Awards. In this recipe for a one-dish meal, adapted from her book *Nathalie Dupree's Shrimp and Grits* (written with fellow Dame Marion Sullivan), Dupree admits her use of cream, butter, and cheese is extravagant, but points out that you can scrimp to your own taste on the butter and the cheese. She also encourages other variations: skip the shrimp and turn the dish into a side dish; or increase the cream to make the grits the consistency of a dip, chop the shrimp and the greens before adding them, and serve the mixture with warm corn chips as an indulgently Southern hors d'oeuvre. And, expert on the subject that she is, Dupree advises that the consistency of grits varies by brand and type, so feel free to add or subtract liquid to suit your taste and application.

Given the grits' origins, start the meal—season permitting—with Fresh Okra Cakes (page 10). For a first course: Vidalia Onion Soup with Bacon Flans (page 86). Fresh Blackberry Cobbler (page 311) is an appropriately Southern ending to the meal.

Prepare Ahead

The whole dish can be prepped ahead, but cook immediately before serving.

4 to 6 servings

- 2 cups whole milk
- 2 cups water
- 1 cup grits, regular or quick (*not* instant)
- 1 clove garlic, chopped
- 1 cup heavy cream
- 2 to 8 tablespoons (¼ stick to 1 stick) unsalted butter
- 1 to 2 cups freshly grated Parmigiano-Reggiano cheese
- 1 pound shrimp (any size), peeled
- ½ to 1 pound baby spinach, baby turnip greens, or arugula, washed well of all grit

Suggested Beverage

An unoaked Chardonnay or a low-tannin red such as an Italian Barbera.

½ teaspoon salt

Freshly ground black pepper

❋ Bring the milk and water to a simmer in a heavy-bottomed nonstick saucepan over medium heat. Add the grits and garlic and bring just to the boil. Reduce heat and cook until the mixture is soft and creamy, whisking now and then, and adding heavy cream as needed to make a loose but not runny mixture. Add as much butter and cheese as desired, stirring to make sure the cheese doesn't stick. Add the shrimp and cook a few minutes more until they are pink. Fold in the greens and remove from the heat. Cover. The greens will cook in the hot grits. Season with the salt and pepper. Serve immediately in large, shallow bowls.

BIG SHRIMP WITH ARMENIAN "PESTO"

Prepare Ahead

You can start the shrimp marinating up to 8 hours before cooking. The Armenian "Pesto" can be prepared ahead and frozen for up to a month. You'll find countless uses for the extra pesto, from dressing vegetables to slathering on sandwiches to tossing with pasta.

Everyone needs a blockbuster way of preparing the iconic big shrimp, all rosy with tails still protruding—to star as an appetizer, to dress up soups and salads, or to just fill the entrée bill with high style. Here's the way Los Angeles Dame Zov Karamardian—restaurateur, chef, and cookbook author—prepares them. She suggests pairing the dressed shrimp with dried bean dishes like the Drunken Beans over Mexican White Cheese— use the version with feta cheese (page 54). Other good partners: Zazu's Backyard Garden Fattoush (page 242) or On-the-Side Fresh Corn and Green Beans (page 215). For an appetizer, Abigail's Crusty Sausage Rolls (page 24); for a first course, choose a seasonal salad or soup; and for dessert, maybe store-bought gelato topped with a homemade sauce (see pages 335–36).

Karamardian learned the food business from her immigrant parents, who had come from the Middle East in 1959 and operated a grocery store in the North Beach neighborhood of San Francisco. Because her father spoke no English, Karamardian as the eldest child was drafted to work in the store and serve as her father's translator. "Now I use the flavors of his homeland and his innate business sense in running my restaurants," says this very successful Southern California businesswoman.

Suggested Beverage

A California Sauvignon Blanc or Argentine Torrontes.

4 main-course servings or 8 to 12 appetizer servings

- ¼ cup (if sautéing rather than grilling the shrimp) plus 2 tablespoons olive oil
- 1 tablespoon chopped parsley
- 1½ teaspoons minced garlic
- ¼ teaspoon salt
- ½ teaspoon freshly ground black pepper
- 24 to 30 (about 1 pound) large shrimp, peeled (except tails) and deveined
- 2 tablespoons freshly squeezed lemon juice
- 1 cup Armenian "Pesto" (recipe follows), divided

✻ Stir 2 tablespoons of the oil, parsley, garlic, salt, and pepper in a medium bowl to blend. Add the shrimp and toss to coat. Cover and refrigerate for at least 15 minutes or up to 8 hours.

✻ If grilling the shrimp, prepare the grill for medium-high heat. Working in batches, grill the shrimp until they are pink and just opaque in the center, about 2 minutes per side, being careful not to overcook. If sautéing the shrimp, heat the remaining oil in a large sauté pan over medium-high heat. Add the shrimp with all the marinade and cook, turning a few times, until just opaque, about 3 minutes.

✻ Place the cooked shrimp (and all the juices if sautéed) in a clean, large bowl and toss with the lemon juice and 2 tablespoons of the Armenian "Pesto." Serve hot or cool to room temperature, if desired. Spoon the remaining pesto into a small bowl and serve on the side.

Armenian "Pesto"

1 cup

½ cup walnuts, toasted in a 350°F oven for about 15 minutes and cooled

¼ cup freshly grated Parmesan cheese

3 cloves garlic, peeled

½ teaspoon salt

½ teaspoon freshly ground black pepper

¼ teaspoon dried red pepper flakes

1 cup packed cilantro leaves

1 cup packed mint leaves

2 tablespoons freshly squeezed lemon juice

⅓ cup extra-virgin olive oil

✻ Place the walnuts, Parmesan, garlic, salt, black pepper, and red pepper in the bowl of a food processor fitted with a steel blade. Process until it forms a thick paste. Add the cilantro, mint, and lemon juice. Blend until the cilantro and mint are finely chopped. With the machine running, gradually add the oil and blend until the mixture is smooth and creamy.

Room-Temperature Foods

Most people agree that "cold" foods taste better at room temperature than straight from the fridge. Yet with growing concerns about food safety, the decision to serve at room temperature is, as Dame Marion Nestle puts it, "a personal decision on how safe you want food to be." A little know-how on seasoning "cold" foods can help. San Antonio Dame Terry Thompson-Anderson advises, "There is an art to seasoning foods that will be served cold. Cold dulls the senses of hot, sweet, salty, and spicy on our tongues. You need to slightly over-season foods that will be served cold. After the food has been chilled it is very hard to adjust the seasonings."

Beef

❈ TUXEDO PHILLY CHEESE STEAK ❈

Short on time? Looking for a sure-to-impress and slightly cheeky entrée? This is it. The dish originated when Philadelphia caterer Dame Lynn Buono conceived of a "black-tie" version of the Philly cheese steak sandwich for a reception honoring President Bill Clinton. She made tiny homemade rolls, stuffed them with sautéed onions and beef tenderloin, and drizzled them with her own "Truffled Cheese Whiz." A month later, *The New York Times* quoted President Clinton as saying, "I broke my diet for those cheese steaks"—the very ones Buono had served him.

For home cooking, we think the combination is best enjoyed as a one-dish entrée—no side dishes needed. In place of the rolls, the meat and onion combo, with its cheese sauce, is served over a thick slice of lightly toasted bread that serves as a giant crouton soaking up the juices. True to the original, Buono stresses that this is a layered combination, "not a stir-fry of beef and onions." She hastens to add that the bit of sautéed spinach, which doubles as a garnish and a vegetable, looks good and tastes good but definitely is not traditional. In fact, the traditional topping is ketchup (for Buono, homemade). "Describing a cheese steak without the ketchup is kind of like explaining a hot dog without the mustard," she says. Appetizers could be Phyllo Fontina Cheese Bites—made well ahead (page 16); the first course, something easy like Prosciutto and Melon in Sambuca (page 62)—season permitting. End with Baked Butterscotch Puddings (page 313).

6 servings

Prepare Ahead

The dish is made easy by doing all the prep hours or even a day ahead.

1½ pounds beef tenderloin tips or beef tenderloin

4 tablespoons olive oil, divided

2 large sweet onions (Vidalia, Texas 1015s, or Walla Walla),
   cut into ⅜-inch crescents (see box, page 52)

1 tablespoon plus ½ teaspoon salt, divided

Six ¾-inch slices artisan-style bread (no larger than 4 inches wide
   and 5 inches long)

2 tablespoons unsalted butter

9 ounces prewashed spinach leaves, rinsed and stemmed

Truffled Cheese Sauce (recipe follows)

Freshly ground black pepper

❊ Place the beef in the freezer for about 2 hours or until the meat is almost frozen (cold meat is easier to cut thinly—see box, page 17). Take the meat from the freezer and cut it against the grain as thinly as possible into ⅛- to ¼-inch slices. The meat can be covered with plastic wrap and refrigerated for up to a day. When ready to proceed, bring the meat to room temperature for about 30 minutes before cooking.

❊ Meanwhile, heat 2 tablespoons of the oil in a large, heavy sauté pan over high heat. Add the onions and ½ teaspoon of the salt, reduce heat to medium, and cook, stirring occasionally, for about 20 minutes. When the onions are golden brown, remove them to an ovenproof dish, cover with foil, and either keep warm in a 250°F oven or reserve for later reheating. No need to wash the sauté pan; you'll use it for the beef.

❊ Lightly toast the bread until golden brown but still soft. This can be done in a toaster, under a broiler, or in a 350°F oven for about 10 minutes. Place in a baking dish and cover loosely with foil. Reserve for later reheating.

❊ In another large sauté pan, place the butter, 1 teaspoon of the salt, and the damp spinach. Reserve to cook immediately before serving.

Suggested
Beverage

A California Cabernet
or a Bordeaux; better
yet, a bottle of each
for a side-by-side
taste comparison.

❊Just before serving, have the onions and bread warm in a 250°F oven and heat the Truffled Cheese Sauce. Place the sauté pan of spinach over medium heat and cook, stirring a couple of times, just until the spinach is wilted. Remove from the heat and reserve. Return the empty sauté pan used for the onions to high heat, add 1 tablespoon of the oil to the pan, and when it is hot, sear half of the meat, stirring quickly, for just a couple of minutes, being careful not to overcook. As soon as the meat is lightly browned, remove it to a plate, and repeat the process with the remaining meat and oil. Season all the beef with the remaining salt and pepper to taste.

❊To serve, place a slice of the toasted bread in the middle of each of 6 plates. Top with a layer of beef, a layer of onions, a generous drizzling of Truffled Cheese Sauce, and a large dollop of wilted spinach. Serve extra sauce on the side.

Truffled Cheese Sauce

For a less dressy dish, skip the truffle oil, but be warned: the unique truffle flavor makes the sauce extra delicious. If you do not have a double boiler, prepare the sauce in a heavy-bottomed saucepan and take extra care while cooking. Or, set the saucepan in a skillet with about an inch of hot water in it.

1½ cups

1 teaspoon cornstarch

2 tablespoons dry white wine

1 cup heavy cream (more to thin if necessary)

6 ounces sharp orange-colored cheddar cheese, grated

1 teaspoon truffle oil, white or black

Salt and freshly ground black pepper

❊Bring 2 cups of water to a boil in the bottom of a double boiler. Meanwhile, dissolve the cornstarch in the white wine. Reserve. Heat the cream in the top of the double boiler over the boiling water until bubbles form around the edge and steam rises off the cream. Slowly whisk in the grated cheese, about ½ cup at a time, waiting until the cheese is fully incorporated before adding more. When all the cheese has been incorporated, whisk in the cornstarch-wine mixture. Remove from the heat. (The sauce can be cooled and stored for a few days at this point. When ready to serve, gently reheat, thinning with extra cream if necessary. If the sauce should "break" or curdle, vigorously whisk in a small amount of hot water until it is smooth.) Add the truffle oil, salt (depending on the saltiness of your cheese, you may not need salt), and pepper to taste.

ASIAN STEAK NORA WITH SHAVED FENNEL SALAD

Prepare Ahead

The meat can marinate up to 12 hours before cooking.

Washington, D.C., Dame Nora Pouillon is delighted with Les Dames d'Escoffier's Green Tables initiative (see box, page 105). Her Restaurant Nora opened in 1979 and became the first certified organic restaurant in America. "Everything I do in the area of food I relate to the environment. I think water is very important. After all, you can't cook without it." Over the years, Pouillon has campaigned strongly for sustainable foods, including seafood. "We need occasional moratoriums to replenish supplies. The ocean is not a bottomless pit," she said, when she supported the 2000 U.S. moratorium on swordfish.

For this recipe, Pouillon favors organic Asian beef. "It is extremely lean and flavorful. Although a bit tougher, it is this very quality that makes it a perfect candidate for marinating. The ginger in the marinade helps with digestion as well as assisting to break down the fibers of the meat. *Tamari* is a soy product, and the benefits of soy have been shown in many studies to aid in the balance of hormones, especially for women. Lastly, with the use of the stronger Asian flavors such as ginger and lemongrass, you don't need extra fat for flavor."

As an alternative to the Shaved Fennel Salad, pair the steaks with the Gingered Sweet Potato–Parsnip Purée (page 232) and Stir-Fried Green Beans and Sunchokes (page 225). For an appetizer, something grand like Smoked Whitefish and Nori Pâté (page 22); for a first course, Basic Greens with an In-Your-Face Dressing (page 68) or, for a more celebratory dinner, Piedmontese Wedding Soup (page 100). Have Bread and Chocolate (page 333) for dessert.

Suggested Beverage

A Rhône Valley blend such as Gigondas or an Italian Chianti Classico Riserva. Interested in pairing red meat with white wine? Give an Alsatian Gewürztraminer or Pinot Gris a try.

4 servings

2 tablespoons tamari or regular soy sauce

2 tablespoons minced garlic

2 tablespoons extra-virgin olive oil

2 tablespoons minced lemongrass, lime leaves, or cilantro

1 tablespoon minced onion

1 tablespoon prepared Dijon mustard

3-inch piece of gingerroot, peeled and minced

4 New York strip steaks, about 8 ounces each *or* 2 pounds of flank, round, or chuck steak

Shaved Fennel Salad (recipe follows)

❈ Make the marinade by combining the tamari, garlic, oil, lemongrass, onion, mustard, and gingerroot in a medium bowl. Whisk to blend. Place the steaks in a nonreactive dish and pour the marinade over them. Marinate for at least 3 hours and no longer than 12 hours, as the meat will become dry and salty.

❈ Preheat the grill or broiler. Grill or broil the steaks on each side until medium rare, about 4 minutes, or until desired doneness. To serve, cut the steaks across the grain into thin slices and place on serving plates with the Shaved Fennel Salad.

Prepare Ahead

The dressing can be prepared hours ahead, but fennel should be sliced and added less than 30 minutes before serving.

Shaved Fennel Salad

4 to 6 servings

1 lemon, zested (remove zest in long strips with zester or use vegetable peeler, then julienne) and squeezed for 1 teaspoon juice

Heaping ½ cup chopped parsley

2 tablespoons minced chives

2 tablespoons water

1 tablespoon extra-virgin olive oil

¼ teaspoon salt

⅛ teaspoon freshly ground black pepper

3 medium (about 2 pounds) fennel bulbs

¼ cup diced and seeded tomatoes or red bell pepper (optional)

✻ In a large bowl, whisk together the lemon zest and juice, parsley, chives, water, oil, salt, and pepper. Remove any brown outer leaves of the fennel, as well as the cores and fronds. Slice the fennel very thinly across the grain, preferably using a mandoline slicer, and add to the lemon mixture as it is sliced. Toss well to coat the fennel. Leave to marinate for approximately 15 minutes, allowing the fennel to soften slightly and absorb the flavors. Add the tomatoes and serve at room temperature.

Storing Gingerroot

Put knobs of gingerroot into a resealable plastic bag and freeze. When you need the ginger, give it 10 minutes at room temperature, and you'll be able to mince and chop whatever amount you need.

SWEDISH MEATBALLS WITH EASTERN-EUROPEAN SAUERKRAUT

Chicago Dame Toria Emas serves her famous meatballs—a Swedish recipe passed down to her by her mother—traditionally with red cabbage, noodles dressed with butter and caraway seeds, and the Swedish drink glögg. Still, Emas—who, as administration director of the Chicago Bar Association, oversees food service for hundreds of occasions every year—is not averse to more adventuresome pairings. Here the meatballs and their sauce team up with an easy and inspired treatment of sauerkraut from Austin Dame Dawn Orsak, who specializes in traditional foodways. Orsak's sauerkraut is a Texas Czech and Polish dish that Orsak's family likes with homemade sausage and a cucumber salad with dill and sour cream dressing. We suggest serving the sauerkraut and meatballs with boiled or mashed potatoes, the entire plate sharing the meatball gravy. For color on the plate: a spoonful of Farmers' Carrots (page 124). Golden Beet Slaw (page 28) makes a lively appetizer. For a first course, wedges of Seasonal Mushroom Galette (page 40) drizzled with a bit of crème fraîche, and for dessert, Gingerbread Dessert Waffles (page 322).

4 to 6 servings (24 meatballs)

¼ cup olive oil, divided

1 apple, peeled, cored, and finely chopped

¼ cup finely chopped onion

¾ pound ground veal

¾ pound ground beef

½ cup fresh homemade fine-textured bread crumbs (see box, page 140)

2 tablespoons water

1 tablespoon prepared horseradish

2 teaspoons freshly ground cardamom (see box, page 101)

1 large egg, beaten

Prepare Ahead

The meatballs are best formed and then firmed up by a few hours or even a night in the refrigerator before frying. The balls can also be made and frozen weeks ahead of serving. Thaw in the refrigerator, then brown and finish in their cooking broth right before serving. Or, make and sauté the meatballs, refrigerate for up to 48 hours, then finish cooking in the broth to serve. This recipe is easily doubled, but you may want to use 2 pans for sautéing the meatballs.

Suggested
Beverage

A dry Riesling or a
red Swiss wine—
Fendant or Dole. For
beer, it's hard to
beat a dark lager.

1 teaspoon salt

10 grinds black pepper

⅔ cup all-purpose flour

**One 14.5-ounce can beef broth or equivalent amount homemade
   broth**

Eastern-European Sauerkraut (recipe follows)

❋ Heat 2 tablespoons of the oil in a large sauté pan over medium heat.
Add the apple and onion and cook until soft but not browned. Remove
from the heat. In a large bowl, combine the veal, beef, bread crumbs,
water, horseradish, cardamom, egg, salt, pepper, and apple-onion
mixture. Shape into round balls about 1½ inches in diameter (you
should have about 24 meatballs total).

❋ Dredge the meatballs in the flour. Using the same sauté pan, heat the
remaining oil over high heat. Add the meatballs, a few at a time, so
as not to crowd the pan. Reduce heat to medium-high and continue
to regulate heat so that the meatballs brown well but not too quickly.
Allow them to brown on one side before gently turning them. To
aid in browning, as you brown each side, press down ever so slightly
to flatten.

❋ As the meatballs appear browned, remove to a paper towel–lined plate.
Don't worry about them cooking completely; they will finish cooking
in the broth. When all the meatballs have been browned and removed

---

In Praise of Stale Bread

I never toss out slightly stale pieces of good bread. Trimmed of crusts (if
particularly crusty) and torn into pieces, they get pulsed to the desired texture
in my food processor. If I don't need the crumbs right away, I freeze them
for later use. If you purchase bread crumbs, Japanese *panko* crumbs with their
light, crunchy texture are a good choice for a crisp coating. Once opened,
store panko in the freezer.

—Washington, D.C., Dame Connie Hay

from the pan, deglaze the pan by adding the broth, bringing it to a boil, and loosening any browned bits that may have accumulated while cooking. Reduce heat to a simmer. Return the meatballs to the pan and cook for about 30 minutes. Serve with Eastern-European Sauerkraut.

Eastern-European Sauerkraut

4 to 6 servings

Prepare Ahead

Sauerkraut can be made 1 or 2 days ahead of serving and reheated.

One 32-ounce can of sauerkraut, or two 1-pound refrigerated packages (such as Boar's Head), drained

1 small apple, cored, quartered, and thinly sliced (no need to peel)

½ cup water

½ cup flat beer or dry white wine

1½ teaspoons caraway seeds

6 slices bacon, cut into ½-inch pieces (to render 2 tablespoons drippings)

1 cup chopped onion

2 tablespoons all-purpose flour

1 teaspoon sugar

1 teaspoon salt

10 grinds black pepper

❋ Combine the sauerkraut, apple, water, beer, and caraway seeds in a large saucepan. Simmer together on low heat for 10 to 15 minutes. In a medium sauté pan, fry the bacon until cooked through but not crisp. Add the onion to the pan and cook until it is transparent. Dust the flour over the bacon and onions and stir well. Cook for about 2 minutes. Add the bacon-onion mixture to the sauerkraut and stir well. Add the sugar, salt, and pepper. Let the mixture come to a boil and then remove from the heat. If the sauerkraut mixture seems too dry, add a little water until it reaches desired consistency. Serve hot.

WINE-DARK BEEF STEW WITH HORSERADISH POTATO PURÉE

Prepare Ahead

Both the stew and the Horseradish Potato Purée can be made a day ahead of serving and reheated.

New York Dame Rozanne Gold began her stellar food career at age 24: she was first chef to New York Mayor Ed Koch. Today, she is chef-director of Joseph Baum & Michael Whiteman Co., the international restaurant consulting firm best known for creating New York City's Windows on the World and the Rainbow Room. She is a columnist for *Bon Appétit* magazine; author of ten cookbooks, including the acclaimed "1-2-3 Cookbook" series; and three-time winner of the prestigious James Beard Book Award. Still, she finds time to dash out yet more recipes and pass along her kitchen wisdom. Of her Wine-Dark Beef Stew, she writes, "You'll never guess the secret ingredient in this voluptuous stew: hoisin sauce! It adds great complexity to the flavor. Use shin meat, also known as shank meat, for the most tender results. Or, buy large pieces of not-too-lean chuck and cut to desired size yourself. Packaged 'stew meat' from the supermarket is usually cut too small and sometimes labeled as chuck when it's top round."

If it's springtime, serve the stew and potatoes alongside Broiled Asparagus with the alternative topping of fried capers (page 218), otherwise, Farmers' Carrots (page 124) are a good choice. Perhaps a few Big Shrimp with Armenian "Pesto" (page 130) could start the dinner, and if it's winter, pass a plate of Tiny Tim Tarts (page 281) for dessert.

6 servings

3 pounds beef shin or chuck *or* 3½ pounds shank meat (bones add weight; cook them with the stew for added flavor)

15 grinds black pepper plus additional as needed

2 tablespoons olive oil

3 heaping cups finely chopped onions

½ cup store-bought hoisin sauce

2 cups Zinfandel or Cabernet Sauvignon, divided

One 14.5-ounce can diced tomatoes with herbs with their juice

5 bay leaves

1 pound slender carrots, peeled and cut diagonally into 1-inch lengths

Salt

1 tablespoon arrowroot

Horseradish Potato Purée (recipe follows)

¼ cup finely chopped parsley

Suggested Beverage

Use the same wine called for in the cooking—a California Zinfandel or a Washington state Cabernet Sauvignon.

✳ Cut the meat into 2½-inch pieces. Season with the pepper and set aside.

✳ In a large Dutch oven or heavy-bottomed pot, heat the oil over medium heat. Add the onions. Cook until the onions are soft and brown, stirring often. Add the meat. Cook over high heat, turning the pieces; as they brown lightly on all sides, remove them to a plate. (The onions will continue to cook with the meat.) When the browning is complete, return all the meat to the Dutch oven and reduce heat to low.

✳ In a medium bowl, stir together the hoisin sauce, 1 cup of the wine, and tomatoes with their juice. Pour over the meat. Add the bay leaves. Cover the Dutch oven and cook over low heat for 1 hour. Add the carrots and cook until the meat and carrots are fork tender, about 1¾ hours.

✳ Transfer the meat and carrots to a large bowl using a slotted spoon. Add the remaining wine to the Dutch oven and cook over high heat until the sauce is reduced to 2½ cups. Add salt and pepper to taste. Dissolve the arrowroot starch in 1 tablespoon water and add to the sauce. Continue to cook over medium heat until the sauce is thick. Pour over the meat and carrots and stir briefly. Remove the bay leaves and reheat before serving over the Horseradish Potato Purée. Garnish with the parsley.

Horseradish Potato Purée

Prepare Ahead

Purée can be prepared hours ahead and reheated, covered, in the oven.

With or without the horseradish, Gold's potato purée is such a great way to mash potatoes—milk, no cream, and butter to your taste.

6 servings

2 pounds Yukon gold potatoes, peeled (if large, cut in half)

2 teaspoons salt plus additional as needed

1½ cups whole milk

1 large clove garlic

¼ cup prepared white horseradish

2 to 6 tablespoons unsalted butter

Freshly ground white pepper

Put the potatoes in a medium pot with cover. Add the salt and water to cover. Bring to a boil, lower heat, and partially cover. Cook the potatoes until tender, about 40 minutes.

Pour the milk into a medium saucepan. Push the garlic through a garlic press and add to the milk. Bring just to a boil. Lower heat and simmer for 10 minutes.

Drain the potatoes, reserving a few tablespoons of cooking water. Put the potatoes in a large bowl and, using a potato masher (or a ricer if you have one), mash thoroughly. Add the hot milk and horseradish, mashing until the potatoes are creamy. Cut the butter into pieces and stir into the potatoes. Add some of the cooking water if necessary. Add salt and white pepper to taste as desired. Serve hot.

ITALIAN-STYLE BRAISED SHORT RIBS WITH ROSEMARY POLENTA

New York Dame Michele Scicolone is an expert on Italian cuisine. She has written thirteen cookbooks—including *1,000 Italian Recipes* and *Entertaining with the Sopranos*—and says that traditionally, short ribs are not a cut of meat used in Italy. Still, because she favors the cut, she likes to prepare them "Italian style." Every time she does, she has guests asking to take home the leftovers. Scicolone especially likes this method of doing short ribs because it allows you to eliminate a lot of the fat before the final reheating and serving.

These short ribs with polenta pair well with Roasted Brussels Sprouts (page 217) in fall and winter and with Basic Wilted Greens (see box, page 228) most any time of year. Begin with an easy starter (see box, page 36) and a first course of cured meat (see box, page 63). Lemon-Cranberry-Pecan Biscotti (page 290) are an appropriately Italian dessert for this meal.

8 servings

8 beef short ribs (about 6 pounds)

1 tablespoon salt

15 grinds black pepper

2 tablespoons olive oil

1 large onion, roughly chopped into ½-inch pieces (2 cups)

3 carrots, peeled and roughly chopped into ½-inch pieces (1 heaping cup)

3 celery ribs, roughly chopped into ½-inch pieces (1 heaping cup)

4 cloves garlic, chopped

2 cups dry red wine

2 cups beef or veal broth, preferably homemade

One 14.5-ounce can Italian peeled tomatoes with their juice

Two 3-inch sprigs fresh rosemary

Rosemary Polenta (recipe follows)

Prepare Ahead

Scicolone advises, "Short ribs are ideal for company since you can make them several days in advance. They reheat perfectly." The polenta can be prepared "almost effortlessly" while the ribs reheat.

❊ Preheat the oven to 325°F. Pat the ribs dry and sprinkle them all over with the salt and pepper. In a large Dutch oven or heavy-bottomed pot, heat the oil over medium heat. Add the ribs in batches, being careful not to crowd the Dutch oven. Cook until the ribs are nicely browned on all sides. Transfer the ribs to a plate as they are done.

❊ When done browning, pour off all but 2 tablespoons of the drippings. Add the onion, carrots, and celery and stir well. Cook for 10 minutes or until golden. Stir in the garlic and cook 5 minutes more. Add the wine, broth, tomatoes with juice, and rosemary. Bring the liquid to a simmer, scraping the bottom of the Dutch oven. Return the ribs to the Dutch oven.

❊ Cover the Dutch oven and place it in the oven. Cook for 2 hours, checking occasionally to see that the liquid is just simmering. Adjust oven temperature accordingly. Remove the cover and cook until the meat is very tender and coming away from the bone, about 1 hour. With tongs, transfer the ribs to a cutting board and let cool.

❊ Degrease the cooking liquid (see box, opposite), discarding the greasy cooked vegetables and rosemary twigs. Return the degreased liquid to the Dutch oven and bring it to a simmer. Cook until thickened to taste. With a sharp knife, trim the ribs and discard any loosened bones. Add the ribs to the Dutch oven. At this point, the mixture can be

---

In Praise of the Lowly Lentil

Instead of fiddling with flours and thickeners before, during, or after making your next beef stew or braised short ribs recipe (or any stewed or braised dish, for that matter), add ½ cup dried red lentils for every 2 cups cooking liquid at the very start of simmering. The lentils will cook down and virtually melt, and you'll have an easy, healthy, thickened sauce. Do *not* use French green lentils; they maintain their firm texture in cooking.

—*Ontario Dame Gail Gordon Oliver*

refrigerated and stored for several days. When ready to serve, prepare the Rosemary Polenta. While it bakes, reheat the ribs in their sauce on top of the stove. Taste for seasoning and serve hot with the polenta.

Suggested Beverage

Definitely Italian: Chianti Classico Riserva or a Super Tuscan (both Sangiovese based).

Rosemary Polenta

8 servings

3 cups water

2 cups milk

1 cup cornmeal (preferably coarsely ground)

1 teaspoon salt

2 tablespoons unsalted butter

1 cup freshly grated Parmigiano-Reggiano cheese

1 tablespoon chopped fresh rosemary leaves

✻ Preheat the oven to 375°F. In a 9- by 13-inch baking dish, whisk together the water, milk, cornmeal, and salt. Bake, uncovered, for 60 minutes. Remove the pan from the oven and whisk the polenta. Stir in the butter,

---

Fool-Proof Degreasing

Dame Scicolone insists that when cooking high-fat meats like short ribs, thorough degreasing is essential. And that includes disposing of the braising vegetables as well. "Even if you degrease the liquid, the vegetables remaining are greasy. Get rid of them. They've done their work in flavoring the sauce." The best way to degrease is to use a large gravy separator (this looks like a large liquid measuring cup with a long spout extending from the base of the cup). Remove the meat from the liquid; pour the liquid into a sieve set over the separator. Dispose of all the solids in the sieve. In the separator, the fat floats to the surface and you pour the fat-free liquid back into the cooking pot. If there is a lot of liquid, you may need to do this in batches. If you don't have a separator, strain the liquid and chill it separate from the meat. Several hours in the refrigerator will produce a sheet of fat you can easily remove, but you will need to allow time for this.

half of the cheese, and the rosemary. Smooth the top and sprinkle with the remaining cheese. Place the pan back in the oven and bake until the cheese is melted and the top is lightly browned, about 10 minutes. Serve immediately.

Poultry

❧ CHICKEN THAI BASIL ❧

Washington, D.C., Dame Nongkran Daks is an expert on Asian cuisine. When she opened her first restaurant, Thai Basil, in Chantilly, Virginia, she named it after this simple, fragrant dish—easy even for those who rarely try Asian recipes. Don't miss it. For appetizers, serve Fresh Vietnamese Summer Rolls (page 26). For dessert, cookies with their own appeal: Raspberry Rosebuds (page 298).

This is a spicy-hot dish; if you prefer a milder heat, use the jalapeño chile peppers instead of the serranos.

Prepare Ahead

Prep all the ingredients hours ahead and the last-minute cooking is simple.

4 servings

- **6 tablespoons vegetable oil**
- **4 cloves garlic, finely chopped**
- **1 pound thinly sliced boneless chicken breast (for easy slicing, firm up meat in the freezer for a few hours; see box, page 17)**
- **1 small yellow onion, cut into ½-inch crescents (see box, page 52)**
- **4 cups thinly sliced cultivated brown or shiitake mushrooms (optional)**
- **4 green onions, cut into 1-inch pieces, both green and white parts**
- **2 tablespoons fish sauce**
- **2 tablespoons oyster sauce**
- **2 tablespoons dark, sweet soy sauce**
- **2 cups (6 ounces, including stems) fresh Thai basil or regular basil leaves, cut in chiffonade (see box, page 59)**
- **3 to 6 fresh serrano or 2 jalapeño chile peppers, cut into diagonal slices**
- **6 to 8 cups steamed rice**

Suggested
Beverage

Off-dry German Ries-
ling or a Thai beer,
such as Singha.

Heat the oil in a wok or a large skillet over medium heat. Sauté the garlic until barely golden. Add the chicken. Stir the meat until it turns white. Add the onion, mushrooms, and green onions. Stir again a few times. Add the fish sauce, oyster sauce, and soy sauce. Mix well. Add the basil and serrano peppers. Mix thoroughly, transfer to a platter, and serve immediately with the rice.

ANNABELL'S OVEN CHICKEN AND SQUASH CASSEROLE

Prepare Ahead

The dish works best
if the casserole is
prepared up to the
final cooking a day
before. The chicken,
too, can be prepared
a day ahead and
reheated in its gravy,
though it is especially
nice when crispy
from the broiler.

Some of our most prized dishes don't come from culinary schools or up-market restaurants. They come from our memories, rich with smells and sounds. These recipes are not rigid formulas, but helpful guides that can tolerate a bit more of this and a bit less of that, such as these two recipes from Charleston Dame Sarah Robinson Graham, who runs her own company representing specialty food lines. For over fifty years, the Annabell of these dishes created what the locals called "famous" midday dinners for Graham's family and friends. Of all Annabell's meals, her Oven Chicken and Squash Casserole lives the most famously in Graham's memory and in her cooking repertoire to this very day.

This is decidedly homey fare. Using whole-grain bread in the casse-role adds more texture and a nuttier flavor. Start with an appetizer of Heavenly Cheddar and Cream Biscuits (page 262), cut cocktail size. The Uncomplicated Green Salad (see box, page 69) is a perfect first course or side dish, though Annabell would certainly have served a creamy cole-slaw. And she would have favored Edna Lewis's Fresh Blackberry Cobbler (page 311) for dessert. We think the Jumbo Ice Cream Sandwiches (page 292) also seem just right to end the meal.

6 to 8 servings

3½ to 4 pounds fryer chicken pieces, skin on (drumsticks or thighs preferred)

3 tablespoons plus 2 teaspoons sea salt, divided

½ teaspoon freshly ground black pepper

2 tablespoons Worcestershire sauce

1 medium sweet onion (Vidalia, Texas 1015, or Walla Walla), cut into ½-inch crescents (see box, page 52)

2 to 3 teaspoons dried herbs: basil, oregano, or thyme, *or* a mixture, plus perhaps a little celery salt or celery seed (total of 1 tablespoon seasoning)

Squash Casserole (recipe follows)

3 tablespoons all-purpose flour

1¾ cups reserved squash cooking liquid (from the Squash Casserole recipe) or chicken broth

2 tablespoons chopped parsley

※ Preheat the oven to 375°F. Put the chicken in a large pot. Cover with cold water and stir in 3 tablespoons of the salt. Let stand at room temperature for 30 minutes, then remove the chicken from the water and place in a shallow metal roasting pan (the bottom of a broiler pan works perfectly). Season both sides of the chicken with the remaining salt and pepper. Place the chicken skin side down. Pour the Worcestershire sauce over the chicken. Distribute the onions evenly over the chicken and sprinkle with the dried herbs. Cover with aluminum foil and cook in the lower third of the oven until the juices run almost clear from the thickest piece of chicken, 25 to 30 minutes—it will finish cooking under the broiler. (The Squash Casserole can be baked at the same time on another shelf.)

※ Take the chicken out of the oven and reserve. Check the Squash Casserole. If it is done, remove it. If not, allow it to finish baking before turning the oven to broil. Remove the foil from the chicken. Turn the chicken skin side up and put under the broiler, 4 to 5 inches below the heat, until skin is crisp and browned, basting once or twice,

**Suggested
Beverage**

A California Chardon-
nay or Viognier, or an
Oregon Pinot Gris.

10 to 20 minutes. You may need to turn the pan halfway through the broiling to brown evenly.

✻ Remove the pan from the broiler and transfer the chicken to a serving platter. Sprinkle the flour over the juices and onions in the pan, mix, and put on the stove over medium-high heat to cook, stirring often, allowing the flour to thicken the juices. As the mixture thickens, slowly add the squash cooking liquid to the pan and allow to cook to desired consistency. Taste for seasoning and serve over the chicken along with the Squash Casserole, topping both with the chopped parsley.

Prepare Ahead

The casserole can
be assembled a day
ahead, then baked
with the chicken.

Squash Casserole

6 to 8 servings

Butter for baking dish

2 cups water

**2 pounds yellow summer squash *or* a mixture of yellow and green
    summer squash, cleaned and cut into ½- to ¾-inch slices**

**1 medium sweet (Vidalia, Texas 1015, or Walla Walla) onion, cut
    into ¼-inch crescents (see box, page 52)**

2 teaspoons salt plus additional as needed

**4 slices good-quality white or whole-grain sandwich bread, toasted
    and torn into ½-inch pieces (3 to 4 cups)**

8 ounces sharp cheddar cheese, coarsely grated

1 tablespoon dried oregano, basil, or thyme (not rosemary)

10 grinds black pepper

2 tablespoons unsalted butter, cut into tiny pieces (optional)

2 tablespoons chopped parsley

✻ Butter a 9- by 13-inch baking dish and set aside. Preheat the oven to 375°F. Put the water, squash, onion, and salt in a large saucepan over high heat. Cook until the squash is just barely soft, 3 to 5 minutes. Do not overcook. Remove from the heat and with a slotted spoon, immediately transfer the vegetables from the cooking water to the prepared baking dish. Fold in the bread, cheese, herbs, and pepper. Taste the cooking liquid—it should be very flavorful, but not too salty. You should have about 2 cups. If necessary adjust the seasoning by adding either more salt or more water and boiling until you have the desired amount. Add about ¼ cup of the liquid to the squash mixture—just enough to make it moist, but not soupy. Reserve the remaining cooking liquid for making the chicken gravy.

❋ Top the squash mixture with the pieces of butter if desired. When ready to serve, bake in the preheated oven (along with the chicken) until the cheese is melted and just beginning to brown, about 30 minutes. If the casserole gets too dry, spoon in a bit more of the cooking liquid or broth. Serve along with the chicken as described, or top with the parsley and serve as you wish.

Making Food Attractive

Among Dames there are many approaches to presenting food. For the most part they are a practical group of cooks; their garnishing style veers toward less, not more. They all value simple things done well. Still, there are Dames who use herb sprigs and edible flowers, artfully placed; Dames who use paper doilies; and Dames who use hollowed bell peppers for containers. Regardless of individual style, all agree that good food makes people want to eat merely by its handsome appearance. And furthermore, they agree that fresh, good food generally has an inherent luster, a glistening brightness about it. Does an appetizer look a little dull? Drizzle it with a bit of your best olive oil. An entrée appears rather monochromatically brown? Shower it with chopped parsley or add a dollop of wilted spinach (see box, page 227). That dessert looks too plain? A sprinkle of confectioners' sugar (kept handy in a sugar shaker) may perk it up.

FILIPINO CHICKEN ADOBO
OVER FRESH GREENS

Prepare Ahead

The dish can be prepared up to the addition of the avocado and the greens 1 or 2 days ahead of serving. When ready to serve, reheat and add the remaining ingredients.

Honolulu Dame Sharon Kobayashi, along with business partner and fellow Dame Ruth Arakaki, is famous for owning the company Latitude 22, which makes and sells a very popular oatcake all over Hawaii under the Akamai Foods label. A former biologist, Kobayashi switched to a career in food by attending the Culinary Institute of the Pacific and doing numerous stints in all sorts of restaurants up and down the West Coast.

This one-dish meal is based on the Filipino classic, chicken adobo. Because it is both easy and tasty, adobo appears often as the "family meal" for restaurant staff in Hawaii, served with steamed rice. Kobayashi lightens up the traditional version by serving it on a bed of fresh greens and topping with chunks of ripe avocado. The steamed rice is traditional but optional. For appetizers, prepare some finger vegetables (see box, page 12); no need for a first course; and for dessert, indulge in the Jam Swirl Brownies (see box, page 296).

4 servings

1½ pounds chicken thighs, boneless and skinless, cut bite size—
   no bigger than 1 inch

One 15.5-ounce can garbanzo beans, drained and rinsed

8 ounces cultivated brown mushrooms, quartered

6 cloves garlic, minced (about 3 tablespoons)

¼ cup red wine vinegar

¼ cup balsamic vinegar plus additional for serving

2 tablespoons soy sauce

6 bay leaves

6 peppercorns, crushed with the back of a heavy pan

⅔ cup chicken broth

¼ cup extra-virgin olive oil plus additional for serving

½ teaspoon salt plus additional as needed

Freshly ground black pepper

6 cups curly cress, watercress, or arugula

6 cups steamed rice (optional)

2 firm but ripe avocados, peeled, diced, and tossed with 1 teaspoon freshly squeezed lemon juice

1 cup red onion cut in crescents (see box, page 52)

Suggested Beverage

A Spanish Albariño or Italian Pinot Grigio (the bitter greens make pairing with a red challenging).

In a large Dutch oven or heavy-bottomed pot, combine the chicken, beans, mushrooms, garlic, vinegars, soy sauce, bay leaves, and peppercorns. Bring to a boil, reduce to medium heat, and cook, uncovered. Stir occasionally until the liquid evaporates and the mixture begins to brown (check it at 25 minutes; it may cook as long as 45 minutes). Remove the bay leaves and add the chicken broth and oil, scraping the bottom to release any residue. Taste and adjust the seasoning with the salt and pepper. Remove from the heat. Distribute the greens on a large serving platter or among 6 plates. Spoon the hot chicken mixture over the greens and place the rice beside them. Top with the avocado and red onion. Drizzle with a little oil to add shine and serve with the extra balsamic vinegar on the side.

Sharing Family Recipes

When a grown child calls home to ask for instructions about how to cook a beloved family dish, it is a special kind of pleasure. Not only does the request affirm that you're a good cook in your offspring's eyes, but it also constitutes a link between the home they came from and the one they are creating for themselves. Sharing recipes from one generation to the next gives a sense of continuity and forges connections built around the pot and the plate.

—*Cleveland Dame Laura Taxel*

BRIE AND BASIL STUFFED TURKEY BREAST

Prepare Ahead

The turkey breasts can be stuffed, wrapped, and refrigerated at least a day before cooking.

Kansas City Dames Karen Adler and Judith Fertig have made a career of celebrating regional food—barbecue, that is. With over a dozen barbecue books to their credit, they share the title "BBQ Queens."

This recipe, adapted from their *BBQ Queens' Big Book of Barbecue*, is their pick for Thanksgiving turkey. It is so versatile and tasty, however, you'll want to make it many times a year. Adler and Fertig prefer to smoke the turkey breasts—either on a stovetop smoker indoors or on a smoker outdoors—but they stress that you can also grill them indirectly or just bake in the oven. Their suggested woods for smoking or grilling are apple, cherry, oak, or pecan. Cook as many breasts as you need, but be sure to make extra: leftovers will be coveted. The meat turns out moist with the melted cheese.

This is casual fare. Good-quality corn chips with a bowl of In-Your-Face Dressing (page 68) make a fun appetizer. During warm weather, serve a first course of Fresh Tomato Soup with Roasted-Corn Guacamole (page 89); during colder weather, Greek Yellow Split-Pea Soup (page 83). For side dishes, consider Greens Braised with Dried Fruits and Nuts (page 226) or Warm Lentils (page 244). For dessert, Shirley's Tunnel of Fudge Cake (page 301), unless, of course, it really is Thanksgiving—then Tiny Tim Tarts are a must (page 281).

8 servings

2 boneless, skinless turkey breast halves, each about 1½ pounds

1 teaspoon salt

10 grinds black pepper

½ pound Brie or Camembert, rind on, cut into 8 medium-thin slices

20 fresh basil leaves

4 ounces prosciutto, thinly sliced, with waxed paper placed between slices to prevent sticking

✳ Start a stovetop or outdoor smoker (preheat to 250°F) or indirect grill, or preheat the oven to 350°F. Make a large pocket-like slit in each turkey breast half. Salt and pepper both halves. Place 4 or 5 slices of cheese evenly inside the slit of each breast half. Tuck half of the basil leaves evenly on top of the cheese. Wrap each breast half with half of the prosciutto—about 3 slices loosely wrapped around each. The prosciutto not only seasons the dish but also serves to hold in the melting cheese. Still, play it safe and place the breast halves on a piece of foil or in a disposable aluminum pan to minimize cleanup.

✳ Cook using one of these methods:

> ✳ Smoke for about 40 minutes on a stovetop smoker over medium-high heat or for 1 hour on an outdoor smoker at 250°F. Use about 1 tablespoon finely ground wood chips in the stovetop smoker and 3 chunks of wood on an outdoor smoker.

OR

> ✳ Cook on an indirect grill with lid closed for 30 to 40 minutes, turning once. For just a "kiss" of smoke, place ½ cup dry wood pellets or wood chips in a smoker box or an aluminum foil packet with holes punched through. Turn one side of your gas grill on high or bank ashed-over coals on a charcoal grill to one side. Place the smoker box or foil packet as close to the heat source as possible. When the pellets or chips start to smolder and give off smoke, put your turkey breasts on the indirect or unheated side of the grill and close the lid.

OR

> ✳ Bake for 35 to 45 minutes in a 350°F oven.

✳ Whatever method you choose, the turkey is done when a meat thermometer inserted into the thickest part of the meat registers 160°F. Let sit for 10 to 15 minutes; the temperature will increase by at least another 5°F. Then slice and serve hot or at room temperature.

Suggested Beverage

Chardonnay, oaked or unoaked, or a fruity Merlot.

DUCK BREAST WITH SAUTÉED POTATOES

Prepare Ahead

The duck must marinate for about 8 hours. You can cook both the duck and the potatoes and prepare the sauce a couple of hours before serving. Just reheat and plate when you are ready.

New York Dame Ariane Daguin tells how she was an expert at deboning ducks and rendering duck fat by the time she was ten. Her father, André Daguin, chef-owner of the Hôtel de France in Auch, Gascony, is famous throughout France for his foie gras and other Gascon specialties.

Yet Ariane did not pursue a career in food until, in 1985, while a student at Columbia University, she and a fellow grad student pooled their resources to launch D'Artagnan—virtually the only purveyor of game and foie gras in the United States at the time. In 2005, Ariane became the sole owner of D'Artagnan, by then a $40-million-a-year business. That same year, she received the Lifetime Achievement Award from *Bon Appétit* magazine, an award previously bestowed on such culinary notables as Julia Child and James Beard. In September 2006, Ariane was awarded the Légion d'Honneur in her native France.

For all her business accomplishments, Daguin still finds time to cook for family and friends. She favors dishes like this duck breast with sautéed potatoes. Daguin points out that duck meat, underneath its fat layer, is actually quite lean, so she marinates the breast in a generous dousing of olive oil and balsamic vinegar. The duck breast with its deglazed sauce is paired with what are possibly the world's best fried potatoes. The secret, you'll find, comes with the duck breast itself. "Nothing fries potatoes to perfection as well as the fat rendered in cooking duck meat," says Daguin.

This is a deliciously rich dish. Modest-sized portions will be pleasing; if you like, accompany them with a bit of raw bitter greens, such as arugula, dressed simply with olive oil, salt, and pepper, or with the Whole Baby Carrots (page 216). For appetizers, serve the Smoked-Salmon Tartare (page 35) with Crostini or Brioche Points (see box, page 30). For a first course, small wedges of Souvenir Eggplant Gratin (page 220). Just "little bites" for dessert: Burgundian Spiced Caramels (page 328) seem appropriately French and easy.

2 to 3 servings

1 whole (about 1 pound) boneless duck breast

½ cup extra-virgin olive oil

¼ cup balsamic vinegar

2 cloves garlic, smashed

½ teaspoon salt plus additional as needed

5 grinds black pepper plus additional as needed

2 fresh rosemary sprigs

2 fresh thyme sprigs

2 medium-size Yukon gold potatoes, peeled and cut into no larger than ½-inch cubes

2 tablespoons veal demi-glace _or_ ½ cup chicken broth

¼ cup heavy cream

4 cloves garlic, skin on

2 tablespoons fresh thyme leaves or chopped parsley

❀ Score the skin side of the duck breast with 1-inch cross-hatch cuts, cutting through the fat and just slightly into the meat.

❀ Mix together the oil, vinegar, smashed garlic, salt, and pepper. Place the mixture, the meat, and 1 each of the rosemary and thyme sprigs in a resealable plastic bag large enough to hold everything (see box, page 160). Marinate in the refrigerator for about 8 hours.

❀ When ready to cook, take out the duck breast, reserving the marinade. Pat excess liquid off the breast with paper towels. In a medium-size heavy sauté pan over medium heat, begin searing duck, skin side down. Sear until skin is nicely browned and crispy, 8 to 10 minutes. Check several times to make sure the skin does not burn, regulating heat accordingly.

❀ As the duck cooks, pour off excess fat into a second large sauté pan with the potatoes and cook over medium-high heat. Regulate heat so that the potatoes brown but do not burn. Once the potatoes begin developing a light brown color, add the unpeeled garlic cloves. Continue

Suggested Beverage

A red Burgundy, a Merlot-driven right-bank Bordeaux, or most any American Merlot.

cooking until potatoes are crispy on the outside and tender on the inside, 12 to 15 minutes. About 10 minutes into the cooking time, add the remaining sprigs of rosemary and thyme. When the potatoes are finished cooking, remove the garlic and herb sprigs. Drain the potatoes on paper towels and return them to the pan to keep warm.

❋ Meanwhile, turn the duck over and continue cooking for 5 to 10 minutes, depending upon how thick the breasts are. You can make a cut into the thickest part to check for doneness. Don't overcook; the meat will continue to cook when it is reheated in the sauce right before serving.

❋ Remove the duck to a plate. Deglaze the cooking pan with the demi-glace, scraping up any browned bits. Add cream and season to taste with some of the reserved marinade, salt, and pepper. If you are using the broth, you will need to continue to cook until the sauce is desired consistency. It should lightly coat a spoon. Just before serving, return the duck and any of its accumulated juices to the sauce to reheat.

❋ To serve, cut the duck across the grain into ¼-inch slices. Serve them in a fan shape alongside the potatoes. Coat the meat with the sauce and sprinkle all with fresh thyme leaves.

How to Marinate in a Bag

Los Angeles Dame Peg Rahn says: When marinating meat, place the meat and marinade ingredients in a resealable plastic bag, just large enough to hold the meat and the marinade. As long as the marinade covers the meat, you won't need to turn the meat while marinating.

Pork

PORK LOIN WITH WINTER CITRUS GRAVY

Somewhere in the annals of food history, someone must have asked, "What's a roast without its gravy?" Here's a seasonal twist on the gravy, as well as the roast. New York Dame Lucy Wing flavors the pork with a rub of fresh tangerine zest, chervil, and cumin, and then uses fresh tangerine juice to turn pan drippings into a sauce that brings new meaning to the word "gravy." Serve the combination with the Horseradish Potato Purée (page 144). Black-Olive Tapenade (page 5) makes a good starter; Creamy Roasted Parsnip Soup (page 94) for a first course; and for dessert, Fran's Original Cheesecake (page 307) or Peach Tree Country Kitchen's Bread Pudding (page 323).

Wing, who is a former magazine food editor for *Country Living*, *McCall's*, and *American Home*, is an outspoken proponent of cooking seasonally. She developed this recipe to take advantage of the availability of winter citrus, as well as chervil, which grows in sunbelt gardens during cool weather.

6 servings

Prepare Ahead

The herb rub for the pork loin can be prepared a day ahead.

One 3-pound center-cut boneless pork loin roast

1 tablespoon finely grated tangerine zest (see box, page 75)

1 tablespoon chopped fresh chervil leaves *or* 2 teaspoons dried chervil or oregano

1 tablespoon olive oil

1 teaspoon salt plus additional as needed

½ teaspoon ground cumin

Suggested Beverage

A Loire Valley Sauvignon Blanc, a Vouvray, or a Beaujolais-Villages.

¼ teaspoon freshly ground black pepper plus additional as needed

One 14.5-ounce can chicken broth plus additional as needed

½ cup (about 3 tangerines) fresh tangerine juice

3 tablespoons all-purpose flour

Chervil sprigs for garnish (optional)

✻ Trim and discard any excess fat from the pork. Place the pork on a wire rack set in a 9- by 13-inch metal baking pan. In a small bowl, combine the tangerine zest, chervil, oil, salt, cumin, and pepper. Rub the herb mixture over all sides of the pork. Set the pork aside for 15 minutes.

✻ Preheat the oven to 350°F. Pour the broth into the baking pan with the pork. Roast the pork until a meat thermometer registers 160°F, about 2 hours. Watch the liquid level and add more broth or water to the pan if necessary.

✻ When the pork is done, transfer to a cutting board and let stand for 15 minutes. In a small bowl, whisk the tangerine juice and flour until smooth. Remove the wire rack from the baking pan. Place the baking pan over medium heat and stir the tangerine mixture into the meat drippings. (If most of the broth has evaporated during roasting, add 1 to 1½ cups water or broth to the pan and heat, stirring to loosen any browned bits.) Heat the tangerine-broth mixture to boiling, stirring until thickened and bubbly. Add salt and pepper to taste. Pour the gravy into a small pitcher.

✻ Cut the pork into thin slices and arrange on a platter. Garnish with chervil sprigs. Serve with the gravy.

SHANGHAI NOODLES WITH SHREDDED PORK AND CABBAGE

If you have only one Asian noodle dish in your repertoire, it should be this one. It's hard to imagine a better flavor (you'll pray for leftovers, which are memorable served at room temperature over shredded raw napa cabbage), and the prepare-ahead instructions make the recipe easy as well. The recipe comes from San Francisco Dame Joyce Jue who grew up in San Francisco's Chinatown and is now an internationally recognized expert on Chinese and Southeast Asian cuisine. Her book *Savoring Southeast Asia* won the 2001 IACP Best International Cookbook Award.

This recipe is one of her personal favorite Chinese noodle dishes. It uses round Shanghai noodles, which are extra thick, dense, and chewy, for absorbing the flavors and seasonings of the braising sauce. These are similar to Japanese udon wheat-flour noodles and can be found in the refrigerator section of Chinese grocery stores. Jue, who contends that Asian menus can be very complicated for the Western cook, suggests that preceding this noodle dish with some nibbly cocktail nuts is "perfectly fine." Skip the first course. A nontraditional but delectably acceptable side dish is Whole Baby Carrots (page 216). And for dessert, fresh fruit accompanied by lychee tea, a Chinese black tea scented with lychee fruit.

4 servings

Marinade

2 teaspoons light soy sauce

2 teaspoons Shao Hsing rice wine or dry sherry

¼ teaspoon sugar

1 teaspoon cornstarch

½ teaspoon Asian sesame oil

½ pound boneless pork loin, partially frozen for ease of slicing

---

Prepare Ahead

Allow about an hour to firm the pork in the freezer before slicing. The pork can be marinated up to 24 hours refrigerated. You can cook the noodles and prep the other ingredients several hours ahead. With all this done, final cooking and assembly are quick and easy.

Noodles

    1 pound fresh Shanghai-style noodles

Braising Sauce

    1½ tablespoons Chinese dark soy sauce

    1½ tablespoons Chinese light soy sauce

    2 teaspoons oyster sauce

    2 tablespoons Shao Hsing rice wine or dry sherry

    1 teaspoon sugar

    Big pinch white pepper

    ¼ cup low-sodium canned chicken broth

    1 teaspoon Asian sesame oil

Stir-Fry

    4 tablespoons corn or peanut oil, divided

    2 cloves garlic, chopped

    1 teaspoon salt

    2 cups shredded napa or regular cabbage

    1 cup garlic chives (*or* 2 leeks, white part only), cut into 1½-inch lengths

To marinate the pork, combine the soy sauce, rice wine, sugar, cornstarch, and sesame oil in a shallow dish large enough to hold the pork. Cut the pork into very thin strips, about ¼ by 1¼ inches. Add the pork to the marinade and toss to coat. Marinate at room temperature for 1 hour or refrigerate for up to 24 hours.

To prepare the noodles, bring 4 quarts of water to a boil in a large pot. Gently pull the noodles apart and add them to the boiling water. Bring to a second boil and cook the noodles until tender but still very chewy, 3 to 5 minutes. Drain. Rinse under cold water and drain again. Set aside.

To make the braising sauce, combine the soy sauces, oyster sauce, rice wine, sugar, white pepper, broth, and sesame oil. Reserve.

For the stir-fry, preheat a wok or large skillet over medium-high heat. When hot, add 2 tablespoons of the oil, garlic, and salt. When the garlic turns light brown, add the pork. Stir-fry until the meat feels firm to the touch, 45 seconds to a minute. Add the cabbage and stir-fry for 45 seconds. Add the garlic chives and stir-fry for another 15 seconds (if using leeks, add them in the next step, described below). Remove the mixture to a bowl and reserve.

Wipe the wok clean with paper towels and reheat until it is hot. Add the remaining oil, and if using the leeks, add them to the hot oil until wilted. Remove and reserve. Add the noodles. Toss until the noodles are coated with the oil. Add the braising sauce; toss together until the noodles are well coated and evenly colored. Simmer over medium-high heat until the noodles have completely absorbed the sauce, stirring frequently for 1 to 2 minutes or until the noodles are "dry"—not dripping with liquid. If needed, add more broth and continue cooking until noodles are tender and chewy. Add the pork and cabbage mixture; toss until thoroughly mixed and hot. Sprinkle with sesame oil. Serve hot.

Suggested Beverage

A spicy New Zealand Pinot Noir, sake, or Asian beer.

✳ PORK RIB GUAZZETTO ✳

New York Dame Lidia Bastianich is one of America's best-known and best-loved Italian chefs. She immigrated with her family to New York from Italy in 1958. She opened her first Italian restaurant in Queens in 1972 and her much-applauded Felidia restaurant in Manhattan in 1981. Today, with her son and daughter, she is involved in three other lauded New York restaurants, plus a Lidia's Kansas City and a Lidia's Pittsburgh. She has published five cookbooks and hosted dozens of television cooking shows.

Of all her recipes, Bastianich chose this fragrant and rich *guazzetto* (braise) of pork ribs as a personal favorite. It is a robust dish, with meat and pasta served together (traditionally the pasta would be served as

Prepare Ahead

The dish is best prepared at least a day ahead. Refrigerate it overnight; then you can skim off any fat that has congealed on the top. Gently reheat to serve.

a first course, the meat as the main course). You can use larger pieces of orange rind, but be aware that the orange flavor can become quite pungent in the *guazzetto*. A starter of cured meats (see box, page 63) would be a good choice, followed by a first course of Little Molds of Roasted Peppers (page 60) alongside lightly dressed salad greens. For dessert, a store-bought gelato with Lemon-Cranberry-Pecan Biscotti (page 290).

6 to 8 servings

3 pounds country-style pork ribs, bone-in, cut into individual ribs

½ cup dried porcini mushrooms

Olive oil to brown meat

¼ to ½ teaspoon salt plus additional as needed

¼ pound bacon, finely chopped (about ½ cup) (see box, page 17)

1 large onion, finely chopped (about 1¼ cups)

2 large stalks celery, finely chopped (about ½ cup)

1 medium carrot, peeled and shredded on the large holes of a box grater (about ½ cup)

2 tablespoons tomato paste

2 to 3 strips orange rind, each ½ inch by 2 inches

1 cup dry red wine

2 to 4 cups hot chicken or beef broth

3 bay leaves

1 sprig fresh rosemary, about 4 inches long, with lots of leaf clusters

Freshly ground black pepper

1 pound dried pasta, such as rigatoni

1 cup freshly grated Parmigiano-Reggiano or Grana Padano cheese

※ Trim any outside fat off the ribs. Discard the fat. Cover the mushrooms with 1½ cups warm water or broth to soak. Film the surface of a large Dutch oven or heavy-bottomed pot with oil and place over medium-high heat. When hot, lay the ribs in and let them sear for a few minutes. (You will probably have to prepare the ribs in two batches. Do not overcrowd the Dutch oven.) When they are colored and slightly crusted, turn them over and brown the other side, cooking 8 to 10 minutes total. Transfer the browned ribs to a platter and sprinkle with the salt. Meanwhile, lift the mushrooms out of the soaking liquid and squeeze the juices into it. Strain the soaking liquid through a coffee filter into a measuring cup and reserve. Chop the mushrooms into small pieces and reserve.

Suggested Beverage

Chianti Classico or Chianti Classico Riserva (serve rustic-style in small tumblers instead of stems).

When the ribs are all browned, add the bacon to the Dutch oven. Lower the heat and stir for a couple of minutes, rendering the fat and scraping up some of the meat crust before it burns. Add the onions, stir well, and let them start to wilt. Stir in the celery, carrot, and reserved mushrooms, and cook over medium-high heat, stirring often, until the vegetables are golden—about 5 minutes. Clear a hot spot, plop in the tomato paste, toast it for a minute on the pan bottom, then blend it into the vegetables. Add the strips of orange rind and stir them in. Return the ribs to the Dutch oven along with any juices they have released. Toss the ribs with the vegetables for a minute or so. Pour in the wine, raise heat, and let boil until wine has almost completely evaporated, turning the ribs over and over in the Dutch oven. Add the reserved porcini juices and as much hot broth as it takes to barely cover the meat. Add the bay leaves, and the rosemary. Lower heat to simmer, cover, and cook until meat is fork tender, about 90 minutes. Add more broth if necessary. When done cooking, remove the orange rind, bay leaves, and rosemary sprig. Season to taste with salt and pepper.

Bring a large pot of salted water to a boil. Cook the pasta al dente and drain.

To serve, toss the pasta with enough of the *guazzetto* juices to coat and top generously with the cheese. Serve pasta alongside the ribs. Spoon a small amount of sauce over the ribs and pass a bowl of sauce as well.

BATALI FAMILY STUFFED ARTICHOKES

Prepare Ahead

Take this one in stages: prepare the meat filling one day (same with the marinara sauce if you're making your own); cook the artichokes the next; assemble and bake the dish for dinner on the third.

Some families are blessed with not one, but many food talents. In the Seattle Batali family, Mario is the celebrity chef, the New York restaurateur, the one who's not only featured in food journals but also profiled in *The New Yorker*. Then there are his parents: as a retired Boeing engineer, Mario's father took up salami making and with Mario's mother opened a salumeria, called Salumi, in downtown Seattle. Now Salumi is a rising brand of artisan-made cured meats, and Mario's sister, Seattle Dame Gina Batali, and her husband have taken over management of the company. It seemed only proper that the family, including Mario, should gather around a well-worn box of family recipes to select one for this book. It was a tie: Noodles with Turkey Fat, or Stuffed Artichokes (both from Grandma Batali).

We chose the artichokes. They are arguably the most fun dish to make in our entire collection, especially if you follow the prepare-ahead notes. The hollowed-out artichokes get splayed like giant blossoms, with the savory stuffing piled in between the petals. The result is dramatic laid on a plate and calls for nothing more than crusty bread and red wine for the entrée course. Start the meal with an extra-easy starter (see box, page 36), followed by a cured meat first course (see box, page 63). Stay with the Italian motif and finish with Chocolate Hazelnut Tart (page 277). The Uncomplicated Green Salad (see box, page 69), served either as a bed for the artichokes or alongside, is strictly optional.

How to Choose an Artichoke

Here's how San Francisco Dame Judy Rodgers puts it in her book, *The Zuni Café Cookbook*: "Choose artichokes as you would flowers. Look for perfect 'blooms' with firm unblemished 'petals.' The freshest artichokes, that have been handled well, feel heavy for their size and make a scrunchy sound when you squeeze them."

For the marinara sauce, homemade is preferred (and a recipe follows), but it's okay to substitute a high-quality store-bought sauce. Note that Grandma Batali seasoned boldly: every seasoning in the pork stuffing is at least a tablespoon, including freshly grated nutmeg. In fact, the dish's balance demands this to offset the rather bland flavor of the artichokes. If you're wary of the amounts, just make sure the measuring spoon is filled to barely level and reduce the salt to 1½ tablespoons. However, don't be too cautious. You don't want to lose the taste of *molto* Family Batali.

4 servings

Stuffing

    1 pound ground pork

    1 medium onion, chopped fine (about 2 cups)

    2 ounces pancetta, chopped fine (about 6 tablespoons; see box, page 17)

    1 cup small pieces of dried white bread (no crusts)

    ½ cup milk

    3 cloves garlic, minced

    ¼ cup freshly grated Parmigiano-Reggiano cheese

    3 tablespoons dried basil

    2 tablespoons salt

    2 tablespoons coarsely ground black pepper

    1 tablespoon freshly grated nutmeg

Artichokes

    4 large artichokes

    1 tablespoon salt

    Juice of 2 lemons

    4 cups Marinara Sauce (recipe follows)

Serving

    ½ cup freshly grated Parmigiano-Reggiano cheese

Suggested
Beverage

A Tuscan red (particu-
larly the Sangiovese
known as Morellino
di Scansano, which
has been called the
best-kept secret in
Tuscany).

✳ To prepare the stuffing, cook the pork, onion, and pancetta in a sauté pan over medium heat until the pork is no longer pink. Let cool. Meanwhile, soak the bread in the milk for 15 minutes. Drain off any extra milk and mix the bread together with the garlic, cheese, basil, salt, pepper, and nutmeg. Add the bread mixture to the pork and mix well, being sure to break up any large chunks of meat or bread.

✳ To prepare the artichokes, cut off the stem and top of each artichoke (you'll be removing about a third of the artichoke). A serrated knife works best. Make sure that the stem is cut so that the artichoke sits level and that all four artichokes are cut to about the same height. With kitchen shears, trim the tips of the remaining thorny leaves. Remove the tiny central leaves from the artichokes and, using a pointed spoon (a grapefruit spoon is ideal—see box, opposite), scrape out and discard the hairy choke, leaving the heart intact. Rinse.

✳ Place the artichokes in a large kettle. Cover them with water and add the salt and lemon juice. Bring to a boil over high heat. Reduce heat, cover, and simmer until the artichokes are tender when you prick them at the stem end, 20 to 25 minutes. Drain the artichokes thoroughly, inverting them and gently squeezing to drain remaining cooking water.

✳ To stuff the artichokes, divide the pork mixture into roughly four equal parts. Gently spread the leaves and with your fingers stuff the pork mixture into the heart and between all of the leaves. This will cause the artichoke to spread out like a big blossom. Spoon 2 cups of the marinara sauce into a baking dish large enough to hold the artichokes. Place the stuffed artichokes in the sauce. Sprinkle with the cheese. Spoon the remaining marinara sauce around and over the artichokes. Cover with foil. The dish can now be refrigerated for up to a day until ready to bake. Preheat the oven to 350°F. Bake the artichokes until just heated through, about 30 minutes. Serve immediately.

Marinara Sauce

If you don't already have a favorite marinara recipe, try this one from Chicago Dame Nancy Brussat Barocci.

4 to 5 cups

½ cup olive oil

Two 28-ounce cans Italian plum tomatoes, drained and roughly chopped

16 fresh basil leaves, finely chopped

1½ teaspoons salt

Freshly ground black pepper

❋ Heat the oil in a saucepan over medium-high heat. Add the tomatoes, basil, salt, and pepper. Simmer over medium-low heat for about 20 minutes. Put the mixture through a food mill or purée in a food processor.

The Useful Toothed Grapefruit Spoon

What a joy to carefully plunge a special spoon with its own tiny teeth into the perimeter of each section of a grapefruit and release the meat in a perfect wedge. However, this is not the only use for the toothed grapefruit spoon. There is nothing handier for hulling strawberries; the tip of the spoon inserted right under the hull is the exact shape needed to easily lift and remove the hull. It is far superior to and much faster than the strawberry huller designed specifically—and quite unnecessarily—for that purpose. When preparing cherry tomatoes for stuffing as an hors d'oeuvre, the grapefruit spoon digs right into the top of the tomato without tearing it and the seed cavity is easily removed. Last but not least, the toothed edges of the spoon are ideal for peeling gingerroot. They scrape off the skin easily without taking extra meat. Such an inexpensive and efficient little tool, the toothed grapefruit spoon.

—Washington, D.C., Dame Susan Belsinger

✣ BREAKFAST-FOR-DINNER SALAD ✣

Prepare Ahead

The vinaigrette can be prepared ahead of time and stored in the refrigerator. Before using, allow it to sit at room temperature for 20 to 30 minutes. Greens can be washed, dried, and measured ahead. The croutons, likewise (quickly reheat before sautéing the bacon). Even the eggs can be cooked ahead and reheated (see box, opposite).

There were many years of cooking school and apprenticing in star-studded kitchens before Los Angeles Dame Mary Sue Milliken teamed up with Dame Susan Feniger in 1981 to open their first of several restaurants. Even now, after all their success in food—including a few hundred episodes of *Too Hot Tamales* for the Food Network—Milliken says, "When it comes to cooking I still feel like a teenager. I cook every day and I enjoy every minute in the kitchen."

Milliken recommends this one-dish dinner for two: fresh greens and poached eggs, which she serves frequently in her household for "breakfast, lunch, or dinner." In summertime, she adds cherry tomatoes and fresh basil leaves to the mix. "If you've forgotten to 'bring home the bacon,' you can substitute canned mackerel, sardines, or anchovies and get those healthy fish oils." In meal planning, she argues for the "eighty-twenty rule—eat 80 percent plant-based foods and 20 percent proteins." This salad fits the rule quite well. Black-Olive Tapenade (page 5; skip the hard-cooked eggs) makes a good appetizer. This dinner doesn't really call for a first course, but do indulge in a rich dessert. A good pick: Fran's Original Cheesecake (page 307).

The recipe can easily be doubled or tripled, especially taking advantage of pre-poached eggs (see box, opposite). Be sure to use very fresh eggs—they have thicker whites and stronger yolk membranes, which help in the poaching process.

2 servings

Torn and Fried Croutons (recipe follows)

4 to 6 thick slices bacon, cut into 1-inch pieces

2 thin slices red onion

¼ cup extra-virgin olive oil

1 tablespoon cider vinegar

1 teaspoon Dijon mustard

2 cloves garlic, minced or put through a garlic press

1 teaspoon freshly squeezed lemon juice

½ teaspoon salt

5 grinds black pepper

2 eggs (see box, page 175)

6 cups assorted salad greens like romaine, escarole, watercress, and arugula

2 tomatoes, seeded and diced

❋ Make the croutons. Using the same skillet as for the croutons, fry the bacon over medium heat until golden and crispy. Remove with a slotted spoon and drain well on paper towels. Or, preheat the oven to 400°F, place the bacon on a foil-lined baking sheet, and bake just until crisp, about 15 minutes. Remove the bacon from the oven, transfer to paper towels and reserve. Meanwhile, soak the onion slices in ice water for 2 to 3 minutes and drain on a paper towel. Separate into rings. Reserve.

❋ In a small jar, combine the olive oil, vinegar, mustard, garlic, lemon juice, salt, and pepper. Shake vigorously to combine.

Poaching Eggs in Advance

Eggs can be poached ahead and reheated at serving time. This process comes in handy whether you need to poach eggs for a crowd or just want to ease last-minute hassle.

Bring 2 inches of salted water to a gentle boil in a wide, preferably nonstick sauté pan. Add a teaspoon of white vinegar per egg to the water to help prevent the eggs from spreading out and forming strings or "feathers." Meanwhile, break each egg into a small individual bowl. When the water is boiling, slip the eggs one by one into the water; reduce heat as soon as the whites begin to set. Simmer eggs gently for 2 minutes and remove with a slotted spoon to a bowl of ice water. The ice water will stop the cooking and retain the runny yolk. Trim any ragged strings with scissors and place back in the ice water. Refrigerate for up to 2 days. To reheat the eggs, place two to three at a time in a strainer and lower them into simmering water; remove after about 35 seconds, drain and serve.

—*San Antonio Dame Pat Mozersky*

Suggested Beverage

Any dry sparkler (Italian Proseccos tend to be good values and have lower alcohol).

❋ Poach the eggs according to the instructions in the box on page 173, but do not cool them on ice water. Rather, simply drain them on paper towels.

❋ Toss the salad greens in a large bowl with the onion, tomatoes, bacon, and croutons. Sprinkle about 3 tablespoons of the dressing on the mixture and toss to coat all ingredients evenly. Add the remaining dressing to taste. Divide the salad onto 2 plates and top each with a warm poached egg. Serve immediately.

Torn and Fried Croutons

3 cups

2 tablespoons olive oil

Two 1-inch slices crusty bread, crusts discarded, torn into ½- to 1-inch pieces (about 3 cups)

½ teaspoon salt

5 grinds black pepper

❋ Heat the oil in a medium skillet over medium-low heat. Add the bread, season with the salt and pepper, and toss to coat. Cook over medium-low heat, stirring frequently, until the croutons are golden, 5 to 10 minutes. Transfer the croutons to a plate.

Small Farm Eggs 101

Supermarket eggs are uniform in size, color, and taste. Even when labeled "organic," they come from huge farms housing tens of thousands of chickens. Supermarket eggs are fine, but they are nothing like the delicious eggs that one can get from a small farmer. Hens that are raised in small flocks, with pasture to forage on, lead active, healthier, and less stressful lives, and that creates eggs that have the best flavor, with saffron-colored yolks sitting on clear, thick jellylike whites. Simply scrambled or fried, these eggs can taste like the finest delicacy. And even premium-priced eggs make very economical meals.

Shell color? This is determined by the breed of chicken that laid the egg. Shell color does not affect flavor. Cleaning? Eggs laid by hens in uncrowded barns are usually clean and don't need washing. Any dirt on the egg can be brushed off as you would a delicate mushroom. Eggs are porous, so vigorous washing can actually do more harm than good. Storing? Refrigerated eggs remain edible for weeks; in fact, supermarket eggs can be over two months old and still be legally sold. However, the eggshell is porous, and over time, as air seeps into the egg, its white becomes thinner, the yolk runnier, and the flavor deteriorates. Eggs keep best in a refrigerator in a closed carton. Is there ever a disadvantage to a freshly laid egg? Only if you want to hard-cook the egg. Wait one week after the egg has been laid, or you won't be able to peel the shell off.

—*Boston Dame Terry Golson*

Golson and her young family keep a backyard flock of twelve hens in suburban Boston. She is the author of several cookbooks, including The Farmstead Egg Cookbook.

Other Meats

❧ VEAL AND WILD MUSHROOM RAGOUT ❧

Here is a dish that Dame Janis McLean likes to teach to busy friends looking for an impressive yet manageable dinner. McLean has been cooking professionally since 1993 and is the executive chef at the Morrison-Clark Inn & Restaurant in Washington, D.C. She normally pairs the dish—which is studded with slices of outsize portobello mushrooms as well as traditional braising vegetables—with spaetzle. She approves, however, when we place one of mentor Anne Willan's Twice-Baked Spinach Soufflés (page 222) at the center of each serving plate and spoon the ragout around it. The creamy pan juices from the soufflés drizzled over the top of the dish make a main course worthy of becoming a tradition.

There's a tiny Italian pasta called *trofie* that is reminiscent of spaetzle. If you can find it, boil about 5 ounces in salted water until tender, toss with a bit of olive oil, then scatter about a half cup around each spinach soufflé before topping with the ragout. If you want simpler sides, consider mashed potatoes or buttered noodles. Whatever you choose, this can be festive fare. Start with Cocktail Potato Latkes (page 33) or Home-Cured Salmon in Phyllo Cups (page 19); Seared Scallops (page 49) for a first course; and for dessert, Lemon Cream Roulade (page 304).

As for veal, McLean says that there are sources for humanely raised veal, but if you prefer, substitute boneless, skinless chicken thigh meat and adjust cooking time (the chicken makes a far less flavorful ragout; oven cooking time will be brief—as little as 15 minutes).

6 servings

Prepare Ahead

Ragout is best prepared at least 1 or 2 days before serving. Prep all ingredients a day ahead of cooking, and the task goes quickly.

2 pounds veal shoulder meat, cut into ¾-inch cubes

1 teaspoon salt plus additional as needed

½ teaspoon freshly ground black pepper plus additional as needed

Vegetable oil, about 3 tablespoons

2½ cups chicken broth

2 cups finely chopped onion

2 teaspoons minced garlic

1 cup dry white wine

½ ounce dried porcini mushrooms, soaked in hot water to cover
for half an hour

Bouquet garni (12 sprigs parsley, 6 sprigs fresh thyme, 2 bay leaves,
all tied together)

3 carrots, peeled

2 leeks, trimmed of roots and tough green ends

4 tablespoons unsalted butter, divided

2 tablespoons olive oil

8 ounces portobello mushrooms, cleaned and stemmed,
caps cut into ⅛-inch slices

½ cup heavy cream

2 teaspoons Dijon mustard

✲ Preheat the oven to 325°F. Pat the veal cubes dry with paper towels and season them with the salt and pepper. Heat a large Dutch oven or heavy-bottomed pot over medium-high heat until hot. Film the bottom of the Dutch oven with the vegetable oil. Carefully add a third to half of the veal cubes, just enough to cover the base of the Dutch oven in a loose single layer (if you crowd the Dutch oven, the meat will not brown). Be careful not to splash yourself with hot oil. Brown, stirring from time to time to make sure you sear all the sides of the meat; each batch will take 15 to 20 minutes. Lift the seared veal out of the Dutch oven with a slotted spoon and reserve on a plate. Repeat until all the meat is browned.

✻ If the drippings are getting too brown, deglaze the Dutch oven: pour about 1 cup of the chicken broth into the Dutch oven, raise the heat, and boil the liquid, scraping loose all the browned bits. Pour the liquid into a measuring cup and reserve. Again, film the bottom of the Dutch oven with vegetable oil and brown the second batch of meat in a similar manner, removing with a slotted spoon to the plate.

✻ Turn the heat down to medium-low and add the onions to the Dutch oven. Cook over medium-low heat until the onions are soft and translucent, 6 to 8 minutes. Then add the garlic and cook until fragrant, about 2 minutes. Add the veal back to the Dutch oven and stir to combine.

✻ Add the wine, turn up the heat and bring it to a boil, then reduce heat to medium and simmer, reducing the wine by two thirds. Check the mushrooms and their water for sand. If the water looks free of grit, add it along with the mushrooms to the veal mixture. If it's not, lift the mushrooms out of the water and add them alone to the veal, discarding the water. Add the chicken broth (including what you may have reserved after deglazing) and bouquet garni. Bring the mixture back to a simmer, then top with a tight-fitting lid and place in the oven. Cook until the veal is tender, about 1 hour, checking occasionally to make sure the liquid covers the meat and is at a bare simmer.

✻ While the veal is cooking, prepare the vegetables. Cut the carrots in half lengthwise and then diagonally into ¼-inch slices; you will have about 2 cups. Cut the leeks in half and then into ¼-inch slices. Cover in water to remove any sand (see box, page 88). Drain. Heat a large sauté pan over medium heat and melt 2 tablespoons of the butter. Add the carrots and sauté over brisk heat until they are barely cooked—still crisp, but lightly browned. Transfer the carrots to a plate and wipe the sauté pan clean.

✻ Melt another tablespoon of the butter and gently cook the leeks over low heat until they are tender. Do not let them brown—if necessary, add 2 tablespoons of water so that they can cook without crisping (if you do this, continue cooking until the water has evaporated).

Suggested Beverage

An earthy Pinot Noir.

When done cooking leeks, transfer them to another plate and reserve separately from the carrots. Wipe the skillet clean again and reheat over medium-high heat. Add the remaining butter and oil. When hot, add the portobello mushrooms and sauté until golden brown on both sides.

❋ When the veal is tender, transfer the Dutch oven from the oven to the stovetop. Add the carrots, portobello mushrooms, cream, and mustard and stir. Cover and simmer over low heat for about 30 minutes to allow the flavors to combine. Remove the bouquet garni before serving and taste for salt and pepper, adding seasoning if desired.

❋ If serving immediately, add the leeks and continue cooking over low heat just long enough to heat them. If serving later, cover the leeks and refrigerate. Place the ragout in the refrigerator to cool, uncovered; cover when chilled. When ready to serve, bring the ragout to a low simmer on the stovetop, cover, and place in a 300°F oven for about 15 minutes. Five minutes before serving, add the leeks and their juices.

❋ Serve as directed in the headnote.

Braising: Some Standard and Unexpected Tips

Dame McLean is a fan of slow-cooked (braised) meat dishes such as her Veal and Wild Mushroom Ragout (page 177), especially since they offer the benefit of being prepared a day or two ahead of serving. She offers several tips for successful braising:

* Select economical cuts of meat—the parts of the animal that move (the shoulder or the leg, for instance, rather than center cuts like tenderloin or rib). This includes chicken—choose legs and thighs, not breasts.

* In trimming the meat, allow at least some of the fat and sinew to remain—it melts into the braise, adding favor.

* Use a heavy bottomed, wide cooking pot. A narrow, tall saucepot is not a good choice.

* Cut vegetables either small enough so they melt into the braise or large enough that they can be scooped out before serving and replaced with more pristinely prepared vegetables.

* The liquid should just cover the meat.

* Avoid boiling: it will toughen the meat. Cooking in the oven more easily keeps the braise at a simmer than cooking on the stovetop.

All this said, McLean adds one unexpected tip you won't want to miss. For a special occasion, elevate the braise to what she calls a "duo" presentation: serve a beef braise with small seared beef tenderloin medallions or a lamb braise with grilled baby lamb chops. "You get the best of both worlds: a luscious rich braise and a medium rare bite of premium meat," says McLean.

LEMON, MUSTARD, AND MINT BUTTERFLIED LEG OF LAMB

If you've never cooked lamb *without* lots of garlic, you'll be pleasantly surprised by this recipe. There's not a clove of garlic in it. Dallas Dame Sue Sims developed it for a luncheon in the Great Room at the Texas State Capitol in Austin. The guest of honor: then–first lady of Texas, Laura Bush.

The lamb can be cooked either under a broiler, which lightly chars the seasoning paste and allows capture of the mixture's flavorful juices, or on a grill, which adds a light flavor of smoke. Either way, the recipe makes a finely seasoned piece of lamb. Pair it with Gingered Sweet Potato–Parsnip Purée (page 232) or Creamy Feta Potatoes from D.C.'s 1789 Restaurant (page 231) and a simple green vegetable such as Broiled Asparagus (page 218). If it's summer, Grilled Gazpacho Salad (page 57) is splendid as either a first course or a side dish to the lamb. The appetizer could be Phyllo Fontina Cheese Bites (page 16), and for dessert, Almond Shortcakes (page 325) is just right.

8 to 10 servings

One 4-pound leg of lamb, boned and butterflied

¼ cup extra-virgin olive oil

3 to 4 lemons, zested for 2 teaspoons grated zest (see box, page 75) and squeezed for 8 tablespoons juice, divided

2 teaspoons to 1 tablespoon salt

10 to 15 grinds black pepper

⅓ cup unsalted butter, at room temperature

¼ cup Dijon mustard

½ cup (about 1 ounce) minced mint leaves

Chicken broth to finish sauce (optional)

✳ Trim the lamb of external fat and pound with a kitchen mallet until roughly of even thickness. Place the lamb in a shallow pan. Brush both sides with the oil and drizzle with 6 tablespoons of the lemon juice. Sprinkle with the salt and pepper. Cover with plastic wrap and let stand at room temperature for 30 to 60 minutes. While the lamb marinates, make a paste of butter, mustard, lemon zest, the remaining lemon juice, and mint. Preheat the broiler or grill to medium-high, 425° to 450°F.

✳ If using the broiler, cover the broiler pan with foil, turning up the edges to catch juices. Remove the lamb from the marinade, reserving the marinade. Place the lamb on the prepared pan. Cook 4 to 6 inches from the flame for 7 to 10 minutes. Turn the meat over and spread the butter paste over it. Cook for 6 to 10 minutes more, depending on thickness of the lamb and desired doneness. The surface of the lamb should be attractively charred and the inside just pink. Try 6 minutes, then test for doneness. The lamb should register 135°F to 140°F on your meat thermometer.

✳ If using the grill, place the lamb on the grill rack and grill for about 7 minutes. Turn the meat and spread it with the butter paste. Grill for another 6 to 8 minutes. Test for doneness as above.

✳ While the lamb is cooking, place the reserved marinade in a small saucepan, bring to a boil, and simmer for a few minutes before removing from the heat and reserving for adding to the cooked lamb juices. When the lamb is done to taste, remove from the broiler or grill. Let rest about 10 minutes, then cut across the grain into ¼-inch slices. Pour any accumulated juices into the heated marinade to make a light sauce. Taste for seasoning. If you have grilled the meat, you will not have accumulated as many juices as when broiling and catching them in the foil, so you may need to add a bit of chicken broth or water to balance out the lemon in the marinade. To serve, drizzle the meat with a bit of the sauce and pass extra sauce on the side.

Suggested Beverage

A New Zealand Pinot Noir or a California Zinfandel.

❊ A FAVORITE MOUSSAKA ❊

Prepare Ahead

You can spread out the preparation over several days, then assemble up to a day ahead.

San Antonio Dame Pat Mozersky has hundreds of well-loved recipes from her career as a cooking school director, television cooking show host, and food columnist for the *San Antonio Express-News*. Still, when it came time to choose a recipe for this book, she didn't hesitate to pick her moussaka, first learned as a young bride from a friend and perfected to take to a Greek-themed potluck: "The other guests were great cooks, and I listened intently as they exchanged recipes and referenced magazine articles. It was a seminal moment for me. The thought that my love for food and cooking could be molded into a professional career first took hold that evening."

This Middle Eastern classic baked dish needs nothing more than heaps of dressed greens on the side, like the Uncomplicated Green Salad (see box, page 69). Consider a platter of Big Shrimp with Armenian "Pesto" (page 130) for appetizers. Or just serve the pesto with warm pita bread, without the shrimp. Do a first course of Winter Salad of Oranges and Pomegranate with Sheep's Milk Cheese, though you may want to omit the pistachios if you serve our suggested dessert: Turkish Apricots Stuffed with Cream and Pistachios (page 327).

Note that broiling the eggplant is a wise alternative to sautéing, by which the eggplant is legendary for sopping up vast amounts of olive oil (oven-baking is another option—see instructions, page 221).

8 to 10 servings

Eggplant

    1 large or 2 small (about 2 pounds) eggplant, cut into ¼-inch slices

    Olive oil for brushing

Filling

    ¼ cup (½ stick) unsalted butter

    1 medium onion, finely chopped (about 1½ cups)

    2 pounds ground lamb, beef, or veal, *or* a mix of these meats

    ½ cup red wine

2 medium fresh tomatoes, chopped (about 1½ cups)

⅓ cup finely chopped parsley

1 teaspoon dried oregano

¼ teaspoon ground cinnamon

¼ teaspoon freshly grated nutmeg

Salt and freshly ground black pepper

Béchamel

3 cups whole milk

¼ cup (½ stick) unsalted butter

¼ cup all-purpose flour

1 teaspoon salt

3 large eggs, beaten

⅛ teaspoon freshly grated nutmeg

Assembly

⅓ cup toasted homemade bread crumbs (see box, page 140)

¾ cup freshly grated Parmigiano-Reggiano cheese, divided

❋ To prepare the eggplant, preheat the broiler and brush the eggplant slices generously on both sides with oil; place on a broiler pan. Broil until golden brown on one side. Turn over and repeat on the other side. Remove and reserve.

❋ To prepare the meat filling, in a large skillet, heat the butter and cook the onion until lightly browned, 6 to 8 minutes. Add the meat and cook, stirring frequently, until lightly browned. Add the wine and tomatoes and stir them into the meat. Add the parsley, oregano, cinnamon, nutmeg, salt, and pepper. Simmer the mixture for 30 minutes, or until most of the liquid has been absorbed.

❋ To prepare the béchamel, heat the milk in a small saucepan to just below the boiling point. In a large, heavy pan, melt the butter over low heat and stir in the flour. Stir frequently, cooking over moderate heat until mixture begins to bubble, about 2 minutes. Remove from the heat

Suggested Beverage

A splendid opportunity to select a wine from the dish's country of origin—a Greek white Moschofilero or a red St. George.

and wait until it stops bubbling. Add the milk all at once to the pan, vigorously beating with a wire whisk until the mixture is smooth. Add the salt, return the pan to the heat, and cook, stirring, until sauce is thickened, 4 to 5 minutes. Spoon out 3 tablespoons of the sauce and stir it into the meat mixture. Whisk the eggs and nutmeg into the remaining sauce.

Preheat the oven to 350°F. Butter a 9- by 13-inch baking dish. Sprinkle bread crumbs evenly over the bottom. Layer half of the eggplant. Cover the eggplant with half the meat mixture. Sprinkle with ¼ cup of the cheese. Add another layer of eggplant, the remaining meat, and ¼ cup of cheese. Over the top, pour the béchamel sauce and sprinkle it with the remaining cheese. At this point, you may cool the moussaka, cover, and refrigerate. Bring to room temperature, then bake the moussaka until the top is golden brown and bubbly, about 1 hour. Let it rest for up to 30 minutes before serving.

Pasta

CATALAN PASTA WITH GARLIC SAUCE

This simple but bold pasta dish is not to be missed. It comes from Seattle Dame Marilyn Tausend, whose name is usually linked to Mexican cooking. For the last twenty years she has worked closely with Diana Kennedy and Rick Bayless—two of the foremost experts on Mexican cuisine—doing culinary trips and writing Mexican cookbooks, including *Cocina de la Familia*, which won the Julia Child Award for Best New American Cookbook in 1997. This recipe, however, comes from Spain. She still keeps the tiny piece of paper on which, many years ago, the cook at a village restaurant serving the dish wrote down its ingredients.

This is a very basic dish: piles of steaming, fragrant *fideos*, tiny bits of pasta into which you swirl the intense, fresh garlic sauce. Traditionally, the dish is made with homemade fish stock (Tausend substitutes bottled clam juice when she doesn't have time to make stock). Traditionally, too, it is served as a first course, but we suggest it as a main course served with a simply dressed green salad or a side of Basic Wilted Greens (see box, page 228)—a most tasty accompaniment, grants Tausend. A very easy (and very Spanish) starter for this meal is toasted almonds and green olives. For a first course have Quail Escabeche (page 51), and for dessert, perhaps the Dark Chocolate Fresh Ginger Truffles (page 330).

4 to 6 servings

Prepare Ahead

The mixture for cooking the fideos can be made several days ahead of serving. The garlic sauce can also be made in advance.

Suggested Beverage

A Spanish red Rioja or for white, an Albariño or a sparkling Cava.

½ cup plus 3 tablespoons olive oil, divided

1 large onion, finely chopped (about 1½ cups)

3 cloves garlic, smashed and peeled

2 medium ripe tomatoes, seeded and finely chopped (see box below) *or* one 14.5-ounce can diced tomatoes, drained

⅛ teaspoon ground cayenne pepper

½ teaspoon freshly ground black pepper plus additional as needed

5 cups bottled clam juice

Pinch of saffron

8 ounces fideos (see box, opposite) *or* 8 ounces angel hair pasta broken into roughly ½-inch pieces

½ to 1 teaspoon salt plus additional as needed

Fresh Garlic Sauce (recipe follows)

❊ Heat ½ cup of the oil in a large Dutch oven or heavy-bottomed pot, and when it shimmers, add the onion. Lower the heat and cook, stirring frequently, until almost caramelized, being careful not to let it burn. Add the garlic and cook another few minutes, then stir in the tomatoes, cayenne pepper, and black pepper, and continue to cook until all of the juices are gone. Add the clam juice and saffron, cover, and simmer for 30 minutes. Reserve. If not immediately completing the dish, refrigerate the tomato–clam juice mixture.

An Easy Way to Peel Fresh Tomatoes: Grate Them

Dame Tausend says that during the winter she uses canned tomatoes for *fideos*, but in late summer she prefers using tomatoes fresh from the garden. An easy way to simultaneously chop and peel fresh tomatoes: first slice them in half through the stem end. With your fingers, remove whatever seeds come out easily. Then simply rub the cut side of the tomato across the largest holes of a box grater resting in a shallow bowl, until you are left with the skin (which you can discard) and lovely pieces of fresh tomato and juice—ready to use.

✳ Just before serving, reheat the tomato–clam juice mixture. Heat the remaining olive oil in a large, heavy skillet or a medium-size paella pan over medium-low heat, and when hot add in the fideos, stirring constantly until very golden (be very careful, as the fideos can easily burn). Add the tomato–clam juice mixture, 1 cup at a time, stirring continuously until the liquid is almost absorbed and the fideos are tender. (The amount of liquid will vary every time you cook this dish. Use whatever amount it takes for the fideos to be tender.) Season with salt and pepper to taste.

✳ Divide the fideos among 4 to 6 dinner plates. Top each serving with about 1 tablespoon of Fresh Garlic Sauce. Pass the rest of the sauce and encourage each person to swirl in more as desired.

If You Can't Find Fideos

The Spanish pasta *fideos*—1- to 2-inch-long very fine strands of eggless pasta (sometimes also labeled *vermicelli*)—may be hard to find. If it eludes you, you can use any good-quality angel hair pasta that is made without egg and lists a 2-minute cooking time; for example, either the 8.8-ounce box of De Cecco angel hair 209 or angel hair pasta that is sold coiled into a "nest." Break the pasta into small pieces, holding the pasta inside the bag as you do, so that pieces don't fly about the kitchen. (Show children this simple technique, and they can enjoy helping you with the preparation.)

Prepare Ahead

If using the raw egg
yolks, prepare the
sauce shortly before
using. If you want to
make it ahead of time,
use the prepared
mayonnaise.

Fresh Garlic Sauce

1½ cups

½ teaspoon salt

6 to 8 cloves garlic, minced

2 large egg yolks, at room temperature*

1 cup extra-virgin olive oil

Or

**Substitute for the raw egg yolks and olive oil 1 cup good-quality
mayonnaise and about ¼ cup olive oil**

✻ Sprinkle the salt in a mortar, add the garlic, and mash together to a paste. Transfer to the bowl of a food processor fitted with a steel blade. Add the egg yolks and briefly process, then with motor running, slowly drip the oil, a few drops at a time, through the feed tube until the mixture turns into a creamy emulsion. Add more oil if necessary. (This garlic sauce is very pungent. If it is too strong for you, blend in a small amount of good-quality mayonnaise to taste; but remember, it will be stirred into the fideos and the flavor will be diluted.) Serve immediately or cover and refrigerate until needed. (What you don't use for the fideos makes an excellent sandwich spread or appetizer dip.)

*Consuming raw or undercooked meats, poultry, seafood, shellfish, or eggs may increase
your risk of food-borne illness especially if you have certain medical conditions, or are
very young or elderly.*

HALI'IMAILE GENERAL STORE
CHICKEN FETTUCCINE CASSEROLE

Before Honolulu Dame Beverly Gannon began her culinary career, she spent five years as road manager for Liza Minelli, Joey Heatherton, and Ben Vereen. Then it was off to London's Le Cordon Bleu. In 1987, Gannon and her husband took over the lease for the old Hali'imaile General Store, once a plantation store for upcountry pineapple workers on the island of Maui. They converted the store into a restaurant of the same name, and it's been a popular island destination ever since. All the while, as one of the twelve original founders of the Hawaii Regional Cuisine Movement, Gannon has spearheaded a move by island chefs to work with local farmers to use seasonal crops in restaurant menus.

This is a popular dish on the General Store's fall and winter lunch menu, but Gannon remembers it best as a casual dinner dish she'd make back when she was a single gal in the entertainment biz. It's a one-dish meal, just right for a buffet, and needs nothing more than something like seasonal tomatoes dressed with a vinaigrette. If it's summer, fry Fresh Okra Cakes for an appetizer; in other seasons, serve Armenian "Pesto" (page 132)—with the shrimp or just with Brioche Points (see box, page 30). At any rate, skip the first course, and for dessert, serve a big platter of freshly baked Glazed Lemon Cookies (page 287) or Chewy Double Chocolate Cookies (page 289).

The chicken broth called for can be made with the carcass of the cooked chicken (see box, page 8).

12 servings

6 tablespoons unsalted butter plus more to grease baking dish

1 cup (3 to 4 ounces) sliced shiitake mushrooms or other mushroom of choice

½ cup chopped onion

¼ cup all-purpose flour

1 cup milk

Prepare Ahead

The casserole can be made several days before baking and serving. Speed up preparation by using a store-roasted whole chicken.

1 cup chicken broth

¼ cup sherry

2 cups sour cream

8 ounces dried fettuccine

12 ounces (about 2 cups) baby spinach leaves, a bit damp from washing

One 3- to 4-pound cooked chicken, skinned, boned, and cut into bite-size pieces

½ cup sliced black olives, drained

¼ cup sliced canned water chestnuts (or up to an entire 8-ounce can, drained)

1 tablespoon dried tarragon leaves

Salt

8 grinds black pepper

1 cup (about 3 ounces) grated Monterey Jack cheese

½ cup (about 1 ounce) freshly grated Parmesan cheese

❀ Butter a 9- by 13-inch baking dish. Melt the butter in a large saucepan. Add the mushrooms and onion. Sauté until the mushrooms are golden and the onions are softened. With a slotted spoon, remove the mushrooms and onions to a medium bowl; reserve. Sprinkle the flour over the remaining fat in the pan. Cook, stirring, for about 2 minutes, to get rid of any floury taste. Stir in the milk and chicken broth and cook until mixture thickens, about 5 minutes. Remove from the heat and stir in the sherry. Fold in the sour cream. Reserve.

❀ Bring a large kettle of salted water to a boil. Cook the fettuccine according to package instructions but for only half the prescribed time—it will continue cooking in the casserole. Drain well and place in the prepared baking dish. Immediately fold in 1 cup of the reserved sauce, being sure to evenly coat the pasta to keep it from sticking together.

❀ Place the spinach in a large sauté pan, cover, and wilt over medium heat for about 5 minutes. Regulate the heat so the spinach does not cook dry before it wilts. Add the spinach to the remaining sauce along with the reserved mushrooms and onions, chicken, olives, and water chestnuts. Stir in the tarragon. Season to taste with salt, and add the pepper. Mix well and pour over the fettuccine mixture. Top with the cheeses. The dish can be made ahead to this point and refrigerated or frozen.

❅ When ready to bake, preheat the oven to 350°F. Bake uncovered until the cheeses are melted and the dish is heated through, about 30 minutes. If the top is beginning to dry before the dish is done, cover with aluminum foil to complete baking. If refrigerated, add about 10 minutes to cooking time; if frozen, add 30 to 45 minutes.

Lids: Heat Management

One of the easiest ways to conserve energy in the kitchen is to cover pots and pans with lids when cooking, especially when boiling pasta. Covering the pot will speed the water to a boil in nearly half the time. Once you add the pasta to the boiling water and the boil drops off, hasten the return by covering the pot again. When the water returns to a boil, remove the lid and turn the burner down to just maintain a steady boil rather than a raging one. (Once the water is at a boil, it does not get hotter with a higher flame.)

Main Courses 193

Vegetarian Dishes

❄ MUSHROOM RAGÙ FOR NOODLES ❄

This is not your typical pasta dish. Rather, it is an aromatic combination of minced vegetables and mushrooms simmered in just a bit of olive oil and cream, then spooned over buttered noodles. Simple to prepare yet highly flavorful, the dish is typical of the dishes that have made its author, Grande Dame Alice Waters, a culinary icon of our times. With the opening of her Berkeley, California, restaurant Chez Panisse in 1971, it's been said that Waters "threw the switch" on food in America, making seasonal and local the standards for ingredients for both restaurants and the food-buying public. Known also for her Edible Schoolyard—a "seed to table" project at a Berkeley middle school—and as the author of eight cookbooks, Waters remains an insistent spirit for all that is good about "good food." She is also renowned for a style of recipe writing that is both approximate and exacting. We've tried to preserve her voice in this recipe.

Prepare Ahead

The ragù can be made 1 or 2 days ahead, then briefly reheated to top the freshly cooked noodles.

4 servings

1 tablespoon olive oil plus additional for sautéing

½ large onion, peeled and finely diced (about 1 cup)

1 carrot, peeled and finely diced (about ½ cup)

1 stalk celery, finely diced (about ⅔ cup)

½ teaspoon salt

3 sprigs thyme, leaves picked from stems

3 sprigs parsley, leaves only, chopped

1 small bay leaf

¼ cup fresh tomato, finely diced

1 pound fresh mushrooms (choose a mixture of two or three types: chanterelles, black trumpets, hedgehogs, cultivated brown or white)

2 tablespoons unsalted butter, at room temperature, plus additional for sautéing

¼ cup heavy cream or crème fraîche (see box, page 20)

½ cup water or chicken broth (if not vegetarian)

8 ounces wide egg noodles (first choice is homemade fresh pappardelle, the classic accompaniment to such a ragù)

¼ to ⅓ cup freshly grated Parmigiano-Reggiano cheese

Freshly chopped parsley

❋ Heat the oil in a large, heavy skillet over medium heat. Add the onion, carrot, celery, and salt. Cook until very tender, but regulate heat to allow little or no browning. Add the thyme, parsley, and bay leaf. Cook for 1 minute and add tomatoes. Cook for another 5 minutes. Remove from the heat and reserve.

❋ Carefully clean and slice the mushrooms, keeping each type separate. If they are very dirty, it will be necessary to wash them (crunching down on dirt and sand is very unpleasant). The mushrooms may take on some water, but it will be thrown off shortly after they hit the hot pan. Heat enough olive oil and butter to lightly coat a small skillet large enough to hold each batch of mushrooms. Sauté each type of mushroom separately. As they cook, the mushrooms will give off liquid; let the juices boil away or tip off the juices and set them aside (the reserved juices can be added back to the sauce later in place of some of the water or broth). Continue cooking the mushrooms until tender and lightly browned (you may need to add a little more oil or butter). Turn each batch of cooked mushrooms onto a cutting board, chop to the size of the cooked vegetables, and combine with the reserved vegetables and herbs in the larger skillet. Repeat this process for all the mushrooms. Then add the cream and water (here you can substitute reserved mushroom juices for any part of the liquid). Bring to a simmer and cook for

15 minutes. Taste for salt and add as needed. Moisten with more liquid if desired, though the ragù is not intended to be soupy. Remove from the heat and reserve.

When ready to serve, bring a large pot of salted water to a boil. Add the noodles and cook until barely tender. While the noodles cook, gently reheat the ragù. When the noodles are done cooking, drain, reserving about 1 cup of the cooking water. Return the noodles to the pot and toss with the butter and cheese and enough of the cooking water to keep the noodles separate and well-coated. Spoon the noodles onto a warm serving platter or 4 individual plates. Top generously with the ragù and a sprinkle of parsley. Serve immediately.

Suggested Beverage

A California Pinot Noir from the Carneros district.

❧ TEXAS CHILES RELLENOS ❧

Prepare Ahead

(Aldaco aptly calls this part of the recipe "getting ahead.") You can prepare the poblano chile peppers and the Crema Poblano Sauce a couple of days ahead. The dish can be assembled up to 2 hours ahead of baking and serving.

A restaurateur for nearly twenty years, Dame Blanca Aldaco—founder, owner, and operator of Aldaco's Mexican Cuisine at Historic Sunset Station and Aldaco's at Stone Oak in San Antonio, Texas—describes herself as a "fiesta in high heels." She serves this recipe not only at the restaurant but also to guests in her own home. Normally it's made with the ham, but the dish is great vegetarian fare without it. The sauce for the dish is also luscious over grilled chicken breasts or shrimp. Note that the heat of the peppers can be varied. Removing the seeds and veins helps moderate them, as do the cheese and cream.

This is a rich dish. Appetizers could be nothing more than warm corn chips. Follow with a first course of Drunken Beans over Mexican White Cheese (page 54); for dessert, serve ice cream or sorbet topped with a drizzle of your best tequila.

6 servings

8 medium to large poblano chile peppers, divided

3 tablespoons olive oil

12 ounces shredded Monterey Jack cheese

Scrambled Egg Filling (recipe follows)

Crema Poblano Sauce (recipe follows)

1½ cups coarsely chopped tomatoes, salted

1½ cups sliced green onions, both green and white parts

❧ Rub the peppers with the oil. Place them on a grill or under the broiler, turning as needed until the skin is evenly charred, about 10 minutes. Set aside 2 peppers for the Crema Poblano sauce. Place the remaining peppers on a plate and top with a damp towel to allow them to steam for about 10 minutes, or until cool enough to handle. Remove the charred skin. To prepare for filling, hold each pepper at the stem and cut a 1-inch slit across and 2 inches lengthwise as in a T, open gently, and carefully remove seeds and veins. Repeat with the remaining peppers. (This can be rather a pesky procedure. Do not worry that your peppers appear a little ragged. Once they are stuffed, sauced, and baked, you'll never notice.)

✳ To assemble the Chiles Rellenos, preheat the oven to 350°F. Place a pepper for stuffing in the palm of your hand with the T slit facing you. Open gently and place 2 tablespoons of the cheese along the bottom. Add 2 heaping tablespoons of the Scrambled Egg Filling, then 2 more tablespoons of cheese. With both hands, firmly reshape the pepper and place in a 9- by 13-inch baking dish or other pan just large enough to hold the 6 peppers. Repeat with the remaining peppers, cheese, and egg filling; if there is any remaining cheese or egg filling, just tuck it into the dish between the peppers. Pour the Crema Poblano Sauce over the top. Bake uncovered until heated through, 13 to 15 minutes. Remove from the oven and top with the green onions and tomatoes.

Scrambled Egg Filling

3 tablespoons vegetable oil

10 large eggs

6 ounces thinly sliced smoked ham, cut into small pieces (optional)

2 green onions, finely chopped, both green and white parts

2 serrano chile peppers, stemmed, seeded, and finely chopped

½ teaspoon salt

✳ Heat the oil in a large skillet over medium heat. In a bowl, combine the eggs with the ham, green onions, serrano peppers, and salt. Add the egg mixture to the skillet and cook, taking care not to overcook. (It's better to undercook as it will be cooked further in the oven.) Remove from the heat and reserve.

Suggested Beverage

Mexican beer or an off-dry German Riesling, or a brut Champagne. Less predictable: a southern Rhône–style blend of Grenache, Syrah, and Mouvèdre.

Crema Poblano Sauce

2 medium poblano chile peppers, roasted (reserved from main recipe)

½ cup milk

1 teaspoon salt

1 to 2 tablespoons vegetable oil

½ medium onion, very thinly sliced

2 large cloves garlic, minced

1 cup heavy cream

❧ Remove the skin, stems, seeds, and veins from the peppers. Place the peppers in a blender or the bowl of a food processor along with the milk and salt. Purée until smooth; reserve.

❧ Heat the oil in a medium saucepan over medium-high heat. Add the onion and garlic; cook until the onions are soft and translucent, 5 to 7 minutes. Add the cream and pepper purée; let simmer, stirring a few times, until flavors blend, 2 to 3 minutes. Remove from the heat and transfer to a bowl.

TOFU WITH SPICY STIR-FRY AND ASIAN GREENS

New York Dame Corinne Trang's career in food journalism started in the mid-1990s with her stint as production editor and test-kitchen director at *Saveur* magazine and has continued with a string of lauded books, including *Authentic Vietnamese Cooking, Essentials of Asian Cuisine*, and *The Asian Grill*. Here she turns tofu and greens into a healthy vegetarian main course.

Trang likes the way the agave nectar blends easily with other ingredients. If you prefer less heat, use the jalapeño rather than the Thai chile pepper. You can also serve the tofu cold without frying it. A side of steamed white rice is recommended but not a must. Start and finish the meal simply with the Cucumber-Sesame Salsa (page 19) served with store-bought rice crackers, and berries topped with Fresh Ginger Cream (page 335).

4 servings

1 pound fresh tofu cake (preferably firm)

¼ cup soy sauce

2 teaspoons dark sesame oil

1 teaspoon raw agave nectar, rice syrup, or brown sugar

2 tablespoons vegetable oil

½ cup peeled and finely julienned (threadlike) gingerroot (see "Prepare Ahead")

1 fresh red Thai chile pepper or jalapeño chile pepper, stemmed and seeded, cut crosswise into thin rounds (see "Prepare Ahead")

3 green onions, finely sliced, both green and white parts

1 cup cilantro leaves

1 tablespoon toasted sesame seeds

Asian Greens (recipe follows)

Steamed rice (optional)

Prepare Ahead

As with most stir-fries, all the time-consuming prep work can be done hours ahead of the last-minute cooking. Two tips from Trang: To finely julienne fresh gingerroot, use a vegetable peeler to make broad slices. Stack the slices and julienne (lengthwise) into fine threads. To seed the Thai chile after you have cut off the stem, roll the pod between your thumb and forefinger to loosen the seeds. Applying some pressure as you roll, allow the seeds to "crawl" out. Slice the pod into thin rounds. You may want to wear rubber gloves when prepping the chile pepper.

**Suggested
Beverage**

New Zealand Sauvi-
gnon Blanc, Italian
Pinot Grigio, or a
slightly effervescent
Portuguese Vinho
Verde—all will
cleanse the palate
between bites.

⁂ Drain and rinse the tofu, then drain again between two double layers of paper towels for 1 hour. Cut the tofu into 5 slices, then again in half, so you have 10 thick squares. Refrigerate until ready to use. Combine the soy sauce, sesame oil, and agave nectar in a small bowl. If using sugar, be sure to stir long enough for the sugar to dissolve in the soy sauce.

⁂ At least 20 minutes before serving, heat the vegetable oil in a large nonstick sauté pan and stir-fry the gingerroot, chile, and green onions until fragrant and lightly golden, about 1 minute. Add the cilantro leaves and stir-fry for 1 minute. Add the stir-fry mixture to the soy sauce mixture and let stand for 20 minutes. Wipe the pan clean.

⁂ Shortly before serving, prepare the Asian Greens and reserve.

⁂ Lightly oil the pan again over medium heat and fry the slices of tofu until golden crisp on both sides, about 5 minutes total. Transfer tofu to a serving platter or distribute between individual serving dishes.

⁂ To serve, top the tofu with just a drizzle of the stir-fry mixture and a sprinkle of sesame seeds. Serve alongside the Asian Greens and rice. Pass the remaining stir-fry mixture on the side for those who want more of its "kick."

Stir-Frying

It is important to stir-fry vegetables over high heat and keep the ingredients moving, so the natural juices evaporate as you cook. Also, do not overcrowd your wok or pan. Stir-fry in two or more batches if necessary. A wet stir-fry is not desirable. Soy sauce, fish sauce, fermented tofu, and dark sesame oil should be back notes. The natural flavor of the vegetables should come to the fore. Accordingly, season with a light hand. Vegetable oil is used generously in Asian stir-fries to keep the vegetables hot when served. Using 2 table-spoons of oil for 1 pound of vegetables is standard. If you want to keep the calories to a minimum, cut the amount of oil by half.

—New York Dame Corinne Trang

Asian Greens

10 to 12 cups

1 pound (10 to 12 cups total) leafy greens: Chinese broccoli, choy sum, water spinach, baby bok choy, chrysanthemum leaves, spinach, or romaine lettuce

1 to 2 tablespoons vegetable oil

2 large cloves garlic, crushed and sliced

1 tablespoon soy sauce or fish sauce

Dash dark sesame oil (optional)

Salt and freshly ground black pepper

To prepare the different greens: For Chinese broccoli, separate the leaves, halve them crosswise, and cut the stems into 1-inch-long pieces. For choy sum, separate the leaves and halve crosswise. For water spinach, cut the leafy stems into 2-inch-long pieces. For baby bok choy, leave whole or halve lengthwise through the stem. For mature bok choy, chrysanthemum leaves, or spinach, separate the leaves. For romaine lettuce, separate the leaves and cut crosswise into 2-inch pieces.

In a wok or large skillet, heat the oil over high heat. Stir-fry the garlic until fragrant and light golden, about 2 minutes. Add the greens and stir-fry until wilted and just tender: 1 to 2 minutes for delicate leaves like chrysanthemum leaves and spinach, 2 to 3 minutes for choy sum or bok choy, and up to 5 minutes for hefty or tough leafy stems such as water spinach or Chinese broccoli. Season with the soy sauce, add a drop or two of sesame oil, and adjust seasoning with salt and pepper just before serving.

Prepare Ahead

Prepare the greens several hours ahead, right up to the final cooking step. Cook at the last minute before serving.

❧ VEGETARIAN CASSOULET ❧

Prepare Ahead

Cassoulet can be assembled up to the point of baking a day ahead.

This is a simple dish to make, even though its provenance is the classic French meat and bean dish that traditionally takes hours to assemble and cook. It comes from Austin Dame Diane Tucker, who has had a varied life in food: she's done cooking stints at numerous restaurants, worked as a personal chef, managed an exotic game ranch, and now, with a master's degree in psychology, she teaches psychology at Texas Culinary Academy in Austin. "The students are required to take the course, but actually, they enjoy hearing what makes things tick in the kitchen: motivation and personality."

Pair the Cassoulet with Whole Baby Carrots (page 216). Start the meal with Golden Beet Slaw (page 28). As this tends to be cold-weather food, end the meal with poached pears in Lemon Verbena Syrup (page 336). Tucker herself is not a vegetarian and developed the dish as a side for a meat course. If you are not a vegetarian, make the cassoulet with meat broth (the richer the better). As a side to roast ham or grilled sausages, you could hardly do better. Feel free to alter the combination of fresh herbs to your taste, perhaps substituting ones that you may have growing in your own garden.

8 servings

2 tablespoons extra-virgin olive oil

1 medium onion, cut into ¼-inch dice (about 2 cups)

2 large carrots, cut into ½-inch dice (about 2 cups)

1 large red potato, cut into ½-inch dice (about 2 cups)

12 cloves garlic, minced, divided

1 tablespoon fresh thyme leaves or 1 teaspoon dried

1 tablespoon chopped fresh sage leaves or 1 teaspoon dried

1 tablespoon chopped fresh rosemary leaves or 1 scant teaspoon dried

Two 15.5-ounce cans cannellini beans, drained and well rinsed

One 14.5-ounce can diced tomatoes with their juice

2 cups vegetable broth

1½ teaspoons salt

15 grinds black pepper

3 thick slices country-style bread, trimmed of crusts and torn into rough pieces

½ cup chopped parsley

1 cup freshly grated Pecorino Romano cheese

Suggested Beverage

Moderate-tannin reds such as Chianti or a regional Pinot Noir from Burgundy; for white, a crisp French Chablis or rosé.

❧ Preheat the oven to 325°F. Oil a 9- by 13-inch baking dish. In a large skillet, heat the oil over medium-high heat. Add the onion, carrots, and potato and sauté for about 5 minutes. Add 6 of the garlic cloves, thyme, sage, and rosemary and sauté another minute. Fold in the beans and tomatoes with their juice; stir in the broth, salt, and pepper. Simmer briefly and taste for seasoning, adjusting if necessary. Spoon the mixture into the prepared baking dish. Bake uncovered for 20 minutes.

❧ To make the bread-crumb topping, place the bread, parsley, and remaining garlic in the bowl of a food processor fitted with a steel blade. Process to make coarse crumbs. Fold in the grated cheese. After the first 20 minutes of baking, remove the baking dish from the oven and top with half of the crumb mixture. Raise oven temperature to 400°F and bake for 15 minutes. Remove the baking dish from the oven and stir well. Top with the remaining crumb mixture and bake until the top is golden brown and the beans are bubbling, about 15 minutes. Serve immediately.

Improving Your Farmers' Market

With farmers' markets burgeoning all over America, there is wide variation in quality and success. Here are some tips from farmers' market gurus Dames Ann-Harvey Yonkers and Abby Mandel for improving your local market.

* Make certain that vendors are growers.

* Expand your market gradually, making sure your original group of farmers is enjoying strong sales before adding vendors.

* Be smart about your product mix. Make the market a place where customers can approach one-stop shopping, from vegetables and fruits to cheeses to dairy to meat to seafood to bread.

* Track farmers' sales by charging them a percentage rather than a flat fee.

* Likewise count customers, so you'll better understand the market's traffic.

* Be sure the market opens and closes on time.

* Make sure vendors provide visible statements on their stalls about their growing and producing practices.

* Use marketing techniques such as fliers, sandwich boards, and weekly e-mails to spread the market's message.

* Integrate local chefs into your market by staging "Chef at the Market" demos and market tours.

* Staunchly preserve the idea that these are farmers selling delicious fresh food direct from the farm to consumers.

❧ LATE SUMMER HARVEST STEW ❧

In 1997, Washington, D.C., Dame Ann-Harvey Yonkers co-founded FRESHFARM Markets, a nonprofit organization that now runs eight producer-only farmers' markets in the Chesapeake Bay region. The markets, linking farmers within a 200-mile radius of Washington, D.C., to both chefs and consumers, have become a veritable gold standard for farmers' markets across the country. Yonkers and her husband, Charlie, tend a nine-acre waterfront farm on the Chesapeake Bay called Pot Pie Farm, complete with one hundred–plus pastured laying hens and organic vegetable beds.

This recipe for a bumper crop stew of garden vegetables "fragrant with heirloom tomatoes, smooth-skinned peppers, just-picked summer squash, and fresh herbs" is typical of the farm cooking the Yonkers favor. Cook up big batches of the stew when the produce is in peak season. The base consists of just four vegetables, but possible additions are almost endless. Whether you serve the stew on pasta or in an omelet, an appealing accompaniment is Basic Greens with an In-Your-Face Dressing (page 68). A Berry Puff Torte (page 315) or Fresh Blackberry Cobbler (page 311) would continue the farmhouse-cooking feel. The yield shown is for the stew served over a pound of pasta generously topped with freshly grated Parmigiano-Reggiano; as an omelet filling or a side dish with meat it serves at least eight.

6 to 8 servings

Prepare Ahead
This dish can be kept in the refrigerator for at least 4 days and frozen for up to 4 months.

¼ cup olive oil

1 large red or yellow onion, cut into thin wedges

5 medium assorted seasonal market peppers (Anaheim, poblano, Hungarian, or bell peppers), cored, seeded, and cut into 1- by 3-inch strips

6 to 8 (1¾ pounds in all) firm zucchini or yellow summer squash *or* a combination, cut into 2-inch pieces

2 cloves garlic, minced

1 to 2 tablespoons salt

4 grinds black pepper

3 pounds ripe tomatoes, peeled, seeded, and chopped *or* if preferred, simply chopped (see box, page 188)

¼ cup chopped fresh basil

1 tablespoon chopped fresh herbs such as sage, oregano, or thyme *or* a combination

Optional

Fresh corn kernels cut from 4 to 6 ears (see box, page 71)

String or roma beans, trimmed and sliced diagonally into 2-inch pieces (about 2 cups)

Chopped hot chile peppers, such as jalapeño or serrano

1 cup pitted black olives, drained

½ cup feta cheese, coarsely crumbled

❋ In a heavy skillet large enough to hold all the vegetables, heat the oil over medium-high heat. Add the onion, stirring to evenly coat. Cook over medium heat, stirring occasionally, until the onion is soft and lightly colored, about 10 minutes.

✻Add the peppers, zucchini, garlic, salt, and pepper. Cook uncovered for about 5 minutes, stirring frequently. Add the tomatoes, cover, and cook until they have rendered their juices. Remove cover and continue cooking, stirring frequently, until the juices have thickened to your preference. Add the basil and other fresh herbs. (At this point add any of the optional ingredients to taste. The beans will require enough time to become tender; the corn, only a brief time in the hot mixture; the olives or cheese, a minute.) Taste for seasoning and adjust if needed. Serve hot or at room temperature as an entrée with cooked pasta, as an omelet filling, or as a vegetable side dish.

Suggested Beverage

An Italian Gavi or an Arneis; if feta cheese is added, serve a young red Valpolicella.

SIDE DISHES

Vegetables and More   The roots of Les Dames are in formal French cuisine, yet even Escoffier favored simple fare. Often the best dishes are simple—and the best side dishes exemplify this. Most sides are in fact *to the side*, out of the spotlight, foils. Occasionally, however, there are dishes that deserve co-star billing: twice-baked soufflés that perfectly enhance a steak; Italian beans and potatoes that only improve a roast. As for ingredients, we urge you to buy organic, local, seasonal, fresh. We like to buy celery with a sharp green color and fresh leaves still on its stalks, our carrots with soil in their creases. We celebrate herbs grown by the kitchen door.

Recipes

On-the-Side Fresh Corn and Green Beans
Kim McElfresh, *Boston Chapter*

Whole Baby Carrots with Star Anise and Orange
Paulette Satur, *New York Chapter*

Roasted Brussels Sprouts
Lisa Ekus-Saffer, *Boston Chapter*

Broiled Asparagus with Lemon Zest
Shirley Corriher, *Atlanta Chapter*

Souvenir Eggplant Gratin
CiCi Williamson, *Washington, D.C., Chapter*

Twice-Baked Spinach Soufflés
Anne Willan, *Washington, D.C., Chapter*

Stir-Fried Green Beans and Sunchokes
Lucy Wing, *New York Chapter*

Greens Braised with Dried Fruits and Nuts
Jen Karetnick, *Miami Chapter*

Fresh Fennel Ratatouille
Carole Brown, *Minneapolis/St. Paul Chapter*

Creamy Feta Potatoes from D.C.'s 1789 Restaurant
Ris Lacoste, *Washington, D.C., Chapter*

Gingered Sweet Potato–Parsnip Purée
Lee Wooding, *New York Chapter*

Tuscan Beans and Potatoes
Nancy Brussat Barocci, *Chicago Chapter*

Marion Cunningham's Simple Side of Orzo
Marion Cunningham, *San Francisco Chapter*

Green Rice
Gail Greene, *Dallas Chapter*

Groaning-Board Wild Rice
Nancy Wong, *Vancouver, B.C., Canada Chapter*

Zazu's Backyard Garden Fattoush
Duskie Estes, *San Francisco Chapter*

Warm Lentils with Walnut Oil and Fresh Lemon Juice
Cynthia Pedregon, *San Antonio Chapter*

Notes

An Alternative Asparagus Topping: Fried Capers

A Dollop of Wilted Spinach

Basic Wilted Greens

Potluck Panic

See also: Best Grits *(page 129)*, Drunken Beans *(page 54)*, Eastern-European Sauerkraut *(page 141)*, Farmers' Carrots *(page 124)*, Fresh Okra Cakes *(page 10)*, Golden Beet Slaw with Fresh Horseradish *(page 28)*, Grilled Gazpacho Salad with Shrimp *(page 57)*, Horseradish Potato Purée *(page 144)*, Julienned Carrots, Fennel, and Sweet Peppers *(page 121)*, Late Summer Harvest Stew *(page 207)*, Mushroom Ragù *(page 195)*, Sautéed Potatoes *(page 158)*, Shaved Fennel Salad *(page 138)*, Squash Casserole *(page 152)*, Three-Sisters Salad *(page 64)*

ON-THE-SIDE FRESH CORN
AND GREEN BEANS

Here's a beguiling combination of summer vegetables from Boston Dame Kim McElfresh, who owns and operates a marketing firm that specializes in the food and hospitality industries. She's also a wife, the mother of two grown children, and employed as a church minister. She remarks that juggling her many roles is typical of what women are especially good at. "'On the side' has more than culinary meaning to me. The words remind me of how women run their lives, juggling career, personal, and family interests. There's always a lot 'on the side.'"

4 to 6 servings

¼ cup olive oil

2 cups green beans, cut diagonally into 1-inch pieces

2⅔ cups fresh corn kernels (cut from about 4 ears—see box, page 71)

4 or 5 green onions, thinly sliced, both green and white parts

Heaping ½ cup chopped mint leaves

2 tablespoons plus 1 teaspoon freshly squeezed lime juice

1 teaspoon salt

10 grinds black pepper

Heat the oil in a large skillet over medium-high heat. Add the beans and sauté for about 2 minutes, shaking pan so the beans do not burn. Add the corn and cook for another minute. Remove from the heat and stir in the green onions, mint, lime juice, salt, and pepper. Serve immediately.

Prepare Ahead

Do all the prepping, including cutting the corn off the cob, hours ahead. Final cooking is quick.

WHOLE BABY CARROTS WITH STAR ANISE AND ORANGE

Prepare Ahead

For convenience, the carrots can be cooked 1 or 2 hours ahead of dinner and briefly, gently reheated to serve.

When it comes to carrots, New York Dame Paulette Satur grows *only* baby varieties on her Long Island farm that supplies many of New York's best restaurants. Though this recipe works for sliced full-size carrots, Satur strongly urges cooking even full-size carrots (young, slender ones) whole. You will need to adjust the cooking time and perhaps the amount of liquid, but it's worth it, Satur says: "I just like the bountiful look of whole vegetables. It's real farmers' market style." Alternatively, you can cut the whole carrots (even baby ones) in half from stem to tip—especially useful if carrots are of varying size. This also makes for a particularly attractive presentation.

In addition, Satur suggests using the multicolored carrots—red ones, yellow ones, purple ones—sometimes found at farmers' markets. "The colored carrots tend to have a more 'carroty' flavor and they look beautiful all layered on a serving platter." Satur concedes that although the optional finely minced shallots taste good, "In my busy farmhouse, I tend not to have a lot of time to slice, dice, and mince"—echoing the thoughts of many of today's busy cooks.

6 servings

½ tablespoon unsalted butter

¼ teaspoon peeled, finely chopped gingerroot (see box, page 171)

¼ teaspoon sugar

3 bunches baby carrots, peeled*, with ¼ inch of green stem remaining *or* 2 bunches of slender full-size carrots prepared like the baby carrots or peeled and cut into ¼- to ½-inch diagonal slices (3 cups)

½ cup freshly squeezed orange juice

⅓ cup finely minced shallots (optional)

1 star anise

½ teaspoon salt

5 grinds black pepper

* Over low heat, melt the butter in a skillet wide enough to hold the carrots in a shallow layer. Add the gingerroot and sugar. Stir until the sugar darkens slightly and begins to caramelize. Add the carrots and toss to coat well. Add the orange juice, shallots, star anise, salt, and pepper.

* Cover the pan tightly and continue to cook over low heat until the carrots are tender, with a slight resistance to the bite. If the liquid is absorbed before carrots are tender, add a very small amount of water until they are finished cooking.

*_"Peeling" baby carrots is usually a matter of lightly scraping them with a paring knife._

ROASTED BRUSSELS SPROUTS

When you mention brussels sprouts, some folks may scrunch up their noses. This recipe is guaranteed to change dislike to delight. Based on Philadelphia chef Marc Vetri's recipe, these sprouts are a staple for Boston Dame Lisa Ekus-Saffer, particularly when she's looking for a quick vegetable side dish. Ekus-Saffer spends her work days running The Lisa Ekus Group, one of the nation's best-known public relations and literary agencies specializing in culinary talent from around the globe.

6 to 8 servings

1 clove garlic, cut in half

1¼ pounds brussels sprouts, cleaned, trimmed, and cut in half lengthwise

2 tablespoons olive oil, divided

2 tablespoons unsalted butter, divided

¼ cup balsamic vinegar

Salt and freshly ground black pepper

Prepare Ahead

The initial sautéing of the sprouts can be done hours ahead. The oven roasting can be done close to serving time. Also note that the sprouts are as good at room temperature as hot out of the oven— perfect buffet food.

✳ Preheat the oven to 425°F.

✳ Rub the garlic half gently over the cut side of the sprouts. Cut any unused garlic into fine slivers.

✳ In a large sauté pan, heat 1 tablespoon of the oil and 1 tablespoon of the butter over medium heat until gently bubbling. Place half the sprouts cut side down in the hot oil and let them cook undisturbed until the bottoms are well browned, 7 to 10 minutes. (Regulate the heat so the sprouts do not burn.) Transfer the sprouts to a shallow, ovenproof baking dish large enough to hold all of them. Repeat the sauté with the remaining oil, butter, and sprouts. When this second batch has browned, return the first batch to the sauté pan. Add in any remaining slivers of garlic. Pour the balsamic vinegar in a circle around the sprouts (this deglazing will cause a big cloud of steam, so make sure your exhaust fan is on). Sprinkle with salt and pepper. Pour the entire mixture, including any browned bits adhering to the sauté pan, back into the baking dish and immediately place in the oven. Roast until the sprouts are tender, crusty, and ready to serve, 5 to 8 minutes.

BROILED ASPARAGUS WITH LEMON ZEST

Prepare Ahead
You can prepare the asparagus up to the point of broiling several hours ahead. Broil right before serving.

Some cooks favor blanching asparagus, as on page 73. Others prefer high-temperature roasting or broiling for keeping the spears snappy yet tender. Regardless of the technique, Atlanta Dame Shirley Corriher's seven-minute rule holds: "The chlorophyll in green vegetables remains bright green if vegetables are cooked less than seven minutes." One caveat: do *not* top the green vegetable with an acid like vinegar or lemon juice, which will turn even perfectly cooked green vegetables an unsavory shade of green.

Here is Corriher's method for Broiled Asparagus. Note that she tops it with lemon zest, which lends fresh lemon flavor without the acidity of the juice turning the green vegetable "yucky army drab."

4 to 6 servings

1 pound fresh asparagus, rinsed in cold water

3 tablespoons olive oil

½ teaspoon salt

½ teaspoon sugar

Finely grated zest of 1 lemon (see box, page 75)

❋ Preheat the broiler and place the oven rack about 3 inches from it. With one hand at the root end of each asparagus stalk and the other hand three quarters of the way up the shaft, gently bend. The asparagus will snap where the tough portion ends. Spread the asparagus out on a baking sheet with sides or on a jelly-roll pan. Drizzle with the oil. Roll the asparagus in the oil to coat. Slip under the broiler and broil for 4 minutes only. Sprinkle with the salt, sugar, and zest; serve immediately.

An Alternative Asparagus Topping: Fried Capers

Do not miss Dame Rozanne Gold's way of garnishing asparagus with fried capers: In a small skillet, heat 2 tablespoons olive oil over medium-high heat. Fry ¼ cup large capers in the oil for about 1 minute. Pour the capers and oil over 1 pound of roasted asparagus (which serves 4 to 6). Gold adds, "Remember to use the startling accent of fried capers to top other dishes as well."

⚜ SOUVENIR EGGPLANT GRATIN ⚜

Prepare Ahead

This recipe can be assembled and baked a day before serving. Reheat in the microwave or covered with foil in a 350°F oven for about 20 minutes.

In 1993 in Monaco, food and travel writer and Washington, D.C., Dame CiCi Williamson was writing an article on Chef Alain Ducasse—the youngest chef ever to be awarded three Michelin stars. Ducasse prepared a special luncheon for Williamson in his restaurant, Le Louis XV, located in the Hotel de Paris across the street from the Monte Carlo Casino. Eggplant Gratin was one of the dishes served at this unforgettable luncheon. This souvenir recipe (translated from the French by Dame Carol Cutler) makes a scrumptious vegetarian entrée, but Williamson mainly uses it as a side dish to roasted and grilled meats. Note in particular that pre-roasting the eggplant uses a minimal amount of oil compared with sautéing.

8 servings

6 to 7 tablespoons olive oil, divided

3 to 4 medium (barely 3 pounds) eggplants

2 large onions, thinly sliced

2 heaping teaspoons finely chopped garlic

2 teaspoons salt

10 grinds black pepper

4 tablespoons chopped parsley, divided

2 teaspoons dried basil, divided

Two 14.5-ounce cans diced tomatoes with their juice, divided

1 cup (4 ounces) coarsely grated mozzarella cheese

¼ cup freshly grated Parmigiano-Reggiano cheese

2 tablespoons fresh homemade bread crumbs (see box, page 140)

✳ Set one oven rack in the center of the oven and the other in the lower third. Preheat the oven to 475°F. Oil a 10- by 14-inch baking sheet *and* a 9- by 13-inch baking dish with 1 tablespoon of the olive oil each; set aside. As an alternative to the dish, you can prepare two 9-inch pie pans (this gives you the option of serving in wedges, which you may prefer; baking time will be slightly shorter).

✳ Cut the eggplants crosswise ¼-inch thick. Place a layer of slices on the oiled baking sheet. Bake on the lower oven rack for 5 minutes; turn the slices over and bake until slices are golden and soft, about 5 minutes. Remove from the baking sheet and repeat, using additional oil as needed, until all the eggplant slices are cooked (several batches will be necessary).

✳ Meanwhile, heat a large skillet and add 1 tablespoon of the oil. Add the onions; cook over medium heat, stirring occasionally, until the onions are soft but not brown, about 15 minutes. Add the garlic near the end.

✳ Reduce oven temperature to 350°F. Place half the cooked eggplant slices in the prepared baking dish. Sprinkle with half the salt and pepper, 2 tablespoons of the parsley, and 1 teaspoon of the basil. Distribute 1 can of tomatoes with their juice over the eggplant. Top with all the onions and repeat layers of remaining eggplant, seasonings, and tomatoes.

✳ Top the gratin with the cheeses and bread crumbs. Bake on the center over rack until the cheeses are melted and juices are bubbling, 30 to 40 minutes. Let cool 10 minutes before serving.

❧ TWICE-BAKED SPINACH SOUFFLÉS ❧

Prepare Ahead

Two days ahead of serving, prepare the ingredients. One day before serving, prepare the soufflés up until their second baking. Ten minutes before serving, finish the soufflés with the final baking.

This recipe comes from Grande Dame Anne Willan, who founded the esteemed bilingual École de Cuisine La Varenne in Burgundy. Willan points out that her twice-baked soufflé method allows the cook to work ahead, thereby eliminating the last-minute stress usually associated with soufflés. After the first baking, you allow the soufflés to cool and deflate. Up to 24 hours later, the only last-minute action required is baking them briefly in the oven a second time, where they infallibly re-inflate. Serve them at a dinner party to accompany grilled steaks or roasted prime rib—the soufflés' velvety sauce can be shared with the meat. We serve the soufflés surrounded by the Veal and Wild Mushroom Ragout (page 177). They also make a dazzling first course on their own.

Depending upon the volume of your egg whites, you may have enough extra mixture for one or two additional soufflés. These can be baked in a second batch once you've removed the initial batch from the roasting pan. The splendid fact is that these soufflés are so forgiving that extras can be reheated even two days after the initial baking (with or without any extra white sauce).

Ten 6-ounce or seven 8-ounce soufflés

Butter for coating ramekins

1 pound spinach, stemmed and washed thoroughly

⅓ cup unsalted butter plus additional for greasing ramekins

1 onion, finely chopped (scant 2 cups)

1½ teaspoons salt, divided, plus additional as needed

Freshly ground black pepper

¼ cup all-purpose flour

1½ cups whole milk

Freshly grated nutmeg

1½ cups half-and-half

5 large egg yolks

6 large egg whites

½ cup (2 ounces) grated Gruyère cheese

❋ For their first baking, the soufflés can be baked in ten 6-ounce rame-kins or seven 8-ounce ramekins. Generously butter the ramekins and chill them.

❋ Pack the damp spinach leaves into a large saucepan, cover it, and wilt the leaves over medium heat, stirring occasionally, 5 to 7 minutes. Drain the spinach and let cool. Squeeze handfuls of spinach in your fists to extract the water, then chop. Reserve.

❋ Melt 1 tablespoon of the butter in the same saucepan, add the onion, and sauté over medium heat until it is soft but not brown, 3 to 5 minutes. Stir in the spinach, ½ teaspoon of the salt, and about 5 grinds of pepper, and continue cooking, stirring, until mixture is quite dry, 2 to 3 minutes. Reserve.

❋ To make the white sauce, melt the remaining butter in a saucepan, whisk in the flour, and cook until foaming but not browned, about 1 minute. Whisk in the milk, a pinch of nutmeg, the remaining salt, and 5 grinds of pepper, and bring to a boil, stirring constantly until the sauce thickens. Simmer for 2 minutes and remove from heat. Transfer about ½ cup of the white sauce into a small saucepan and pour the half-and-half on top so it makes a layer to prevent a skin from forming. Reserve.

❋ Stir the spinach into the remaining sauce and heat until very hot, stir-ring. Remove from the heat, taste, and adjust the seasoning; it should be well seasoned to make up for the bland egg whites. Beat in the egg yolks a bit at a time so they cook in the heat of the sauce and thicken it slightly. Cover the saucepan with plastic wrap to prevent a skin form-ing on the spinach mixture.

❋ Preheat the oven to 350°F. Bring a heavy-duty roasting pan (large enough to hold the ramekins) of water (deep enough to come about two thirds of the way up the sides of the ramekins) to a boil on the stove (see box, page 314).

✳ Add a pinch of salt to the egg whites and beat in a bowl until stiff but not dry. Warm the spinach mixture gently until the saucepan is hot to the touch. Add about a quarter of the beaten egg whites and stir until well mixed. The heat of the mixture will cook the whites slightly. Add this mixture to the remaining whites and fold them together as lightly as possible.

✳ Fill the chilled ramekins with the mixture, smoothing the tops with a metal spatula. Run a thumb around the edge of each dish to detach the mixture so the soufflé rises straight. Gently lower the ramekins into the roasting pan of hot water, bring it back to a boil on the stove, and carefully transfer it to the oven. Bake until the soufflés are puffed, browned, and just set in the center, about 15 minutes for 6-ounce soufflés, 20 to 25 minutes for 8-ounce soufflés. They should rise well above the rims of the ramekins. Take the ramekins from the roasting pan and leave them to cool 15 to 20 minutes—the soufflés will shrink back into the ramekins, pulling away slightly from the sides. When cooled, use a paring knife to nudge the batter back in from the rim of the ramekin, then run the tip of the knife around the edge of each soufflé to loosen it and carefully turn the soufflé out. Place browned side up in a gratin dish large enough to hold all the soufflés.

✳ Whisk the reserved sauce and layered half-and-half until smooth, place on medium-high heat, and keep whisking; bringing it just to a boil. Season to taste with salt, pepper, and nutmeg, and pour on top of the soufflés, letting it pool around the sides. Sprinkle the soufflés with the cheese. The soufflés can be held, covered with plastic wrap, for up to 24 hours in the refrigerator.

✳ To finish the soufflés, heat the oven to 425°F. Bake the soufflés until they are browned, slightly puffed, and the sauce is bubbling, 7 to 10 minutes. Serve them at once.

STIR-FRIED GREEN BEANS AND SUNCHOKES

Though New York Dame Lucy Wing has made a career out of being a food editor (for *Country Living*, *McCall's*, and *American Home*), she likes to say she has a double major: food and gardening. This recipe showcases sunchokes (also known as Jerusalem artichokes), an underutilized root vegetable that grows prolifically in her Pennsylvania farm garden. Edible tubers of a perennial sunflower plant, sunchokes resemble potatoes and taste like water chestnuts. Wing says she stores the sunchokes in perforated plastic bags that she recycles from grocery store grapes. Tucked in the refrigerator vegetable drawer, the chokes will keep for months, handy for spur-of-the-moment use—often oven-roasted like potatoes and served with a little dressing of olive oil, salt, and pepper, or puréed and made into soups. If you don't have sunchokes in your garden, you can find them in many supermarkets nearly year-round.

6 servings

Prepare Ahead

As with most stir-fries, all the prep work can be done hours ahead. Cooking, however, should be done at the last minute.

    2 tablespoons vegetable oil

    1 pound green beans, tips trimmed, snapped into halves

    ½ pound sunchokes, well scrubbed and cut into ¼-inch slices

    1 small onion, halved and sliced into ¼-inch crescents (see box, page 52)

    ½ cup vegetable broth, divided

    2 tablespoons reduced-sodium soy sauce

    2 teaspoons sugar

    1 teaspoon cornstarch

    1 clove garlic, finely chopped

In a large skillet or wok, heat the oil over high heat. Add the beans and stir-fry for 2 minutes. Add the sunchokes and onion; stir-fry for 1 minute. Reduce the heat to medium. Add half of the broth. Cover and cook until the beans are tender but crisp, about 5 minutes.

※ Meanwhile, in a small bowl or cup, mix the remaining broth with the soy sauce, sugar, cornstarch, and garlic. When the beans are tender-crisp, stir in the cornstarch mixture and continue to cook until the sauce bubbles. Serve immediately.

GREENS BRAISED WITH DRIED FRUITS AND NUTS

Prepare Ahead

Greens can be washed and trimmed a couple of days ahead. Final chopping and cooking should be done right before serving. Or follow Karetnick's lead: cook and freeze, thaw, and reheat.

Many Dames are involved in community-supported agriculture cooperatives in which consumers contract with small local farmers to purchase the season's harvest. Miami Dame Jen Karetnick, a freelance food and travel writer, is a site host for Redland Organics, the South Florida vegetable cooperative. One season, the co-op yielded such a plethora of leafy greens that after a while members simply refused to take home their bunches of kale, chard, and mustard greens. Left with piles of leafy "extras," Karetnick devised this recipe, which she repeatedly doubled and tripled, giving batches to neighbors and freezing in tubs to serve later, tossed with wide noodles or as a side dish to grilled meats.

4 servings

½ pound (about 5 cups) fresh greens (mustard greens, Swiss chard, kale, or napa cabbage *or* a mix)

2 tablespoons olive oil

1 shallot, finely chopped

¼ cup raisins

¼ cup chopped dried apricots

¼ cup pine nuts

¼ cup slivered almond

2 cubes vegetable bouillon (Knorr brand preferred)

¼ cup dry white wine

2 cups hot water

1 teaspoon salt

10 grinds black pepper

✻ Wash the greens in several changes of water. If the stems are thick, remove and chop into ¼-inch dice. Reserve. If the leaves are big, pull them off the stem, roll them up, and roughly slice them into ¼- to ½-inch ribbons. Chop any remaining stems as above and add to the reserved stems.

✻ In a large, heavy saucepan over medium heat, warm the oil and sauté the shallot until aromatic. Add the raisins, apricots, pine nuts, almonds, and reserved stems. Stir until the nuts are lightly browned and the fruit plumps up. Add the bouillon cubes, smashing them into the mixture. Add the white wine and boil for a minute or two. Add the greens and toss. Add the hot water. Season with the salt and pepper. Stir and cook over low heat for 8 to 10 minutes or until the greens are wilted, the stems are tender, and the liquid has reduced to a slightly syrupy consistency. The dish will remain brothy.

A Dollop of Wilted Spinach

Dallas Dame Renie Steves uses baby spinach leaves to add color to otherwise brown dishes, like cooked grains and rice. To top 6 servings, place about 9 ounces of baby spinach leaves (leaves still damp from washing, stems removed) in a sauté pan with 2 tablespoons butter and ½ teaspoon salt. Right before serving, place the pan over medium heat and cook, stirring a few times, just until the spinach is wilted, about 2 minutes (spinach will be very green and shiny). Remove from the heat immediately and dollop atop any otherwise plain-looking entrée or side dish. You've made a vegetable side dish and garnish all in one.

Basic Wilted Greens

Farmers' market advocate Ann-Harvey Yonkers claims there is probably no more typical market staple these days than fresh greens in many varieties. Once washed, they're easy to cook, making a versatile side dish full of vitamins and iron. Choose the freshest greens possible (whether from your own garden or the market) and combine varieties. Yonkers likes to make nests of wilted greens, then top them with farm-fresh eggs fried quickly in olive oil. Here is her way with greens. (See also Asian Greens, page 203.)

6 to 8 servings

> 2 pounds fresh greens (baby or mature) such as chard, kale,
>
> dandelion, collards, mustard, spinach, and escarole
>
> 3 tablespoons olive oil
>
> 1 cup finely diced onion
>
> 2 to 3 cloves garlic, finely minced
>
> 1 teaspoon salt
>
> 10 grinds black pepper

* Prepare the greens as in the recipe for Greens Braised with Dried Fruits and Nuts on page 224. Baby greens will not need their stems removed or leaves cut.

* In a sauté pan large enough to hold all the raw greens (they will shrink as they wilt, so the pan can be full to overflowing to start), heat the oil over medium heat. Add the onion and sauté for 3 to 5 minutes, stirring occasionally. Add the garlic and any chopped stems, and continue cooking for 3 to 5 minutes. Add the greens, stir well, and cook, covered, until the leaves are wilted and the stems are soft, about 5 minutes. Taste for tenderness and season with the salt and pepper. Serve immediately.

❧ FRESH FENNEL RATATOUILLE ❧

Fresh fennel adds texture, as well as an additional layer of subtle flavor, to the classic French ratatouille. Minneapolis Dame Carole Brown, a free-lance food writer and a cooking-school teacher, commends the dish for its versatility: its rich vegetable flavors pair well with most any meat (she often adds grilled pork or lamb sausage to the finished ratatouille, turning it into a one-dish meal). The dish can be served either hot or at room temperature, and its ingredients are generally available year-round.

8 to 10 servings

½ cup olive oil, divided, plus more as needed

1 pound (1 medium) eggplant, cut into 1-inch pieces

1 medium onion, cut into 1-inch pieces

1 medium green bell pepper, cored, seeded, and cut into 1-inch pieces

1 medium red or yellow bell pepper, cored, seeded, and cut into 1-inch pieces

1 medium fennel bulb, cored and cut roughly into 1-inch pieces (reserve fronds)

6 cloves garlic, thinly sliced

4 sprigs parsley

4 sprigs fresh thyme *or* 2 teaspoons dried

½ teaspoon red pepper flakes

2 tablespoons red wine vinegar

1 cup red or white wine *or* chicken broth

One 28-ounce can whole tomatoes with their juice

½ pound (2 medium) zucchini, cut into ½-inch slices

2 bay leaves (Mediterranean or Turkish preferred; see tip, page 53)

½ teaspoon salt plus additional as needed

Freshly ground black pepper

½ cup chopped fresh basil leaves

Prepare Ahead

The ratatouille can be prepared several days ahead of serving. Reheat gently over medium heat, stirring frequently. Do not add fresh basil and fennel fronds until right before serving.

✳ In a large Dutch oven or heavy-bottomed pot, heat 2 tablespoons of the oil over medium-high heat and add half of the eggplant cubes, spreading them in a single layer. Lightly brown them on all sides, then transfer to a plate. The browning will be uneven. Use a flexible metal spatula to keep the cubes from sticking to the Dutch oven. Repeat with 2 more tablespoons of the oil and the remaining eggplant, transferring to the plate when browned.

✳ Heat the remaining oil and add the onion to the Dutch oven. Cook over medium heat until the onion begins to soften, 3 to 5 minutes. Add the peppers, fennel, and garlic; cook for 5 minutes. Add additional oil if necessary to keep the vegetables from sticking. Cover the Dutch oven if necessary to keep the vegetables moist and to prevent them from browning, but don't let them get watery. Tie the parsley and thyme together and add to the Dutch oven. Add the red pepper flakes, vinegar, and wine. Add the tomatoes with their juice by holding each tomato over the Dutch oven and tearing it into roughly 1-inch pieces before dropping into the vegetable mixture. Pour in any remaining juice left in the can. Return the eggplant to the Dutch oven, and add the zucchini, bay leaves, salt, and pepper.

✳ Cover the ratatouille with a round of parchment paper. Cover the Dutch oven and cook over low heat until the vegetables are cooked and the flavors have blended well, 1 to 1½ hours. Add more liquid (wine, broth, or water) if necessary to keep a nice stewlike consistency. Stir gently from time to time.

✳ Remove the parsley bundle and bay leaves before serving. Add salt and pepper to taste. Stir in the fresh basil and the reserved fennel fronds as desired, and serve.

CREAMY FETA POTATOES FROM D.C.'S 1789 RESTAURANT

Celebrity chef and Washington, D.C., Dame Ris Lacoste served these Creamy Feta Potatoes with a rack of lamb and a red-pepper purée throughout the decade she was executive chef at the celebrated D.C. restaurant 1789. Lacoste, after graduating from the University of California at Berkeley with a degree in French, went off to Paris to practice the language. She happened to take a part-time typing job at the École de Cuisine La Varenne. The school's founder and president, Grande Dame Anne Willan, spotted the young Lacoste's flair for food and proposed that she be her personal assistant by day and a full-time cooking student at night. Two years later, Lacoste finished her La Varenne training, and she's been working as a chef ever since.

6 to 8 servings

2 tablespoons unsalted butter

4 cups finely diced onion

2 cloves garlic, minced

8 ounces imported Greek feta cheese, crumbled

Butter to grease pan

1¼ cups heavy cream

1 cup whole milk

½ teaspoon salt

2 pounds (about 3 large) russet potatoes, peeled and covered with water

Freshly ground black pepper

½ cup fresh homemade bread crumbs (see box, page 140)

Melt the butter in a large skillet. Add the onions and cook until soft but not browned, about 5 minutes. Add the minced garlic and cook 1 minute longer. Remove the skillet from the heat and cool. Stir in the feta cheese. Reserve.

Prepare Ahead

All the ingredients can be prepared at least a day ahead, including peeling the potatoes. That leaves only slicing the potatoes, assembly, and baking (quite unattended) prior to serving. Baking time is about 90 minutes. The dish can be assembled an hour before that, so 2½ hours before serving, your work, other than tending the oven, is done.

✻ Preheat the oven to 350°F. Butter a 9- by 13-inch baking dish. Put the cream, milk, and salt in a saucepan and heat to just under a boil. Remove from the heat and reserve.

✻ To avoid discoloration, slice the potatoes one at a time, as you need them, to create each layer. Slice 1 of the potatoes—either on a mandoline, or with a 2-mm slicing blade on the food processor, or by hand—into ⅛-inch slices and line the bottom of the dish. Season the layer with about 8 grinds of black pepper (do *not* salt the layers).

✻ Cover with one third (about 1 cup) of the onion-feta mixture. Repeat two more layers, leaving enough sliced potatoes for a top layer. Pour the hot cream mixture over the top layer. The cream should reach to the top of the potatoes but not cover them. Add another 8 grinds of black pepper. Do not cover the dish for baking.

✻ Bake for 20 minutes. Remove the pan from the oven and use a large spoon or a bulb baster to baste the top potatoes with the cream from the corners. Return the pan to the oven and bake for 40 minutes. Sprinkle the top with the bread crumbs. Continue to bake until the crumbs brown, 15 to 20 minutes longer. The potatoes should be fork tender and the cream nearly absorbed. Let sit for up to 20 minutes before serving (if necessary, briefly reheat).

GINGERED SWEET POTATO–PARSNIP PURÉE

Prepare Ahead
Prepare the purée hours ahead and reheat to serve.

Most any roasted meat will be enhanced when situated with this delicately flavored vegetable. The recipe comes from New York Dame Lee Wooding, a veteran of test kitchens and avocational cooking schools, who especially favors the purée for accompanying fall and winter meals of roast turkey, pork, or duck.

1 pound sweet potatoes, peeled and cut into 1-inch pieces

½ pound parsnips, peeled and cut into ½-inch pieces

3 quarter-size slices peeled gingerroot

1½ teaspoons salt, divided (Wooding, like most Dames, is insistent on kosher or coarse sea salt—"I find traditional table salt has a very metallic taste"; see explanation, page xxv.)

¼ cup half-and-half

1½ tablespoons unsalted butter, divided

¼ teaspoon freshly ground white or black pepper

Pinch of cayenne pepper

1 teaspoon finely grated lemon zest

Put the sweet potatoes, parsnips, and gingerroot in a large saucepan. Add water to cover by 1 inch and add 1 teaspoon of the salt. Bring to a boil, then reduce heat and simmer until the vegetables are tender, 15 to 20 minutes. Drain, reserving ½ cup of the cooking liquid.

Add the half-and-half, ¼ cup of the reserved cooking liquid, and 1 tablespoon of the butter to the vegetables and purée with an immersion blender (see box, page 101) until smooth and creamy, adding more of the cooking liquid as needed. (Or, the purée can be made in the bowl of a food processor fitted with a steel blade or with an electric hand mixer, but the texture will not be as smooth.) Season with the remaining salt, white pepper, and cayenne pepper. If serving immediately, top with the remaining butter and the lemon zest. If not serving immediately, butter a shallow baking dish and spoon purée into it. Top with the remaining butter and lemon zest. Cover with foil. Refrigerate until ready to serve. Reheat in a preheated 350°F oven until hot, about 20 minutes.

❋ TUSCAN BEANS AND POTATOES ❋

Prepare Ahead

The dried beans can be cooked a couple of days ahead and the potatoes prepared hours ahead. Combine the two for the final cooking right before serving.

This dish is typical of Chicago Dame Nancy Brussat Barocci's way with Italian food. It's simple, yet refined. It's adaptable to most any time of year. And it's handsome in an old-world, homey way. Barocci especially likes it to serve with grilled steaks and chops. It's equally suited to sautéed sausage or roasted chicken. For a tad dressier dinner, accompany with Barocci's Little Molds of Roasted Peppers (page 60).

Barocci uses an extra-virgin Tuscan olive oil to top the dish with a crowning flourish of flavor.

10 to 12 servings

2 pounds new potatoes, peeled and cut into ½-inch cubes

¼ cup olive oil

¼ cup (½ stick) unsalted butter

4 cloves garlic, minced

½ teaspoon salt plus additional as needed

¼ pound pancetta, finely diced (about 1 cup) (see box, page 17)

1½ cups chopped shallots

1½ cups chopped red onions

4 cups cooked white beans, preferably cannellini or Great Northern (about ½ pound dried; for cooking instructions, see page 54), *or* two 15-ounce cans white beans, drained and rinsed

1 cup beef broth

12 fresh sage leaves, chopped, plus about 1 tablespoon for topping

Freshly ground black pepper

Condiment-quality olive oil to drizzle over the dish

❋ Pat the potatoes as dry as possible with paper towels. Heat the oil and butter in a heavy skillet large enough to hold the potatoes in a single layer (or divide the oil and butter between 2 skillets). Add the potatoes and sauté over moderate heat, shaking the pan from time to time to keep them from burning, until they are golden on all sides, about

25 minutes. When the potatoes are just seconds from being done, add the garlic and salt. Lift the potatoes and garlic out of the pan with a slotted spoon and drain on paper towels. Reserve.

❋ Add the pancetta to the same skillet, sautéing over medium heat until crisp (if necessary, add a little extra oil to keep the pancetta from sticking). Add the shallots and onions, reduce heat to medium-low, and cook until the vegetables are very soft, 10 to 15 minutes.

❋ Add the reserved potatoes to the pan, along with the beans, broth, and sage. Season with salt and pepper to taste. Cook over medium heat, stirring gently to combine, until hot. Spoon onto a serving platter or individual plates, top with the tablespoon sage, and drizzle with the oil.

Potluck Panic

Every cook can recall a humiliating moment, like the Jell-O mold that didn't, hollandaise that parted like the Red Sea, or the roast so dry it shattered on the plate. But one tale that arouses an empathetic groan among cooks is a potluck dish that returns home untouched, unsampled, uneaten. Completely overlooked. Even the most accomplished cook eats a slab of humble pie when her carefully crafted Sardine à la Terrine is cold-shouldered by everyone except the host's cat. That's when it hits you: you have just made leftovers—or worse, fodder for gossip among cooks.

On the other hand, maybe your potluck contribution has been the same for years. It's always eaten, the serving dish scraped clean. Yet recently you overhead someone say, "Oh, spinach dip. I guess Marilou must be here." This is a classic symptom of potluck predictability.

There is a serious, if unspoken, element of competition among cooks at potlucks. These are perfect venues to show off and show up your pals. Winners leave with empty bowls and plates. Losers leave pretty much the way they arrived except for that big dent in their culinary ego.

To rise above the ordinary and humbly shout, "I'm more special than you," it's good to know what "sells" at a potluck and how to sell it. Abandon your recipes for layered-bean anything—which go from fun to frightening in no time—or casseroles with cheese toppings that dry to a leathery hide. For the Fourth of July potluck table, resist producing a big bowl of chocolate mousse, which has a funny way of turning into a murky brown puddle on a hot day.

Make sure the ingredients are easily identifiable at a glance, unless you plan on standing next to your Feng Zhao Con Guacamole à la Mode with an explanation (and an apology).

Nothing says "eat me" like embellishment. Flowers, shrub-sized herb sprigs, and blizzard-like dustings of powdered sugar are great smokescreens for mediocre dishes. And remember, anything on a frilly toothpick is a sure winner.

Market your dish to increase desirability and decrease anxiety (namely yours). Have trustworthy family or friends mill around the gathering testifying loudly to the virtues of your Thai Rice Krispie Croquettes. If that doesn't work, personally take them to the guests and plunk them on their plates. Even if they aren't eaten, you'll be saved the embarrassment of leaving with much of what you brought. Most important, remember, there's always the trash can in the ladies' room.

Even though I am a food writer, culinary instructor, and cookbook author, the phrase "bring a covered dish" makes me panic, too. Before I choose, I always look for all the components of a successful potluck dish: easy to prepare, can be prepared a day ahead of time, can be held unrefrigerated for several hours, is filled with ingredients everyone knows and loves, and is full of color and texture.*

—*Cleveland Dame Marilou Suszko*

*Using Suszko's criteria, we suggest making the "Two-Sisters" version (no squash) of the Three-Sisters Salad (page 64) for your next potluck. Doubling the recipe should give you a dish impressive enough for a potluck table. If cutting kernels from 8 ears of corn daunts you (or the season does not permit), substitute 6 cups of good-quality frozen corn.

MARION CUNNINGHAM'S
SIMPLE SIDE OF ORZO

Prepare Ahead

The orzo, like all pasta, is best served immediately after it is dressed; however, it can be prepared up to the addition of fresh herbs and reheated successfully, covered, in the oven. Add the fresh herbs right before serving.

Seattle Dame Sharon Kramis received rough notes for this recipe in a handwritten note from Grande Dame Marion Cunningham. We've added directions, and we recommend the recipe for both its simplicity and its versatility. Kramis first met Cunningham at James Beard's summer cooking school in Gearhart, Oregon, in 1972. It was Beard who recommended to publisher Alfred A. Knopf that Cunningham become the "new Fannie Farmer" and completely revise the classic *Fannie Farmer Cookbook*. Cunningham went on to publish a half dozen of her own cookbooks, including award-winner *The Breakfast Book*. Recently, author, pastry chef, and all-around food authority David Lebovitz called Cunningham "the last of the great, classic American cooks." Kramis was always struck by her desire "to bring families back to the table, to daily share good food and good stories." And she especially takes note of Cunningham's business card. It reads simply: "Cook."

In her book *Learning to Cook*, Cunningham offered a recipe similar to this one, but substituted chopped cilantro leaves for the basil. She also suggested adding about two cups frozen peas (just thawed) and, in another menu, about a cup of chopped mint leaves and a cup of dried currants, adding the currants to the orzo while it was still in the hot cooking water.

8 servings

1 tablespoon salt plus additional as needed

2 cups orzo pasta

4 to 8 tablespoons unsalted butter, at room temperature

6 to 8 tablespoons freshly grated Parmigiano-Reggiano cheese

Freshly ground black pepper (not too fine, not too coarse—Kramis insists on at least 2 teaspoons)

1 cup snipped fresh basil leaves (optional)

Toasted pine nuts (optional)

❧ Bring a large pot of water to a boil. Add the salt. When the water has returned to the boil, add the orzo and cook until it is very tender with no crunchy centers, about 10 minutes. Drain well and return to the pot. Toss with the butter and cheese. Season with salt and pepper to taste. Right before serving, fold in the basil and pine nuts to taste. Serve hot.

❧ GREEN RICE ❧

Dallas Dame Gail Greene is a home economist and food stylist who has done a lot of recipe development for the American Heart Association. This dish is typical of her work: a healthy side dish with just enough flavor of its own to complement, but not compete with, the foods it accompanies.

Prepare Ahead

Everything except the final cooking of the rice can be done hours ahead of serving.

4 to 6 servings

2 cups water

2 poblano or pasilla chile peppers, cored, seeded, and coarsely chopped

1 small onion, quartered

½ cup chopped parsley

½ cup chopped cilantro leaves

2 tablespoons canned diced green chiles, drained, *or* 1 fresh serrano chile pepper, chopped (about 1 tablespoon)

2 cloves garlic, coarsely chopped

1 teaspoon salt plus additional as needed

5 grinds black pepper

2 tablespoons vegetable oil

1 cup long-grain white rice

In the bowl of a food processor fitted with a steel blade, place the water, poblano peppers, onion, parsley, cilantro, green chiles, garlic, salt, and black pepper. Cover and blend on medium-high speed until smooth, about 30 seconds. Strain, reserving liquid (about 2 cups) and vegetable pulp separately.

Heat the oil in a medium saucepan over medium heat. Cook the rice in the oil, stirring frequently, until the rice is well coated, about 1 minute. Pour the reserved liquid over the rice. Heat the rice mixture to boiling, stirring once or twice; reduce heat. Cover and simmer for 15 minutes. *Do not lift cover or stir.* Remove from the heat and fluff rice lightly with a fork. Cover and let steam for 5 to 10 minutes. Taste for salt and fold in reserved vegetable pulp to taste (it will add a bright green color to the rice). As a bonus, any remaining pulp can be seasoned with chiles, salt, and cumin to taste and folded into plain yogurt for a dip or sauce. (The pulp freezes well for later use, too.)

✤ GROANING-BOARD WILD RICE ✤

Prepare Ahead

The rice can be prepared a day ahead and reheated.

Many Dames favor recipes passed to them from family members. British Columbia Dame Nancy Wong, who runs her own public relations firm specializing in restaurant clients, remembers well the celebratory dinners her mom would make for gatherings of fifty or more. "Our dining room table really was a 'groaning board,' and there was a separate table for desserts as well." One of Wong's favorite dishes was made with the wild rice (which actually is not a rice, but a grass) that to this day is harvested by hand in the swampy areas of central Canada and the northern United States. She points out that twenty years ago, the rice was considered a rare luxury, but now, it is quite commonly available in most specialty food stores.

Here is Wong's way with wild rice, just as her mom taught her. Wong attributes the dish's inimitable texture to first presoaking and not overcooking the rice. Yes, the recipe does call for a full stick of butter—don't skimp. The butter makes the nutty rice quite sumptuous, and when the mushrooms are the extravagant wild variety, the dish is especially remarkable for its taste and texture.

4 to 6 servings

1 cup wild rice

3 cups boiling water

¼ cup dried currants

2 tablespoons Cognac or brandy

½ cup (1 stick) unsalted butter

3 large shallots or 1 small onion, diced (about 1 cup)

6 medium cultivated brown or white mushrooms, sliced (wild mushrooms make the dish even more festive)

Salt (at least ¼ teaspoon)

Rinse the rice in a colander under cold running water. Put the rice in a medium saucepan and add the boiling water. Cover and boil for 5 minutes *only* (be careful not to boil a second longer). Remove from the heat and let the rice sit covered for 1 hour. Meanwhile, soak the currants in the Cognac for 1 hour.

Preheat the oven to 300°F. In a medium Dutch oven or heavy-bottomed pot, heat the butter over medium-high heat. Add the shallots and cook until just translucent. Add the mushrooms and continue cooking, stirring occasionally, until the mushrooms are wilted and just barely golden. After the rice and currants are done presoaking, drain the rice and add it along with the currants and the Cognac to the sautéed shallots and mushrooms. Cover and place in the oven for 45 minutes. The texture of the rice should be tender but definitely crunchy. Most of the grains should puff, but not open. Season to taste with salt. Serve immediately.

ZAZU'S BACKYARD GARDEN FATTOUSH

Prepare Ahead

All the steps of the recipe can be done hours ahead, except for the final tossing of the vegetables, herbs, and bread. Do that immediately before serving so that the bread remains slightly crunchy.

This Middle Eastern herb and bread salad is typical of San Francisco Dame Duskie Estes' wine-country cooking. She and her husband, who is also a chef, grow all the fresh herbs needed for it in the backyard garden of their Santa Rosa, California, restaurant, Zazu Restaurant and Farm. Estes, who after graduating from Brown University worked in a number of big-name restaurants before opening her own, especially likes the *fattoush* served with simple grilled salmon, quail, or lamb. Ingredients like sumac (a tart-tasting spice made from the red berries of a decorative bush common in the Middle East and parts of Italy) and pomegranate molasses (a syrupy mixture made from the juice of fresh pomegranates) is typical of Estes' generation of chefs. In the last twenty years, ingredients once thought of as unusual have become more and more commonly available. If you can't find them in your local supermarkets or ethnic markets, you can obtain them over the Internet. Estes won't go as far as calling them "optional," but admits that the dish can be enjoyed without them—but only if you must.

6 servings

Two 10-inch pita breads, cut roughly into 1-inch squares

½ cup plus 2 tablespoons olive oil, divided

½ teaspoon ground sumac, divided

1 teaspoon salt plus additional as needed

10 grinds black pepper plus additional as needed

2 tablespoons sherry vinegar

2 tablespoons freshly squeezed lemon juice

1 tablespoon pomegranate molasses or balsamic vinegar

1 tablespoon brown sugar

1 small English or 2 lemon cucumbers, peeled, seeded, and diced into ¼-inch pieces (1 heaping cup)

1 red bell pepper, cored, seeded, and cut into ¼-inch dice
(about ¾ cup)

½ cup coarsely hand-torn parsley leaves

½ cup coarsely hand-torn fresh basil leaves

½ cup coarsely hand-torn mint leaves

½ cup feta cheese (preferably Bulgarian), crumbled

✼ Preheat the oven to 350°F. In a large bowl, toss the pita with 2 table-spoons of the oil, ¼ teaspoon of the sumac, salt, and pepper. Spread the pita mixture in a thin layer on a baking sheet. Bake until golden and crisp, 10 to 15 minutes. In a large bowl, make the dressing by combining the vinegar, lemon juice, pomegranate molasses, brown sugar, and remaining sumac. Whisk in the remaining oil. Season to taste with salt and pepper.

✼ Immediately before serving, add the cucumber, bell pepper, parsley, basil, and mint to the dressing. Toss to coat, then fold in the toasted pita pieces and top with the feta.

WARM LENTILS WITH WALNUT OIL AND FRESH LEMON JUICE

Prepare Ahead

The lentils can be prepared up to the addition of the lemon juice and walnut oil hours ahead. Complete and reheat at mealtime.

San Antonio Dame Cynthia Pedregon—who owns and operates a popular restaurant in Fredericksburg, Texas, called The Peach Tree—suggests choosing this warm French green-lentil dish when, as she puts it, "you want your entrée to command the attention." Not only is the dish a perfect companion to entrées, it also can be adapted in so many ways: add sautéed pancetta, diced roasted red pepper, julienned arugula or spinach, or crumbled cheese—feta, fresh goat, or pecorino. Pedregon also notes that the dish is easily doubled. "Leftovers make a splendid room-temperature salad."

4 to 6 servings

- **5 cups chicken broth or a combination of broth and water**
- **1¼ cups French green lentils (lentils *du puy*), picked over and rinsed**
- **1 bay leaf**
- **1 tablespoon fresh thyme leaves or 1 teaspoon dried thyme**
- **1 tablespoon olive oil**
- **1 cup thinly sliced green onions, both green and white parts**
- **1 clove garlic, minced**
- **½ cup coarsely chopped parsley**
- **1 to 2 tablespoons freshly squeezed lemon juice**
- **3 tablespoons walnut oil**
- **Salt and freshly ground black pepper**
- **½ cup chopped walnuts, toasted**

✳ In a medium saucepan, bring the broth to a boil. Add the lentils and return the liquid to boil. Skim off any foam, then add the bay leaf and thyme. Reduce heat to medium and cook the lentils until tender, 25 to 30 minutes. Be careful not to overcook—French lentils should still hold their shape and not become mushy. Remove the bay leaf and drain the lentils, reserving ½ cup of the broth. You can use the remaining broth for soups.

✳ In a medium skillet, heat the olive oil over medium heat. Add the green onions and garlic and sauté for 1 to 2 minutes. Add the parsley and cook just until wilted. Add the cooked lentils and the reserved broth to the skillet. Stir until heated through. Add the lemon juice, walnut oil, and salt and pepper to taste. Top with the walnuts and serve.

Breakfast-for-Dinner Salad

page 172

Whole Baby Carrots with Star Anise and Orange

page 216

Roasted Brussels Sprouts

page 217

Creamy Feta Potatoes from D.C.'s 1789 Restaurant

page 231

Scandinavian Cardamom Braid

page 260

Chocolate Chunk Coffee Cake Muffins

page 268

Passion Fruit–Macadamia Nut Tart

page 284

Berry Puff Torte

page 315

BAKED GOODS

A Sampling from the Pros Les Dames d'Escoffier includes many of the country's best-known artisan bakers. In city after city they have literally shaped the excellent breads and baked goods that today mark our national cuisine. Baking, however, is different from the rest of cooking—so different that we assigned a special team of Dames (together they have published hundreds of their own recipes for baked goods) to test the recipes in this section.

From the Dames who bake comes this message: You, too, can bake at home, with far less effort or loss of nerve than you'd expect; try crusty loaves, dimpled loaves, braided loaves—even loaves that need no kneading. There are also cinnamon buns, biscuits, muffins, and a coffee cake. And what you bake at home may well taste even better than anything you can buy at a bakery—even one of ours.

Recipes

One-Day Artisan Bread
Leslie Mackie, *Seattle Chapter*

No-Knead Foccacia
Suzanne Dunaway, *Los Angeles Chapter*

Challah to Teach the Kids
Joan Nathan, *Washington, D.C., Chapter*

Scandinavian Cardamom Braid
Beatrice Ojakangas, *Minneapolis/St. Paul Chapter*

Heavenly Cheddar and Cream Biscuits
Beth Allen, *New York Chapter*

Cinnamon-Nutmeg Buns
Flo Braker, *San Francisco Chapter*

Chocolate Chunk Coffee Cake Muffins
Deborah Mintcheff, *New York Chapter*

Buttermilk Berry Coffee Cake with Lemon Spice Topping
Carol Prager, *New York Chapter*

Notes

The Best Method for
Freezing Bread

Eating Bread Hot
from the Oven

Homemade Jams and
Food Safety

A Simpler Way to
Grind Spices

❧ ONE-DAY ARTISAN BREAD ❧

Daily in Seattle, Dame Leslie Mackie's Macrina Bakery makes hundreds of loaves of artisan-style breads—crusty, knobby, crackly loaves shot through with irregular air bubbles; new-world breads baked in old-world style.

Even with all this bread, Mackie still wanted a single loaf steaming out of her own home-kitchen oven. This is the recipe for that loaf—an easy-to-make, rough-shaped, flattish bread with a wonderfully thick crust and moist interior—a loaf that Mackie says is "delightful smelling and just right for slicing and dipping in extra-virgin olive oil."

Prepare Ahead

With risings, allow about 8½ hours from start to finish, mostly unattended.

1 loaf

¾ cup warm milk (105°F to 115°F)

¾ cup warm water (105°F to 115°F)

2 teaspoons active dry yeast

2 tablespoons olive oil

2¾ cups all-purpose flour plus additional for shaping

2 teaspoons salt

❧ Combine the milk and water in a large metal bowl. Sprinkle in the yeast and whisk until dissolved. Let stand until cloudy and slightly foamy, about 10 minutes.

❧ Add the oil and combine. Add the flour and salt and mix with a wooden spoon for 2 to 3 minutes. Be very careful not to overmix the dough. The mixture will not look like bread dough. It will be very wet and loose—"shaggy" in Mackie's words.

❧ Cover the bowl with plastic wrap and place in a warm area (approximately 75°F). Let stand (proof) until doubled in size and filled with bubbles, 2 to 2½ hours.

❧ At this point, remove the plastic wrap and dust the top of the dough with flour. With your fingertips, release the outer edge of the dough all around the bowl. Then with floured fingers, make a turn in the dough by stretching it in four directions, then flipping it over. To accomplish this maneuver, imagine the four points of a cross. Starting at the top (the dough farthest away from you), lift the dough, stretch it up, and place in the center of the bowl. Now take the base of the cross, stretch it up, and place it in the center of the dough. Repeat this with the left and right sides. Now invert the whole mass of dough. Cover the bowl with plastic wrap and let stand (proof) at 75°F for 30 minutes, then refrigerate for 4 hours.

※ Take the dough from the refrigerator and remove the plastic wrap. Dust the top of the dough with flour. Release the edges of the dough again, then invert the dough onto a heavily floured baking sheet. With well-floured hands, shape into a rectangle about 1 inch deep (the dough will be loose, sticky, and hard to shape). Cut a piece of plastic wrap large enough to cover the dough and spray it with nonstick cooking spray. Cover the dough and let it rest at room temperature for 30 minutes.

※ Meanwhile, place a baking or pizza stone or a very large cast-iron skillet in the middle of the oven and preheat to 400°F. Invert the loaf onto the preheated stone (the dough will *not* form a neat shape). Bake for 15 minutes, spraying the loaf three times with water to add steam to the oven. Bake until the loaf is golden to deep brown and sounds hollow when tapped on the bottom, 25 to 35 minutes longer. Transfer to a wire rack to cool before serving.

The Best Method for Freezing Bread

Cool the loaf completely, double-wrap in foil, and place in a heavy-duty sealable plastic bag. To serve, allow time for bread to thaw at room temperature; depending on the size of the loaf, this could take an hour or more. Then remove wrapping and reheat in a preheated 325°F oven for 10 to 15 minutes.

❋ NO-KNEAD FOCACCIA ❋

Want a dependable, forgiving dough that can be made on one day and baked the next, needs no kneading, and can be used to make many styles of bread? This is it. Los Angeles Dame Suzanne Dunaway became famous for her bread-making talents before she and her husband sold their Southern California baking company, Buona Forchetta Hand Made Breads, and moved to Europe, dividing their time between Italy and France. Although the company was loved especially for its slender baguettes seasoned with hazelnuts, pecans, olives, or fresh rosemary, Dunaway's favorite recipe was her focaccia dough. She featured it in her book, *No Need to Knead: Handmade Italian Breads in 90 Minutes*. In it, she describes how the dough can also be used for loaves of bread and for dinner rolls. Here's the focaccia version.

Although the Fleischmann's dry yeast packet stipulates the water should be 105°F to 115°F, Dunaway says it can be lukewarm, "like tepid bathwater—easy and encouraging." To make this a breakfast focaccia, mix 1 teaspoon cinnamon with 1 cup coarse brown or turbinado sugar and sprinkle over the dough in place of the rosemary.

Prepare Ahead

Note that there is both a same-day and an overnight method

1 large or 2 small focaccia sheets

2 cups lukewarm water

2 teaspoons active dry yeast

4 cups all-purpose flour, divided, plus additional as needed

2 teaspoons salt

2 to 3 teaspoons olive oil

2 tablespoons chopped fresh rosemary leaves

1 teaspoon kosher or coarse sea salt

❋ Measure the water into a large bowl. Sprinkle the yeast over the water and stir until dissolved. Stir in 2 cups of the flour and the salt and stir briskly until smooth, about 2 minutes. With a strong wooden spoon (Dunaway says a large one with a big hole in the middle of its bowl is just right for working flour into a stiff bread dough), stir in the remaining flour for about 2 minutes longer, just until the dough pulls away from the sides of the bowl and the flour is incorporated. The dough will be fairly wet and sticky, but when it pulls away from the sides of the bowl and forms a loose ball, you'll know the dough has been stirred sufficiently. If necessary, stir in an additional ¼ to ½ cup of flour.

※ **Same-day method:** Cover the bowl with plastic wrap and let the dough rise in a warm place until doubled in volume, 30 to 40 minutes. Proceed with the shaping instructions.

※ **Overnight method:** Cover the bowl and refrigerate overnight. The dough will rise in the refrigerator and acquire extra flavor from the slower yeast action. Remove the dough 30 minutes before shaping and let stand, covered, in a warm place. The dough will rise for the second time. Proceed with the shaping instructions.

※ To shape the focaccia: Preheat the oven to 500°F. Oil a 17- by 13- by 1-inch nonstick baking sheet for large focaccia or 2 baking sheets if making 2 small focacce. Pour the dough onto the sheet(s) without deflating the dough, scraping it from the sides of the bowl with a silicone spatula. Brush the dough with 2 teaspoons of the oil. To make the traditional focaccia with indentations, dip your fingers into cold water and thrust them straight down through the dough to the metal pan. Pull the dough to the sides about 1 inch at a time. Pull the holes at random to form little craters all over. The holes will fill in a bit as the focaccia awaits baking. As you work, stretch the dough into a 1-inch-thick oval. (If you are using a single baking sheet, the focaccia will cover almost the entire sheet.) Brush the focaccia with another teaspoon of the oil and sprinkle with the rosemary. The focaccia does not need to rise, but if you get called away from it for a few minutes, don't worry. It will bake beautifully despite a little neglect.

To bake the focaccia: Just before placing the focaccia in the oven, sprinkle with the coarse salt. Place the focaccia in the oven and reduce heat to 450°F. Bake until the focaccia turns a golden-brown color mixed with a little darker brown around the indented area, 15 to 25 minutes. Remove the focaccia from the pan and cool on a wire rack. Cut the focaccia into wedges or rectangles and serve warm.

Eating Bread Hot from the Oven

As enticing as it seems, bread hot from the oven is still giving off gases and, if consumed, will likely give you a stomachache once the joy of eating hot bread has passed. Properly cooled on a rack, the loaf reabsorbs its moisture into its interior and the crust stays crusty. It's not unlike letting a roast rest before carving: if you carve it immediately out of the oven, it bleeds its juices. Both roasts and loaves need to rest to properly reabsorb their natural juices. For the bread, allow about an hour—the larger the loaf, the longer the time.

—Seattle Dame Leslie Mackie

Homemade Jams and Food Safety

What could be better than homemade bread and jam? For breakfast, for a snack, for a dessert to end a Sunday supper? Maybe they provide cause enough to invite in guests with no need to cook an entire dinner—"Come over, I'm just opening a jar of homemade jam."

Home canning, like home baking, was once thought to have gone the way of backyard clotheslines and the icebox, but now preserving seasonal fruits and vegetables has become a tenet in the sustainable food movement, embraced by Les Dames d'Escoffier. The most important tip for making jam and other preserved foods: "Safety, safety, safety," says San Diego Dame Karen Ward, author of *Canning and Preserving for Dummies*. To help ensure a safe, bacteria-free product, Ward prescribes basic canning gear. Usually when you purchase a water-bath canning kettle with a jar rack (jars are never placed directly on the bottom of the kettle or touching each other), the other items you need are included: jar lifter (different from tongs, which do not securely hold the jar level and, if used to pick up the jar by the band, can disturb the vacuum seal), bubble freer, lid lifter, wide-mouth funnel. You may also want to purchase a foam skimmer, as the holes in a slotted spoon are too large to adequately remove the foam quickly so that the hot product can be transferred immediately to the jars).

The following recipe is for one of Ward's favorite summer fruit preserves. Frozen blueberries or raspberries may be used in place of fresh: thaw them in their container and use all of the resulting juice.

PLUM-BLUEBERRY JAM

(Or substitute raspberries for Plum-Raspberry Jam)

6 to 7 half-pints

7 half-pint canning jars with two-piece caps

4 cups (about 2½ pounds) finely diced pitted plums, skin left on

1½ cups (about 10 ounces) fresh or frozen blueberries (if frozen, thaw and reserve juices)

¼ cup water

6 cups granulated sugar

2 tablespoons freshly squeezed lemon juice

2 teaspoons grated orange zest

One 3-ounce pouch liquid fruit pectin

* Prepare your canning jars and two-piece caps according to the manufacturer's instructions. Keep the jars and lids hot in simmering, not boiling, water. Fill a canning kettle with water and bring the water to a boil over high heat. In a 6- to 8-quart nonreactive pot, combine the plums, blueberries, and water. Bring to a boil over high heat; reduce heat and simmer, covered, for 5 minutes. Add the sugar, lemon juice, and orange zest. Return the heat to high and, stirring constantly, bring to a full rolling boil (a boil that cannot be stirred down); boil hard for 1 minute, stirring constantly. Remove the pot from the heat and add the pectin all at once; stir to combine. Remove any foam from the surface with a foam skimmer.

* Immediately ladle the hot jam into the prepared jars, leaving ¼ inch of headspace. Wipe the jar rims with a clean paper towel. Seal the jars with the two-piece caps and hand-tighten the bands. Place the filled jars in the canning kettle with boiling water to cover them by 1 to 2 inches. Process the jars for 15 minutes after the water returns to a boil. Remove from water with a jar lifter and place on a clean kitchen towel away from drafts. Cool completely overnight or up to 24 hours. Test the seals. If there are jars that have not sealed, refrigerate them and use the jam within 2 months. Store the jars *without* the screw bands in a cool, dark place. Storing without the bands allows you to see if a vacuum seal has broken or if there is any seepage from the jar, which indicates a spoiled product and would be hidden by a screw band. Ward emphasizes: *do not use or even sample any spoiled product.*

* After opening a jar, refrigerate any unused jam, securing the lid with a screw band, for up to 3 weeks. Unopened sealed jars will keep in a cool, dry, dark place for up to 1 year.

✢ CHALLAH TO TEACH THE KIDS ✢

Prepare Ahead
Allow 2½ hours
for rolls to be
ready to bake.

Some years ago Washington, D.C., Dame Joan Nathan started a new family tradition. When the daughters and sons of her friends celebrate their bat and bar mitzvahs, *The New York Times* food writer and cookbook author invites them to meet in her kitchen, and she teaches them to make the Jewish bread challah, including a lesson in how to braid the dough (sometimes honing braiding skills with balls of different-colored Play-Doh). The same challah dough can be made into these enviable dinner rolls. This recipe is adapted from her book *The New American Cooking*.

If the yield seems too much, keep in mind that leftover challah makes marvelous French toast or bread pudding.

24 dinner rolls

2 packages active dry yeast

½ cup plus 1 tablespoon sugar, divided

1¾ cups warm water (105°F to 115°F)

½ cup flavorless vegetable oil, such as canola

2 large eggs, beaten, plus 1 egg lightly beaten for egg wash

1 tablespoon salt

7½ to 8 cups all-purpose flour

Poppy or sesame seeds (optional)

✢ Sprinkle the yeast and 1 tablespoon of the sugar over the water in a large bowl; whisk until dissolved. Let stand until slightly foamy, about 5 minutes. Whisk the oil and eggs into the yeast mixture, then whisk in the remaining sugar and salt. With a wooden spoon, gradually stir in 7 cups of the flour to form a soft dough. Turn the dough onto a well-floured surface and knead until smooth and elastic, about 10 minutes, working in enough of the remaining 1 cup flour to just keep the dough from sticking. (Or, use a stand mixer with the paddle attachment for the initial mixing, then switch to the dough hook for the final mixing and kneading.)

✳ Shape the dough into a ball and place in a greased bowl, turning the dough to coat it on all sides. Cover the bowl tightly with plastic wrap and let the dough rise in a warm place (80°F to 85°F) for about 1½ hours. When the dough has doubled in volume (if you press a finger into the dough, the indentation will remain), punch it down to remove all of the air. Shape the dough into a neat ball and return it to the bowl. Cover and let rise in a warm place for 30 minutes.

✳ Grease 2 large baking sheets. Divide the dough into 24 equal pieces (about 2 ounces each) and shape each into a ball. To finesse the shape, take each ball of dough and roll it around on a work surface under a cupped hand until a neat round ball forms. Place 12 rolls on each of the prepared baking sheets. Brush with the egg wash, then cover and let rise in a warm place until they double in volume, about 20 minutes. Meanwhile, place oven racks in the lower and middle sections of the oven and preheat the oven to 350°F. Brush the rolls again with the egg wash and sprinkle with poppy seeds. Bake until nicely browned on the top and bottom, about 20 minutes, rotating the baking sheets halfway through the baking time. Transfer the rolls to wire racks to cool.

✣ SCANDINAVIAN CARDAMOM BRAID ✣

Prepare Ahead

This bread is a natural for mixing ahead of time, as it needs to be chilled at least 2 hours or overnight.

Minneapolis Dame Beatrice Ojakangas simplifies this Scandinavian classic by chilling the dough after mixing. She says this eliminates tedious kneading and makes the dough easy to shape into braids. The other secret to this egg- and butter-rich bread is using freshly ground cardamom seeds. Preground cardamom loses so much flavor that, "regardless of brand, you will hardly taste it in the finished bread," says Ojakangas, who has been honored by the James Beard Hall of Fame for her expertise in Scandinavian cooking.

Two 18-inch loaves

2 packages active dry yeast

1 cup warm water (105°F to 115°F)

½ cup (1 stick) unsalted butter, melted

½ cup nonfat dry milk

1 teaspoon freshly ground cardamom seeds (1 to 2 tablespoons cardamom pods, seeds removed and finely ground—see box, opposite)

½ cup granulated sugar

4 large eggs, divided

1 teaspoon salt

4 to 4½ cups all-purpose flour

1 teaspoon milk

Sugar cubes crushed into coarse pieces to make ¼ cup *or* ¼ cup turbinado or raw sugar

✣ In a large bowl, dissolve the yeast in the water and let stand about 5 minutes or until the yeast foams. Whisk in the butter, dry milk, cardamom, granulated sugar, 3 of the eggs, and salt.

✣ Stir in 3½ cups of the flour, 1 cup at a time, until the dough is very stiff but still moist (the amount of flour you need will vary depending on the time of year and humidity). Add the remaining flour, ½ cup at a time, until the dough begins to pull away from the side of the bowl. Cover the bowl with plastic wrap and refrigerate at least 2 hours or overnight.

❋ Cover 2 baking sheets with parchment paper. On a lightly floured surface, divide the chilled dough into 2 pieces. Divide each of the pieces into 3 equal balls. Shape each ball into a rope about 20 inches long and 1 inch wide. Pinch the strands together at one end, then gently spread them apart. Move the right strand over the middle strand, then bring the left strand over the new middle strand. Continue until all the strands are braided, tucking the ends underneath the loaf. Repeat for the second loaf. Place the loaves on the baking sheets. Gently stretch and shape each loaf until it is 18 inches long. Cover each with a clean kitchen towel and set in a warm place (80°F to 85°F). Let rise until puffy, 45 minutes to 1 hour.

❋ Arrange the oven racks to divide the oven into thirds. Preheat the oven to 375°F. Beat together the remaining egg and milk for the glaze. Brush the loaves with the glaze and sprinkle with the crushed sugar. Bake the loaves, switching the pans between the racks halfway through, until golden, 25 to 30 minutes. Cool completely on wire racks.

A Simpler Way to Grind Spices

The fully equipped kitchen these days may well have a dedicated spice grinder—separate from the coffee grinder so that spice oils do not end up in your morning cup. However, there are simpler ways, and for some applications they work fine. As Ojakangas says, "Before I had a coffee grinder, I used a mortar and pestle, and before that, I put whole spices in a heavy-duty plastic bag and hit them with a rolling pin until they were pulverized."

HEAVENLY CHEDDAR AND CREAM BISCUITS

Prepare Ahead

Although the biscuits are best made and cut right before baking, they may be covered with a clean tea towel and held for up to 30 minutes at room temperature before baking and serving hot out of the oven as a "Texas-style treat."

Home economist and New York Dame Beth Allen grew up in a Texas home, where hot bread with supper every night was customary. Since then, her career has included long stints with many big consumer brands—*Reader's Digest*, Campbell Soup, Corning Glass, and Pillsbury Company—as well as co-authoring the *Good Housekeeping Great American Classics Cookbook*. Still, even now, living with her husband in New York City, at every meal she makes she insists on including at least one Southern specialty from her past. These sumptuously rich biscuits are often on Allen's menus.

Southern Dames are almost unanimous in their choice of biscuit-making flour: White Lily, a flour from Memphis that's milled entirely from soft winter wheat. If you can find it, use it (for these biscuits use only *all-purpose* White Lily flour). If you'd prefer plain biscuits, omit the cheese; the recipe works without it. This recipe is also easily doubled.

12 dinner or 30 tea biscuits

2¼ cups sifted all-purpose flour (not self-rising)

1 tablespoon baking powder

1 teaspoon salt

½ cup (1 stick) cold unsalted butter, cut into ¼-inch cubes

¼ cup vegetable shortening

½ cup (2 ounces) finely grated aged sharp or extra-sharp cheddar cheese, chilled (cheese needs to be grated on the very smallest holes, preferably with a Microplane—see box, page 75)

¾ to 1 cup heavy cream

Sweet paprika

Place oven racks in the upper and lower thirds of the oven and preheat to 425°F. Butter 2 baking sheets or line them with parchment paper. In a large bowl, mix the flour, baking powder, and salt. Using a pastry blender or knives, cut the butter and shortening into the flour until the mixture resembles coarse crumbs or grains of rice. Stir in the cheese.

✳ Make a well in the center of the mixture and pour in ¾ cup of the cream all at once. Using a wooden spoon or a silicone spatula, mix just until the flour disappears and the mixture is evenly moistened (the mixture will be crumbly). Turn the mixture out onto a lightly floured surface and knead with the heel of your hand three or four times, just until the mixture holds together and a soft dough is formed. Add a little more cream (not much more than 1 tablespoon) if necessary. Continue to knead—eight to ten times or for about 30 seconds, then pat (do not roll!) the dough into a ¾-inch-thick round. For dinner biscuits, use a floured 2½-inch round biscuit cutter; for small tea biscuits, use a floured 1¾-inch round biscuit cutter (a fluted one is especially nice). Cut out the biscuits, gathering and re-patting out the scraps of dough as you go. To encourage rising, push the cutter straight down into the dough, then lift up quickly without twisting. Work fast and re-flour the cutter often.

✳ Place the biscuits 1 inch apart on the baking sheets and brush the tops with about 2 tablespoons of cream and lightly sprinkle with paprika. Bake the biscuits, switching the pans between the racks halfway through, just until they are puffy and golden, 12 to 15 minutes for the dinner biscuits, 8 to 10 minutes for the tea biscuits. Watch closely and do not let them get too brown. Serve hot. You probably will not need additional condiments such as butter or honey; however, Allen often serves the biscuits generously stuffed with small pieces of warm baked ham.

✣ CINNAMON-NUTMEG BUNS ✣

Prepare Ahead

The dough can be prepared a day ahead of assembling and baking the buns. Buns are best eaten the day of baking. Store any leftover buns, covered with aluminum foil, at room temperature, or freeze in a resealable freezer bag. Thaw buns at room temperature for about an hour. To freshen after thawing, preheat the oven to 325°F, wrap buns in parchment paper or foil, place on a baking sheet, and heat just until warm, 7 to 10 minutes.

"Baking with yeast epitomizes comfort food. A little patience and a bit of practice, and baking with yeast will pay off big time," says San Francisco Dame Flo Braker. A cookbook author, cooking teacher, and for eighteen years the "baker columnist" for the *San Francisco Chronicle*, Braker combined parts of several old family recipes from her childhood to make this recipe "especially for Les Dames." The bold amounts of nutmeg, allspice, and cloves give the buns a sophisticated spin, but the aroma of yeast dough baking is indisputably homey. Don't let the recipe length scare you away—these buns are worth it.

20 buns

Dough

4½ to 4¾ cups all-purpose flour, divided, plus additional for kneading

¼ cup granulated sugar

1 tablespoon (1 envelope plus ¾ teaspoon) instant yeast

1 teaspoon ground cinnamon

½ teaspoon salt

¼ teaspoon freshly grated nutmeg

¼ teaspoon ground allspice

⅛ teaspoon ground cloves

1 cup plus 2 tablespoons (9 fluid ounces) whole milk, divided

6 tablespoons (¾ stick) unsalted butter

2 tablespoons honey, preferably orange blossom

¼ cup water

2 large eggs, at room temperature

2 large egg yolks, at room temperature

1 teaspoon pure vanilla extract

Streusel Filling

  1½ cups packed light brown sugar

  ¾ cup all-purpose flour

  5 teaspoons ground cinnamon

  ¼ teaspoon salt

  1 cup (2 sticks) cold unsalted butter, cut into ½-inch slices

  1 cup chopped walnuts

  1 cup chopped pecans

Sugar Glaze

  ⅔ cup confectioners' sugar

  2 tablespoons milk, whole or low-fat

  ½ teaspoon pure vanilla extract

  ½ teaspoon freshly grated nutmeg

  ⅛ teaspoon salt

❋ To make the dough, in the bowl of a stand mixer stir together 2½ cups of the flour with the sugar, yeast, cinnamon, salt, nutmeg, allspice, and cloves; set aside.

❋ In a small heavy saucepan, heat 1 cup of the milk with the butter over low heat until most of the butter melts. Off the heat, stir in the honey, water, and the remaining milk. Set aside to cool until just warm (120°F to 130°F), 1 to 2 minutes.

❋ Pour the milk mixture over the flour-yeast mixture and use a silicone spatula to mix well until the dry ingredients are moistened. Attach the bowl to the mixer and fit the mixer with the flat paddle attachment. Add the eggs and egg yolks, one at a time, mixing on low speed just until each egg is incorporated. Add the vanilla in the final moments of mixing. Stop the mixer, add another cup of the flour, and resume mixing on low speed until smooth, 30 to 45 seconds. Gradually add 1 cup of the flour and resume mixing on medium-low speed to make a soft, smooth, yet slightly sticky dough, about 45 seconds.

✻ Sprinkle the work surface with about 1 tablespoon of the flour, turn out the dough onto it, and sprinkle another tablespoon of the flour over the dough. Knead until the dough is smooth and not too sticky, about 1 minute. While kneading, add additional flour, up to ¼ cup if necessary. (The dough will remain sticky. For a tender bun, you want just enough flour—not too much.) Rather than adding more flour, slip a pastry scraper under the dough to release it from the surface and slap it down. Repeat this slapping action five times to strengthen the dough.

✻ Divide the dough in half and place each portion in a separate large bowl. If not baking that day, place a piece of plastic wrap directly on the surface of each piece of dough. Cover each bowl tightly with additional plastic wrap secured by a rubber band and refrigerate for up to 24 hours. If baking the same day, cover the bowl securely with plastic wrap and set aside in a warm place—about 70°F—until almost doubled, about 1 hour. The dough is ready for shaping if an indentation remains when the dough is poked with a finger.

✻ To shape the buns, lightly coat two 9- by 13-inch metal baking pans with nonstick cooking spray and line the bottom of each pan with a sheet of parchment paper; set aside. (*Metal* pans are preferable to glass in this case because glass retains more heat than metal and the buns could overbake.)

✻ To form the buns, gently deflate the dough in each bowl and let rest at room temperature for 30 minutes. Meanwhile, prepare the streusel filling. In a large bowl, combine the brown sugar, flour, cinnamon, and salt. Cut in the butter with a pastry blender or knives until the mixture is crumbly. With fingertips, blend in the nuts. Refrigerate until ready to use.

✻ Roll out each piece of dough on a lightly floured surface into a square approximately 12½-inches on each side. A lightly floured flexible cutting board helps immensely in manipulating the dough. Sprinkle half of the streusel filling over each square of dough. Roll up, jelly-roll fashion, and pinch the seams to seal the rolls. Gently roll each cylinder back and forth on your work surface to shape uniform logs about 14 inches long.

※ With a serrated knife, carefully cut each log into 10 even slices (a scant 1½ inches thick), using a slow sawing motion to preserve the buns' round shape. Place the buns from one of the logs, cut side down, in one of the prepared pans, leaving about 1 inch of space between the buns. Repeat, placing the remaining buns in the other prepared baking pan. Loosely cover the pans with plastic wrap or cotton towels and let rise at room temperature until puffy and doubled in size, 60 to 75 minutes (time may be longer if the dough has been refrigerated). At least 30 minutes before baking, place a rack in the center of the oven and preheat to 350°F. (Braker stresses that successful baking requires a stable, non-fluctuating heat. The oven needs to have all the elements up to desired heat, so don't shortcut the preheating.) To test whether the buns have risen enough, gently press a finger into the dough; once the indentation remains, the buns are ready to bake.

※ Bake the buns until pale golden brown, 25 to 30 minutes. For even baking, rotate the pans 180 degrees halfway through.

※ While the buns bake, prepare the sugar glaze. In a small bowl, mix the confectioners' sugar, milk, vanilla, nutmeg, and salt until creamy and smooth.

※ Transfer the pans of baked buns from the oven to wire racks. With a clean pastry brush, brush the glaze over the buns while still warm. If the glaze is too thick, add more milk, about ½ teaspoon at a time, until of a spreading consistency.

※ Cool the buns for 10 to 15 minutes, then place a rack on top of one of the pans of buns and invert the pan onto the rack. Lift off the pan and remove; discard the paper. Place a platter on the buns and invert the rack. Remove the wire rack. Repeat the procedure for the other pan of buns. (Don't worry about the glaze. You're moving quickly enough that it shouldn't stick to the rack.) Serve warm or at room temperature.

CHOCOLATE CHUNK COFFEE CAKE MUFFINS

New York Dame Deborah Mintcheff specializes in editing and writing "packaged books"—cookbooks that carry a brand name or are subject-driven rather than author-driven. Along the way, she's always, always cooking—her own recipes and others'. She developed the recipe for these muffins, each a sort of individual streusel-topped sour cream coffee cake, for a New Year's Day brunch party menu. Their feather-light texture is dotted with melted chocolate and fragrant with cinnamon sugar.

12 muffins

1¼ cups sugar, divided

1½ teaspoons ground cinnamon

2 cups all-purpose flour

2 teaspoons baking powder

½ teaspoon baking soda

½ teaspoon salt

¾ cup (1½ sticks) unsalted butter, at room temperature

2 large eggs, at room temperature

1½ teaspoons pure vanilla extract

1 cup sour cream, at room temperature

1 cup chopped walnuts

4 ounces bittersweet or semisweet chocolate, chopped into ¼-inch pieces

⁂ Place a rack in the middle of the oven and preheat to 400°F. Generously grease 12 regular muffin-pan cups, including the entire rim of each cup.

⁂ In a small bowl, whisk together ½ cup of the sugar and the cinnamon. Reserve. In a medium bowl, whisk together the flour, baking powder, baking soda, and salt.

In the large bowl of an electric mixer, cream the butter and the remaining sugar on medium speed until light and fluffy, about 2 minutes. Beat in the eggs, one at a time, scraping the bowl occasionally. Beat in the vanilla. (The mixture will appear curdled.) On low speed, add the flour mixture alternately with the sour cream, beating just until blended and beginning and ending with the flour mixture. The batter will be very thick.

Spoon half of the batter into the prepared muffin cups, dividing it evenly and spreading it into a layer. Sprinkle ¼ cup of the cinnamon sugar over the batter, then top with half of the walnuts and all of the chocolate. Spoon the remaining batter on top. (It won't look perfect and it doesn't have to cover completely.) Top with the remaining walnuts, then sprinkle with the remaining cinnamon sugar. The cups will be filled high above their rims.

Bake the muffins until a toothpick inserted into the center comes out clean, about 20 minutes. Place the muffin pan on a wire rack and let cool for 10 to 15 minutes. Invert a jelly-roll pan over the muffin pan and invert both together. Lift off the muffin pan. Place the muffins right side up on the wire rack. Serve warm or at room temperature.

BUTTERMILK BERRY COFFEE CAKE
WITH LEMON SPICE TOPPING

Prepare Ahead

The cake keeps well for days, but you can also prepare this using the container method (see "Prepare Ahead," page 268) and enjoy coffee cake hot from the oven.

New York Dame Carol Prager is currently the food editor for *Weight Watchers* magazine and also the author of *365 Great Cakes and Pies* and *100 Great Chicken Dishes*. Out of her hundreds of recipes, this coffee cake is not only a classic, but also an easy way to take advantage of frozen berries you may have saved from the summer season.

8 servings

½ cup (1 stick) unsalted butter, at room temperature, plus additional to grease pan

1 cup sugar

2 large eggs

1 teaspoon pure vanilla extract

1⅔ cups all-purpose flour

½ teaspoon baking powder

½ teaspoon baking soda

¼ teaspoon salt

½ cup buttermilk

1½ cups fresh or frozen blueberries *or* raspberries (if using frozen, include juices)

2 teaspoons freshly squeezed lemon juice

Lemon Spice Topping (recipe follows)

Lightly butter a 9-inch springform pan. Preheat the oven to 350°F. In a large bowl, beat together the butter and sugar with an electric mixer on medium-high speed until light and fluffy, about 2 minutes. Add the eggs, one at a time, beating well after each addition. Beat in the vanilla.

❋ Sift together the flour, baking powder, baking soda, and salt. With the mixer on low speed, alternately add the flour mixture and buttermilk to the butter mixture, beginning and ending with the flour mixture, and beating only until blended.

❋ Turn half of the batter into the prepared pan. In a medium bowl, toss the berries with the lemon juice. Sprinkle the berries on top of the batter. Cover with the remaining batter. Sprinkle the Lemon Spice Topping over all. Bake the coffee cake until a cake tester inserted into the center comes out clean, 65 to 70 minutes. Transfer to a wire rack and let cool 15 minutes. Remove the side of the pan. Serve the cake warm or at room temperature.

Lemon Spice Topping

½ cup packed brown sugar

⅓ cup flour

¾ teaspoon ground cinnamon

½ teaspoon grated lemon zest

3 tablespoons unsalted butter, at room temperature

❋ In a medium bowl, combine the brown sugar, flour, cinnamon, and lemon zest. With a pastry blender or a fork, cut in the butter until the mixture resembles coarse crumbs.

DESSERTS

Familiar and Uncommon All the favored flavors are here—chocolate and vanilla, lemon and strawberry, blackberry and butterscotch. Nostalgic favorites as well—puddings, thumbprint cookies, brownies, ice-cream sandwiches, berry cobbler. You'll also meet what are likely to be new tastes in your kitchen: the inimitable taste of passion fruit, of cacao nibs, of cheesecake made with Brie, of a cream puff so big it holds three heaping cups of berries. You'll find all the recipes clear and encouraging. You, too, can "roll" sponge cake around a luscious lemon filling, produce no-fail chocolate soufflés, and bake a dramatic cake that feeds twenty-four. That's the spirit of Les Dames.

Recipes

TARTS

Chocolate Hazelnut Tart
Carole Bloom, *San Diego Chapter*

Tiny Tim Tarts
Jane Mengenhauser, *Washington, D.C., Chapter*

Passion Fruit–Macadamia Nut Tart
Abigail Langlas, *Hawaii Chapter*

COOKIES

Glazed Lemon Cookies
Gale Gand, *Chicago Chapter*

Chewy Double Chocolate Cookies
Gale Gand, *Chicago Chapter*

Lemon-Cranberry-Pecan Biscotti
Karen Stiegler, *Palm Springs Chapter*

Jumbo Ice Cream Sandwiches with Fresh Raspberry Sauce
Patricia Ward, *Philadelphia Chapter*

Praline Brownies
Susan Westmoreland, *New York Chapter*

Raspberry Rosebuds
Susan Fuller Slack, *Charleston Chapter*

CAKES

Shirley's Tunnel of Fudge Cake
Shirley Corriher, *Atlanta Chapter*

Lemon Cream Roulade
Carole Walter, *New York Chapter*

Fran's Original Cheesecake
Fran Bigelow, *Seattle Chapter*

OTHER DESSERTS

Fresh Blackberry Cobbler
Edna Lewis, *Atlanta Chapter*

Baked Butterscotch Puddings
Sharon Hage, *Dallas Chapter*

Berry Puff Torte
Linda Lau Anusasananan, *San Francisco Chapter*

Notes

Chopping Chocolate

Why Bother with Dessert Wines?

An Introduction to Port

Give the Gift of Port

Cookie-Baking Tips

Jam Swirl Brownie Variation

Dip and Sweep

Preparing Pans to Prevent Turn-Out Trauma

Safety Tips for Hot-Water Baths

Percentages on Chocolate Packages

Test Your Thermometer

Pairing Seasonal Fruits with Cheese

Recipes

Bittersweet Chocolate Soufflés with Nibby Cream
Alice Medrich, *San Francisco Chapter*

Gingerbread Dessert Waffles
Charlotte Ann Albertson, Ann-Michelle Albertson, and Kristin Albertson, *Philadelphia Chapter*

Peach Tree Country Kitchen's Bread Pudding with Jack Daniel's Caramel Sauce
Nancy Fitch, *San Antonio Chapter*

Almond Shortcakes with Strawberry-Rhubarb Sauce
Ingrid Gangestad, *Ontario, Canada Chapter*

See also: Winter Salad of Oranges and Pomegranate *(page 76)*

LITTLE BITES

Turkish Apricots Stuffed with Cream and Pistachios
Sheilah Kaufman, *Washington, D.C., Chapter*

Burgundian Spiced Caramels
Jennifer Lindner McGlinn, *Philadelphia Chapter*

Dark Chocolate Fresh Ginger Truffles
Pam Williams, *British Columbia, Canada Chapter*

Bread and Chocolate: A Little Dessert Bruschetta
Bev Shaffer, *Cleveland Chapter*

SAUCES

Fresh Ginger Cream
Susan Fuller Slack, *Charleston Chapter*

Lemon Verbena Syrup
Ann-Harvey Yonkers, *Washington, D.C., Chapter* and Paulette Satur, *New York Chapter*

See also: Jack Daniel's Caramel Sauce *(page 324)*, Nibby Cream *(page 320)*, Strawberry-Rhubarb Sauce *(page 325)*

Tarts

❧ CHOCOLATE HAZELNUT TART ❧

San Diego Dame Carole Bloom studied pastry making and confectionery arts in Europe before returning home to California to start writing cookbooks and teaching cooking classes. Her eighth cookbook, *The Essential Baker*—a comprehensive guide organized by main ingredients rather than type of dessert—immediately received acclaim for its unusual approach. Her work appears regularly in *Bon Appétit*, *Gourmet*, and *Food & Wine*. Of her hundreds of recipes, this one, learned in 1978 when training at E. Rosa Salva Pasticceria in Venice, Italy, is among her very favorites. The tart is fragrant with fresh orange zest and, typical of Italian desserts, not overly sweet.

One 11-inch tart or two 8-inch tarts

Tart Shell

  1¾ cups all-purpose flour

  ⅓ cup sugar

  2 teaspoons finely grated orange zest (see box, page 75)

  ½ teaspoon baking powder

  ⅛ teaspoon salt

  10 tablespoons (1¼ sticks) unsalted butter, cut into pieces and chilled

  1 large egg, at room temperature

  2 teaspoons pure vanilla extract

Filling

  1¾ cups hazelnuts (preferably raw)

  3 tablespoons sugar

Prepare Ahead

The pastry dough can be made up to 4 days in advance and kept tightly wrapped in the refrigerator, or it can be frozen for up to 4 months. If frozen, be sure to defrost in the refrigerator before using. Should you want to make just 1 smaller tart, make the full recipe of the dough and freeze half. Then make half a recipe of the filling and reduce baking time about 5 minutes; repeat the process when you make the second tart. The finished tart can be covered with aluminum foil and stored at room temperature for up to 4 days.

5 ounces bittersweet (70 to 72 percent cocoa content) or milk chocolate *or* a combination, finely chopped (see box below)

6 tablespoons (¾ stick) unsalted butter, at room temperature

½ cup sugar

2 large eggs, at room temperature

2 teaspoons finely grated orange zest (see box, page 75)

1 tablespoon all-purpose flour

1 tablespoon pure vanilla extract

Serving

1 cup heavy cream, flavored with 1 teaspoon pure vanilla extract and whipped

❋ To make the tart shell, in the bowl of a food processor fitted with a steel blade, combine the flour, sugar, orange zest, baking powder, and salt. Pulse a few times to blend. Add the chilled pieces of butter and pulse the mixture until the butter disappears into the flour, about 30 seconds.

❋ In a small bowl, lightly beat together the egg and vanilla. With the food processor running, pour the mixture through the feed tube. Process until the dough forms a ball, about 30 seconds.

Chopping Chocolate

It's not easy to chop chocolate, and hardly anyone advises using the food processor. Most say "do it the old-fashioned way"—with a large chef's knife on a cutting board, no more than 6 ounces at a time, and not too vigorously, or else the chocolate may fly about the kitchen. It helps to have the chocolate at room temperature. Thin slabs are easier to chop than thick chunks (you might choose your chocolate for chopping accordingly). Once you have the chocolate roughly chopped, you can pulse it briefly in a food processor with a steel blade to get more uniformity.

✳ Alternative: To mix the dough without a food processor, soften the butter and beat it with a mixer until light. Add the sugar and orange zest and cream together. Combine the baking powder and salt with the flour and add to the butter in two stages, blending well after each addition. Beat the egg and vanilla together and add to the dough, mixing gently until blended.

✳ Shape the dough into a flat disk and wrap tightly in a double layer of plastic wrap. Chill until firm, at least 2 hours. Let it stand at room temperature to become pliable before rolling; if the dough is very cold it will splinter when rolled out.

✳ Roll out the dough between sheets of lightly floured waxed paper to a 14-inch circle. (If rolling out half portions of dough for an 8-inch tart, roll each to about a 10-inch circle.) Gently place the dough circle over the rolling pin and unroll into a 1-inch-deep, fluted-edge tart pan with a removable bottom. Carefully lift up the sides of the dough and ease into the bottom and sides of the tart pan. This helps prevent the dough from shrinking as it bakes. Trim off any excess dough around the edge of the pan. If the dough sticks or cracks, you can repair it by hand-pressing trouble spots into the pan. Place on a baking sheet and chill for 30 minutes.

✳ To make the filling, center a rack in the oven and preheat to 350°F. Place the hazelnuts on a jelly-roll pan and toast in the oven for 15 to 18 minutes, until the skins split and the nuts are a light golden brown. Remove the pan from the oven and transfer the hazelnuts to a clean tea towel. Wrap the towel around the hazelnuts and rub them together to remove most of the skins (a few remaining skins are fine). In the bowl of a food processor fitted with a steel blade, pulse the hazelnuts with the sugar until the nuts are finely ground, about 2 minutes. Add the chopped chocolate and pulse about 30 seconds to break up any larger pieces of chocolate.

❊ Using an electric stand mixer with the flat beater attachment or a large mixing bowl and a hand-held mixer (preferable for the half-batch version), beat the butter until fluffy, about 1 minute. Add ½ cup of the sugar and continue beating, stopping occasionally to scrape the sides and bottom of the bowl with a silicone spatula, until thoroughly combined.

❊ Lightly beat the eggs and add the orange zest, then add to the butter mixture. Use a silicone spatula to help mix evenly. Add the flour, hazelnut-chocolate mixture, and vanilla, and blend together thoroughly.

❊ Transfer the filling to the chilled pastry shell, spreading it evenly over the pastry. Bake the tart until the filling is puffed and set and the crust is golden brown, 25 to 30 minutes. Remove from the oven and transfer to a rack to cool completely. When the tart is cool, gently remove the sides of the pan.

❊ To serve, cut the tart into wedges and top with a dollop of whipped cream.

Why Bother with Dessert Wines?

At the end of an indulgent meal when everyone is bracing for the trip home, the pleasures of dessert wines can be overlooked. Yet they present infinite delights. Our team of beverage experts offers a sampling of them in this section. Charleston Dame Debbie Claypoole Marlowe, who owns and operates The Wine Shop and Marina Liquors in downtown Charleston, says that a memorable dessert wine served in small quantities can leave a lasting impression. She also notes that dessert wines can dress up a simple supper and eliminate the need for time-consuming desserts. "They're just so easy. Pull the cork and pour 3 to 4 ounces into small glasses," says Marlowe.

❄ TINY TIM TARTS ❄

Washington, D.C., Dame Jane Mengenhauser writes, "After holding this recipe close to my apron pocket during my many years as a newspaper food editor, it was in retirement that I let it go for others to enjoy. My conscience got the best of me while writing a freelance article titled 'The Art of Recipe Sharing.'" Originally, Mengenhauser says, these two-bite tarts were a Christmas dessert. "But the ingredients are almost always in my kitchen cupboard, and I'm tempted to make them for any holiday—Christmas, Easter, or the Fourth of July! What kind of New Englander would I be without a stash of cranberries in the freezer year-round?"

These are easy to make, but there are variables, says Mengenhauser. If you find you do not have enough dough for 24 tarts (everyone presses out dough a little differently), then make 23, but don't cram the extra filling in. "Just lick the bowl!" The tarts should be golden brown, but every oven is different. So keep an eye on the tarts while they bake. Mengenhauser stresses, "Never be tempted to put more than three cranberries in each cup; one berry too many can force a tiny fruit eruption during baking."

24 tarts

Prepare Ahead

The tarts freeze perfectly, so you can make them weeks ahead of serving.

Crust

½ cup (1 stick) unsalted butter (chilled if using a food processor; at room temperature if using an electric mixer)

One 3-ounce package cream cheese, at room temperature

1 cup all-purpose flour

Filling

1 large egg

¾ cup sugar

2 tablespoons unsalted butter, at room temperature

1 teaspoon pure vanilla extract

½ cup finely chopped walnuts or pecans

1 cup (4 ounces) fresh or frozen cranberries (about 72 berries)

Suggested Beverage

A German Riesling Auslese with high acidity and good dose of sweetness matches well with the Tiny Tims' sweet-tart taste.

Preheat the oven to 325°F. Have ready a nonstick mini-muffin pan with cups that measure ⅞ inch deep and 1¾ inch wide and that will accommodate 24 tarts, or bake in two 12-tart batches. Spray the pan with nonstick cooking spray, or butter and flour the cups. Alternatively, line the muffin cups with mini-muffin papers and spray them with nonstick cooking spray.

To prepare the crust, in the bowl of a food processor fitted with a steel blade, process the butter, cream cheese, and flour until a ball of dough forms. This can also be done in a bowl with an electric mixer. The dough should be fairly moist and come together easily.

Cut the dough into 24 roughly even pieces and place a piece in each muffin cup. Using fingertips, press the dough over the bottom and all the way up the sides of each cup. Refrigerate the pan with the dough while you make the filling.

To make the filling, using an electric mixer on medium speed, combine the egg, sugar, butter, and vanilla in a medium bowl. Mix well. Stir in the nuts. Place 3 cranberries (if the cranberries are large, you may have room for only 2) in each cup and spread some of the nut mixture over the berries, filling each cup so the berries are barely covered. Be very careful not to overfill: any filling that dribbles over the edges will cause the baked tarts to stick.

Bake until well browned, 20 to 25 minutes. Transfer the pan to a wire rack to cool entirely. Run the tip of a knife around the edge of each tart to loosen, then slip the tarts out of the pan.

An Introduction to Port

When it comes to dessert wines, port is a good place to start. Here are a few tips:

* Restaurants are great for exploring port, as they often offer several varieties by the glass.

* Vintage port is the most expensive. Age these for at least 15 years. Decant before serving. The classic pairing is with Stilton cheese.

* Late-bottled vintage port (LBV) is essentially a "baby" vintage, aged in oak 4 to 6 years before bottling. LBVs are a nice compromise when a vintage port is either not ready to drink or just too expensive. They pair nicely with chocolate.

* Tawny port offers great value for price. Look for 10- and 20-year styles and serve with a variety of desserts, particularly anything with caramel, brown sugar, or nuts.

* Most vintage ports and LBVs come with a regular cork and will keep after opening about the same time as any other wine—less than a week. Ports with a T-top cork (embedded in the cap—most tawny ports have these) will keep for several weeks after opening.

—*Houston Dame Robyn Tinsley, Co-founder and Managing Editor, WineSkinny.com*

PASSION FRUIT–MACADAMIA
NUT TART

Prepare Ahead

The dough, which needs to be refrigerated for at least 2 hours before using, can be made several days ahead. It also can be frozen for several weeks. The tart shell can be baked early in the day and the tart can be assembled several hours before serving.

If you haven't already discovered it, it's time to experience a new flavor: passion fruit. This tropical fruit has an inimitable taste absolutely worth the extra effort to obtain. If you have fresh passion fruit, you can make your own juice: for ½ cup of juice, allow 5 to 6 passion fruit (depending on their juiciness). Scoop the pulp of the fruit, including the seeds, into a coarse strainer placed over a large measuring cup. Press pulp though the strainer; you will have a very thick juice. Discard seeds.

There are several sources of frozen unsweetened passion-fruit juice. Goya brand (www.goya.com) makes a frozen passion-fruit "pulp" that is available at Latino markets (passion fruit in Spanish is *maracuya*). Perfect Purée of Napa Valley (www.perfectpuree.com) also makes a passion-fruit concentrate that can be obtained from some local markets or from www.amazon.com. (Both the "pulp" and the concentrate can be used in place of fresh juice.) Meanwhile, urge your local specialty grocer to stock passion-fruit frozen concentrate. Avoid sweetened products or blends with other fruits, such as those marketed by Boiron.

You'll find numerous uses for this tropical treasure, which you can keep ready in your freezer (divide the concentrate into half-cup containers and refreeze). Arguably, the best use will be this tart, created by Hawaii Dame Abigail Langlas. Langlas was born and raised in Hawaii but trained as a pastry chef in Europe. She now runs her own bakeshop in Honolulu and loves to use local Hawaiian ingredients in classic pastries. This recipe is a conversion of the lemon tart she learned to make as a student in Lyon, France. If you cannot obtain fresh passion fruit or the frozen concentrate, consider filling the macadamia nut tart shell with a lemon or grapefruit curd filling. Note that the filling is meant to be very tart. If you desire a sweeter taste, add up to an extra tablespoon of sugar when making the filling.

One 9-inch tart

Tart Shell

¾ cup (4 ounces) roasted macadamia nuts, salted or unsalted

⅛ teaspoon salt (optional)

½ cup (1 stick) unsalted butter, at room temperature

¼ cup sugar

1 large egg yolk

¼ teaspoon pure vanilla extract

1¼ cups all-purpose flour plus additional for rolling dough

Filling

½ cup unsweetened passion-fruit juice (or frozen concentrate, thawed but *not* diluted)

¾ cup granulated sugar plus additional as needed

¾ cup (1½ sticks) unsalted butter, cut into rough pieces for melting

3 large eggs

Serving

Confectioners' sugar

Heavy cream, whipped and lightly sweetened

Fresh berries (optional)

❋ To make the tart shell dough, place the nuts and salt (if the nuts are *un*salted) in the bowl of a food processor fitted with a steel blade. Process until finely ground, being careful to stop short of puréeing the nuts completely. Remove the nuts from the bowl and reserve. Put the butter and sugar in the same food processor bowl, and process until mixture just starts to get light and fluffy. Add the egg yolk and vanilla. Add the flour and ground nuts, processing until all dry ingredients are combined; the dough will be crumbly. Remove the dough and form into a flat disk. Wrap in plastic wrap and chill for at least 2 hours. The dough should feel firm to the touch. If you refrigerate it longer, let it sit at room temperature until it becomes slightly pliable for rolling, about 15 minutes.

Suggested Beverage

An Alsatian late-harvest Gewürztraminer or Australian late-harvest Pinot Gris complements the tropical fruitiness of the dessert.

To form and bake the shell, preheat the oven to 350°F. On a generously floured surface, roll out the dough to ¼ inch thick (about an 11-inch round). Lay the dough over a 9-inch, 1-inch-deep tart tin with removable bottom. Gently fit it down the sides, pressing the dough firmly into the corners and against the tin's sides. Should the dough crack (and it often will), just pat the pieces into the pan (the dough is very forgiving). (If you have a second tart tin of the same size, you can press the second removable bottom over the tart to help smooth the bottom). Make sure the dough is snug against the bottom edge of the tin.

Bake the tart shell until golden brown, 18 to 25 minutes (do not underbake; the taste of the well-browned shortbread against the rich tart filling is what makes this dessert so impressive). Remove from the oven and cool on a rack for at least 1 hour, then loosely cover and set aside for up to 24 hours.

To make the filling, bring the passion-fruit juice, sugar, and butter to a boil in a large saucepan, stirring occasionally, until the butter is melted. Meanwhile, whisk the eggs until well blended. Slowly drizzle about a third of the boiling liquid into the eggs, whisking constantly. Pour the egg mixture into the saucepan with the remaining hot liquid; cook over medium heat, stirring slowly and continuously with a wooden spoon until the mixture returns to a boil (the liquid should thicken enough to coat the spoon with a creamy layer). Remove immediately from the heat and strain through a sieve into a large measuring cup to remove any bits of cooked egg. Pour the filling into the cooled tart shell. Using the back of a large soup spoon, make swirls in the filling. Refrigerate for at least 1 hour before serving. The tart will hold well, refrigerated, for up to 8 hours.

To serve, slip off the rim of the tart tin and slide off the metal bottom (if you're nervous about the strength of your tart shell, you can leave the metal bottom in place). Dust the edges of the tart with confectioners' sugar. Dollop with whipped cream and garnish with fresh berries.

Cookies

❧ GLAZED LEMON COOKIES ❧

"One of our greatest living pastry chefs"—that's the essence of what journalists keep calling Chicago Dame Gale Gand, executive pastry chef and partner at the much-lauded Chicago restaurant Tru. Gand, who first worked as a silversmith and goldsmith before studying pastry at La Varenne in Paris and doing stints with well-known chefs such as Alfred Portale and Charlie Trotter, has many cookbooks, a James Beard Award, and a long-running Food Network show to her credit. These cookies, which bake into sandy-textured balls of bright lemon flavor, stand a good chance of becoming a "must" in any baker's repertoire, professional or home cook.

Testers and tasters of this recipe, all of whom were unanimous in their love of the cookies, were divided on whether to glaze or not. You might want to sample an unglazed cookie before proceeding with this step. To achieve this cookie's inimitable texture, bake in a convection oven. If you must use a conventional oven, increase the oven setting to 350°F and bake as instructed.

24 cookies

Cookies

¾ cup (1½ sticks) unsalted butter, at room temperature

1 cup sugar

2 tablespoons finely grated lemon zest

2 tablespoons freshly squeezed lemon juice

2 cups plus 2 tablespoons all-purpose flour

¾ teaspoon baking powder

¼ teaspoon salt

Prepare Ahead

If you'd like, freeze the cookies after baking and cooling, then defrost them as needed. Or, freeze the unbaked balls of dough and bake and defrost as needed. If the balls are frozen, increase baking time by about a third.

Suggested Beverage

A German Riesling Auslese or a pot of freshly steeped lemon verbena tea.

Glaze

3 tablespoons freshly squeezed lemon juice

2 cups confectioners' sugar

❀ Preheat a convection oven to 325°F. Line 2 baking sheets with parchment paper.

❀ In a mixer with a paddle attachment (or in a large bowl with an electric hand mixer), beat the butter and sugar on low speed till smooth. Do not try to incorporate any air—just blend the ingredients. Add the lemon zest and juice and continue to mix on low only until incorporated. Add the flour, baking powder, and salt. Mix on low for 1 to 2 minutes. Stop and squeeze the dough in your hand. It should be crumbly but still form a ball. If necessary, beat for up to a minute longer. Do not overbeat.

❀ Using either a number 100 ice cream scoop (about an inch in diameter), a melon baller, or a mounded teaspoon, scoop the dough onto the baking sheets. (The ice cream scoop gives the cookies a very appealing ridged texture.) Bake until the edges start to turn a light golden brown, about 8 minutes. *Do not* let the cookies get golden brown all over or they will be too dry. Transfer the cookies to a rack and let cool.

❀ If you opt to glaze the cookies, blend the lemon juice into the confectioners' sugar until the mixture is smooth. Dip the tops of the cooled cookies into the glaze.

CHEWY DOUBLE CHOCOLATE COOKIES

Here's another astonishingly good Gale Gand cookie, in the running for best chocolate cookie ever: crackly on the outside, exquisitely gooey in the center.

30 cookies

2½ cups semisweet chocolate chips, divided

¼ cup (½ stick) unsalted butter, cut into 4 pieces

¼ cup all-purpose flour

¼ teaspoon baking powder

¼ teaspoon salt

2 large eggs

¾ cup sugar

In a small bowl over simmering water, melt 1¾ cups of the chocolate chips and butter together. Meanwhile, in a separate bowl, mix together the flour, baking powder, and salt. In a mixer with a whip attachment or in a bowl with an electric hand mixer, whip the eggs and sugar until light and fluffy. Add the chocolate mixture. Mix in the dry ingredients and the remaining chocolate chips. Let sit at room temperature for 30 minutes to set up. Line 2 baking sheets with parchment paper. With a number 30 ice cream scoop or a tablespoon, scoop dough onto the baking sheets. Freeze for a minimum of 30 minutes.

Preheat the oven to 375°F. Bake the cookies, straight from the freezer, until the tops are shiny and cracked, 7 to 10 minutes. Do not over-bake. The cookies will be very soft. Allow them to firm up for about 15 minutes before serving.

Prepare Ahead

Since the cookies are baked straight from the freezer, they lend themselves to being served fresh from the oven. Be sure to clear space in your freezer for the pans of cookies. Once frozen, the cookies can be removed from the pans and stored in resealable plastic bags. The cookies also freeze well after baking.

Suggested Beverage

Banyuls (a fortified, port-like red wine from southern France) or Malmsey Madeira.

LEMON-CRANBERRY-PECAN BISCOTTI ⁑

Prepare Ahead

You may prepare the dough ahead of time and freeze it until you are ready to begin baking. Note that the dough must chill at least 3 hours before baking, and that the use of parchment paper is essential. The shelf life of fresh biscotti is 6 months. Store them in an airtight container. If they become too soft, recrisp them in a 250°F oven for a few minutes. If they become too hard, place them in a micro- wave set on low for 30 seconds

The case can be made that no cookie (other than perhaps the chocolate chip cookie) has been so abused by commercial production as that twice-baked Italian wonder, the *biscotto*. Palm Springs Dame and Cordon Bleu–trained Pastry Chef Karen Stiegler decided to recapture the essence of the crunchy classic and add her own combination of ingredients. Follow her basic formula, but vary the choice of nuts and dried fruits as you like.

48 biscotti

3 cups all-purpose flour

1 teaspoon salt

1 teaspoon baking powder

¼ teaspoon baking soda

10 tablespoons (1¼ sticks) unsalted butter, at room temperature

1⅓ cups granulated sugar

1½ tablespoons finely grated lemon zest (see box, page 75)

3 large eggs, divided

3 tablespoons freshly squeezed lemon juice

1½ cups dried cranberries

1½ cups chopped pecans

Raw or turbinado sugar for sprinkling

⁑ Whisk together the flour, salt, baking powder, and baking soda in a medium bowl. Using an electric mixer, beat the butter, granulated sugar, and lemon zest in a large bowl until blended. Add 2 of the eggs, one at a time, beating just to blend after each addition. Beat in the lemon juice, then the flour mixture. Stir in the cranberries and pecans.

⁑ On a lightly floured surface, divide the dough into 3 equal portions. With lightly floured hands, form each portion into an 8-inch-long log and flatten it to 2½ inches wide; place each log on a piece of plastic wrap large enough to cover the dough. Wrap securely in the plastic wrap and chill for at least 3 hours or up to 3 days.

Suggested Beverage

An Italian Vin Santo (the mere word "biscotti" conjures up this unmatched pairing).

❋ Position oven racks in the upper third and middle of the oven. Preheat the oven to 325°F. Line a heavy, rimmed baking sheet with parchment paper. Unwrap the logs of dough, leaving them sitting on the plastic. Beat the remaining egg well to make a glaze. Brush the top of the logs with the egg glaze and sprinkle with the raw sugar. Lift the logs from the plastic wrap and transfer to the lined baking sheet. Space them evenly 2 to 3 inches apart; the logs will spread during baking. Bake on the upper rack until golden brown and just firm to the touch, 45 to 50 minutes. Transfer to a cooling rack and reduce oven temperature to 300°F. Let the logs cool completely, about 1 hour.

❋ For the second baking, line 2 heavy, rimmed baking sheets with parchment paper. With a long serrated knife, carefully cut the logs crosswise into ½- to ¾-inch slices (the thinner slices require a little more care). Arrange the biscotti on the baking sheets; place the end pieces cut side down. Bake on the upper and middle racks until golden brown around the edges, about 25 minutes (you may want to turn the biscotti over after the first 15 minutes for more even drying). Cool completely; the biscotti will continue to crisp as they cool. Store in an airtight container at room temperature.

Give the Gift of Port

Palm Springs Dame Zola Nichols recommends port as a gift for a newborn. "I think the old English custom of buying a vintage port at the birth of a child with the idea of putting the wine down for at least twenty years is a wonderful gift idea."

JUMBO ICE CREAM SANDWICHES
WITH FRESH RASPBERRY SAUCE

Prepare Ahead

The ice cream sandwiches can be made 2 days in advance and stored in the freezer.

Have kids (most any age) at home? They like ice cream? Want a dessert that's not too tricked out—just right for backyard barbecues and pool parties? Try this one from Philadelphia Dame Patricia Ward, who has spent thirty years in recipe development, cookbook writing, and food styling—pleasing art directors, marketing managers, and food photographers. For this recipe, she jumbo-sizes the icebox cookies she learned to make as a young girl, then turns the cookies into ice cream sandwiches, drizzled with melted chocolate and served in a pool of fresh raspberry sauce. You'll love Ward's jaunty presentation and the fact that preparation takes place well ahead of dinnertime. Although you might be tempted to skip straining the sauce, Ward grimaces at the thought of seeds in her sauce: "I guess the food stylist in me won't go away."

4 ice cream sandwiches

8 Brown Sugar Icebox Cookies (recipe follows)

1 pint vanilla ice cream (or other flavor), slightly softened so it is spreadable

2 ounces dark bittersweet or semisweet chocolate, roughly chopped into ½-inch pieces

Fresh Raspberry Sauce (recipe follows)

Confectioners' sugar

Prepare the cookies. Cut 4 pieces of aluminum foil large enough to wrap the finished sandwiches. Place a cookie, upside down, in the middle of each piece of foil. Using a number 10 ice cream scoop or a half-cup measure, place a heaping scoop of ice cream on the bottom of each cookie. Using a metal spatula, spread out evenly. Top each with another cookie, bottom side down. Fold foil up over each of the sandwiches and place them in the freezer until firm.

Place the chocolate in a microwave-safe cup. Microwave on medium until the chocolate turns shiny, about 1 minute. Stir until smooth. Microwave in 10-second increments if more time is necessary. Remove the sandwiches from the freezer. Unwrap, but leave them sitting on the foil sheets. Drizzle each sandwich with melted chocolate and return to the freezer, leaving the foil open until the chocolate sets. Then close the foil securely over the sandwiches and freeze for up to 2 days before serving.

To serve, cut the sandwiches into halves. Place a half sandwich on each serving plate and lean the second half against the first. Spoon the raspberry sauce over the sandwiches, letting it pool around them. Using a sieve or sugar shaker, shower each plate lightly with confectioners' sugar and serve immediately.

Brown Sugar Icebox Cookies

36 four-inch cookies

3½ cups all-purpose flour

1 teaspoon baking soda

2 cups packed brown sugar

1 cup (2 sticks) unsalted butter, melted

2 large eggs

1 teaspoon pure vanilla extract

1 cup chopped walnuts or pecans

Mix together the flour and baking soda; set aside.

In a large mixing bowl, using an electric hand mixer at medium speed, beat together the brown sugar and butter until well blended. Add the eggs, one at a time, beating well after each addition. Beat in the vanilla. Using a large spoon, stir in the flour mixture, mixing well. Stir in the walnuts. Cover the bowl and chill in the refrigerator for 1 hour.

Suggested Beverage

The sweetness of ice cream rarely requires a beverage pairing. A good pairing would be: a sweet Oloroso sherry or an ultra-sweet PX sherry.

Prepare Ahead

The cookie dough can be refrigerated up to 2 weeks or frozen for a couple of months.

On a lightly floured surface, shape the dough into a 9-inch-long roll about 3 inches in diameter. Wrap the roll in plastic wrap. Chill in the refrigerator for at least 4 hours or up to 2 weeks.

Preheat the oven to 375°F. Line 2 baking sheets with parchment paper. Cut the roll into ¼-inch slices and place about 2 inches apart on prepared baking sheets. (You can make just enough for the Ice Cream Sandwiches and freeze the remaining dough for later use, or bake up all the dough and have a supply of cookies for munching.) Bake until golden brown, 10 to 12 minutes. Remove from the baking sheets; cool on racks.

Fresh Raspberry Sauce

1½ cups

Two 6-ounce packages fresh raspberries

½ cup sugar

2 tablespoons freshly squeezed lemon juice

Place the raspberries, sugar, and lemon juice in the bowl of a food processor fitted with a steel blade. Cover and process until mixture is smooth and the sugar is dissolved. Press the mixture through a sieve or food mill to strain out seeds. Discard the seeds and refrigerate the sauce, covered, until ready to serve. The sauce keeps well refrigerated for several days.

Cookie-Baking Tips

* Any cookie can be made big or small. Just remember to shorten the baking time accordingly—use ice cream scoops of all sizes for easy, even portioning. A small cookie is often enough to satisfy your sweet tooth.

* Make batches of dough, scoop cookies, and freeze. This way you can always have freshly baked cookies for family and guests.

—San Francisco Dame Emily Luchetti, Pastry Chef at the celebrated Farallon restaurant

❧ PRALINE BROWNIES ❧

New York Dame Susan Westmoreland is *Good Housekeeping* magazine's food director. The job includes managing the famed test kitchen and planning and producing the magazine's food pages, special issues, and cookbooks. In 2001 she was named the James Beard Foundation's Editor of the Year. Although her job is to develop new material to tempt consumers, her personal cooking relies heavily on old favorites, like this brownie, which she developed when she needed something to serve her prospective (Southern) in-laws. "The brownies were a rave with the Southerners and the Yanks. I've been making them ever since for everything from afternoon teas to cocktail parties to baby showers." It's a nice touch to serve them in paper or foil petit four cups, but not a must.

Prepare Ahead

The brownies can be baked and iced up to 2 weeks in advance and frozen. Westmoreland says they're "delicious at room temperature, refrigerated, or even frozen."

64 bite-size brownies

¾ cup (1½ sticks) unsalted butter

4 ounces unsweetened chocolate

4 ounces semisweet chocolate

2¼ cups sugar

6 large eggs

2 teaspoons pure vanilla extract

½ teaspoon salt

1¼ cups all-purpose flour

Praline Topping (recipe follows)

¾ cup coarsely chopped and toasted pecans

❧ Preheat the oven to 350°F. Line a 9- by 13-inch metal baking pan with foil, letting the foil hang over the edges of the pan by several inches (this will make for easy removal of the brownies). Grease the foil.

❧ In a large, heavy saucepan over low heat, melt the butter and chocolates, stirring frequently. Remove the saucepan from the heat. With a wire whisk, beat in the sugar, then the eggs, until well blended. Stir

Suggested Beverage

A ruby port or a fruity California Zinfandel (the acid in both will help cut the richness of the chocolate). Or, infuse milk with a coffee cream liqueur like Bailey's— serve either warm in a mug or on the rocks in a tall glass.

in the vanilla, salt, then the flour just until blended. Spread the batter evenly in pan.

❋ Bake until the top is set, 32 to 35 minutes (do not overbake—a toothpick inserted in brownies will *not* come out clean). Cool the brownies in the pan on a wire rack. To frost, with a metal spatula, spread the Praline Topping over the cooled brownies; sprinkle with the pecans. Cover loosely with foil and refrigerate or freeze for longer storage. (As the brownies are meant to be rather creamy, refrigerating them makes them easier to cut.)

❋ When ready to cut, using the overhanging pieces of foil, carefully lift the sheet of brownies out of the pan. Cut the brownies lengthwise into 8 strips, then cut each strip crosswise into 8 pieces.

Jam Swirl Brownie Variation

Phoenix Dame Eileen Spitalny is an expert on brownies. She owns the country's largest mail-order brownie company, Fairytale Brownies. For one of her best-selling brownies, she swirls raspberry jam over the brownie batter before baking. Here's how to turn the rather adult and boozy Praline Brownie into a Jam Swirl Brownie for the kids (or the kid in all of us). Be warned: these are deliciously easy. Spitalny uses only Callebaut chocolate in Fairytale Brownies.

You'll need 1 cup of jam—raspberry or any other flavor (chunkier preserves may need sieving). Prepare Praline Brownies up to the point of placing them in the oven to bake. After spreading the batter evenly in the pan, spread the jam in three equally spaced stripes (⅓ cup jam in each stripe) across the batter. Then draw a knife vertically through the stripes at 2-inch intervals, creating a sort of "swirl" pattern. Bake according to Praline Brownie directions. Allow the brownies to cool, then refrigerate before cutting into bars.

Praline Topping

½ cup (1 stick) unsalted butter, cut into 8 pieces

½ cup packed dark brown sugar

¼ cup bourbon

3 cups confectioners' sugar

☀ In a medium saucepan over medium-low heat, heat the butter and brown sugar until the mixture melts and bubbles, about 5 minutes. Remove the saucepan from the heat. With a wire whisk, beat in the bourbon, then the confectioners' sugar until mixture is smooth.

✻ RASPBERRY ROSEBUDS ✻

Prepare Ahead

The formed cookies can be baked at once, or covered and chilled several hours. Increase baking time for chilled cookies by 2 to 3 minutes

When Charleston Dame Susan Fuller Slack, a food stylist and cookbook author (*Japanese Cooking for the American Table*; *Fondues & Hot Pots*), was researching Martha Washington's heirloom cookbooks at the Mount Vernon archives, she discovered an intriguing little "cake" (cookie) made with cornstarch and flavored distinctively with rose water. It became her inspiration for a rolled and cut white cookie she developed for a luncheon honoring First Lady Laura Bush. The cookie, cut and decorated in all sorts of fanciful ways, has been one of her signature recipes ever since. However, Slack—like most Dames these days—knows that home cooks with busy schedules need shortcuts to exciting food. With that in mind, Slack has converted her recipe into a "thumbprint" cookie—easy to prepare (even little kids can help) yet it maintains the exquisite texture and taste of the original.

Rose water is made from a distillation of rose petals. It can be purchased in Middle Eastern and Indian food markets and even some supermarkets. You can substitute rum, but the flavor will be less exotic. You can also disregard the recipe title altogether and use other flavors of fruit preserves.

Note that bleached flour is preferred for this recipe; the bleaching process helps break down the flour's gluten and contributes to the cookies' fine texture. The butter should be cut when cold and left at room temperature until just slightly softened—*not* to the point that it feels oily and begins to lose shape.

30 cookies

⅓ cup slivered almonds

1¼ cups all-purpose flour, preferably bleached, measured by the "dip and sweep" method (see box, page 300)

¾ cup cornstarch, measured by the "dip and sweep" method (see box, page 300)

½ teaspoon salt

1 cup (2 sticks) unsalted butter, cut into small pieces and barely at room temperature

½ cup confectioners' sugar

2 tablespoons plus 1 teaspoon rose water (see headnote), divided

1 teaspoon pure almond extract

¼ cup seedless raspberry preserves

Rose Water Glaze (recipe follows)

In the bowl of a food processor fitted with a steel blade, process the almonds until finely ground. Add the flour, cornstarch, and salt; pulse on and off quickly to blend the ingredients. Set aside.

In the mixing bowl of an electric mixer, beat the butter and confectioners' sugar on medium speed until the mixture has a light, creamy appearance. Beat in 2 tablespoons of the rose water and almond extract. On the lowest speed, gradually add the flour-almond mixture, beating until the ingredients come together to form a smooth, slightly soft dough. The dough can be shaped at once; if it is too soft, cover the bowl and chill for up to 30 minutes.

Preheat the oven to 350°F. Line the bottom of 2 large, heavy baking sheets with parchment paper. For each cookie, heap a tablespoon or a number 100 ice cream scoop with dough. Roll the dough into balls. If necessary, dust your hands and the tablespoon lightly with flour to prevent sticking. Place the dough balls on the baking sheets about 1½ inches apart.

Bake 1 pan of cookies at a time just until the cookies are set, about 12 minutes. Remove from the oven. With the end of a wooden spoon (¼ to ½ inch in diameter), gently press straight down into the center of each rounded cookie. Rotate the pan; return to the oven until the cookie bottoms turn golden brown, 3 to 4 minutes. Remove from the oven; cool for 3 to 4 minutes. With a thin metal spatula, carefully lift the cookies to a wire rack to finish cooling.

Put the raspberry preserves and the remaining rose water into a small bowl; stir until smooth. Spoon about ¼ teaspoon of the preserves into the center of each cookie, then drizzle the glaze in a decorative lacy pattern over the tops.

❋ Let the cookies stand until the glaze and preserves are set, about 1 hour. Arrange the cookies, in a single layer, in an airtight container. Frozen cookies can be layered between sheets of waxed paper for up to 1 month.

Rose Water Glaze

1 tablespoon unsalted butter, at room temperature

1 cup sifted confectioners' sugar

1 tablespoon rose water or rum

2 teaspoons heavy cream or milk

❋ In a small mixing bowl, whisk together the butter, confectioners' sugar, rose water, and cream until smooth, adding extra cream as needed. The glaze should be thin enough to drizzle over the cookies.

Dip and Sweep

This is the ideal way to measure flour (and other fine, powdered ingredients) for many baked goods. Lightly stir flour in its storage container. Dip a dry measuring cup into the container to fill. To level top, sweep the back of a knife blade across the rim of the cup, returning excess flour to the container.

Note: This method is *not* recommended for fine-textured cakes, because flour measured by this method can weigh as much as 25 percent more than flour lightly spooned or sifted directly into a measuring cup. This is enough extra flour to make a perfectly balanced cake dry and heavy.

—*Charleston Dame Susan Fuller Slack*

Cakes

❧ SHIRLEY'S TUNNEL OF FUDGE CAKE ❧

Atlanta Dame Shirley Corriher, a trained chemist, writes recipes like no one else. Nearly every recipe she publishes begins with "What This Recipe Shows" and goes on to give the reader the hows and whys of making the particular dish. She's made a career of being a "food sleuth," solving cooking problems for everyone from large corporations to chefs to home cooks. When her book *CookWise* came out, fellow Dame Flo Braker wrote, "*CookWise* is for the kitchen what the dictionary is for the library."

Her redo of the famous Tunnel of Fudge Cake—the 1966 Pillsbury Bake-Off recipe that, according to Corriher, "literally 'made' the Bundt pan"—appeared on the front page of not the *food* section, but the *science* section of *The New York Times* (December 28, 2004). The article explained each Corriher alteration: she substituted 2 yolks for 1 of the eggs and oil for part of the butter to make the cake more moist; dark brown sugar replaced some of the white sugar to give the cake an even fudgier flavor; and she made the point that the nuts were vital to make this cake "fabulous." Corriher serves the cake either at room temperature or cold. When cold, the center becomes firm like a piece of fudge with nuts.

So get out your 12-cup Bundt pan. Note: You will need an accurate oven thermometer. You can't use the toothpick test for doneness—this cake has so much sugar that the center is not going to set but remains a "tunnel of fudge"—so you are dependent on a correct oven temperature and the 45-minute cooking time.

24 servings

Prepare Ahead

The cake can be baked a couple of days before serving cold or at room temperature.

2½ cups (10½ ounces) chopped walnuts *or* walnuts and pecans

2 tablespoons unsalted butter, cut into roughly 8 pieces, plus 1¼ cups (2½ sticks) unsalted butter, cut into tablespoon-size pieces

⅛ teaspoon plus ½ teaspoon salt

Nonstick cooking spray

1 cup granulated sugar

¾ cup packed dark brown sugar

1 teaspoon pure vanilla extract

⅓ cup vegetable oil

2 large egg yolks

2 cups confectioners' sugar plus additional for topping

¾ cup natural cocoa powder (Corriher prefers: Ghirardelli and Scharffen Berger)

4 large eggs

2¼ cups bleached all-purpose flour

⁂ Make sure your oven thermometer is installed in the oven. Arrange a shelf in the lower third of the oven with a heavy baking sheet or pizza stone on it and preheat the oven to 350°F. On a large baking sheet, roast the nuts for 10 minutes. Pour into a bowl, add 2 tablespoons of the butter and ⅛ teaspoon of the salt, and toss well to distribute the butter. Reserve.

⁂ Spray a 12-cup Bundt pan generously with nonstick cooking spray. (Wine expert Gil Kuler, who makes this cake frequently, heats the empty pan for about 5 minutes just before he sprays it and then pours in the batter. This ensures that he gets a good ¾-inch base of well-set cake to hold the fudge center.)

⁂ With an electric mixer, beat the remaining butter to soften, then continue to beat until it reaches the fluffy stage. Add the granulated sugar, then the brown sugar, and continue to cream until airy. While creaming, feel the bowl; if it does not feel cool, place it in the freezer for 5 minutes, then continue creaming. Beat in the remaining salt and vanilla. Blend in the oil and egg yolks. Stir in the confectioners' sugar, then the cocoa. Stir the eggs into the batter by hand, one at a time, with minimum stirring just to blend them into the batter well.

※ In a large mixing bowl, stir the flour and nuts together. Then fold the flour-nut mixture into the batter by hand. Pour the batter into the prepared pan. Bake for 45 minutes exactly.

※ When you remove the cake from the oven, it will have a runny fudge core with an air pocket above the fudge. Without your intervention, this air pocket will become a hole under the fudge when the cake is chilled. Therefore, about 20 minutes after you take the cake out of the oven, to minimize this hole, press the inside and outside edge of the cake bottom down all the way around. This will press the whole bottom down and reduce the air pocket. Leave the cake in the pan on a rack until completely cooled (about 3 hours—this is important). Invert onto a platter and gently lift off the pan. Sprinkle the cake with confectioners' sugar. Serve at room temperature or cold.

Suggested Beverage

Nuts and cocoa powder suggest a Bual or Malmsey Madeira.

❧ LEMON CREAM ROULADE ❧

Prepare Ahead

The roulade can be made up to 24 hours ahead of serving.

If you want to master one new show-stopper dessert, this could be your chance. The recipe is from master teacher, New York Dame, and pastry chef Carole Walter, who has been teaching hands-on cooking classes for over thirty years. She guesses she's worked with over twenty-five thousand students. Along the way, Walter has won numerous awards for her cookbooks on cookies, cakes, pies, and tarts. She favors this roulade because it has always been popular with her students; it is especially appealing for its good looks and not-too-sweet taste, and the fact that the only butter used in the recipe is for greasing the pan.

The encouraging teacher in Walter comes out: "Roulades are made of sponge-cake batters that are baked in shallow pans, and then rolled while still hot and flexible. Don't be intimidated by rolling roulades; the technique is very easy to master." And keep in mind that for all its impressiveness, the roulade need not be reserved for elegant meals. If you don't have a platter long enough for the roulade, Walter suggests serving it on an attractive (sanitized) wooden bread board.

10 to 12 servings

Sponge Cake

　Butter for greasing pan

　6 large eggs, separated

　¾ cup sugar

　2 to 3 lemons, zested for 2 teaspoons grated zest (see box, page 75) and squeezed for 3 tablespoons juice

　¾ cup sifted cake flour

　½ teaspoon cream of tartar

　¼ teaspoon salt

　4 tablespoons confectioners' sugar, divided

Filling

¾ cup sugar

⅓ cup all-purpose flour

2 to 3 lemons, zested for 4 teaspoons grated zest (see box, page 75) and squeezed for ⅓ cup juice

1 large egg plus 1 large egg yolk, lightly beaten

1½ cups well-chilled heavy cream

Serving

Fresh seasonal berries

❋ Position a rack in the center of the oven and preheat to 350°F. Butter the bottom of a 12- by 17- by 1-inch jelly-roll pan. Line the bottom with parchment paper and butter the parchment.

❋ Using an electric mixer fitted with the whip attachment, beat the egg yolks on medium speed until lightened in color. Add the sugar in four additions and beat until thick. Blend in the lemon zest and juice. Reduce the mixer speed to low and mix in the flour. Transfer the batter to a large mixing bowl.

❋ In a clean mixer bowl with a clean whip attachment, beat the egg whites on medium speed until frothy. Add the cream of tartar and salt. Increase the speed to medium-high and beat just until firm, moist peaks form. Using a large silicone spatula, fold one quarter of the whites into the batter, then gently fold in the remaining whites. Spoon the batter into the prepared pan and smooth the surface with a metal offset spatula.

❋ Bake until springy to the touch and golden brown on top, about 15 minutes. While the cake is baking, lay a large sheet of baking parchment on a flat surface. Place 2 to 3 tablespoons of the confectioners' sugar in a fine-mesh strainer and thoroughly dust the parchment, covering an area at least 3 to 4 inches larger than the size of the jelly-roll pan.

Suggested Beverage

A Canadian or New York State ice wine.

※ When the cake is done, remove from the oven and release the edges with a paring knife. Immediately invert the cake onto the parchment and peel off the baking paper. Roll the cake tightly in the dusted parchment, working from the long side. Place on a wire rack and cool with the seam side down for about 30 minutes. While the cake is cooling, make the filling.

※ In a medium bowl, thoroughly whisk together the sugar, flour, lemon juice and zest, egg, and egg yolk. Place over simmering water and cook, stirring occasionally, until thick, about 15 minutes. Set aside to cool until tepid. In a chilled bowl with chilled beaters, whip the cream into soft peaks. Fold one third of the whipped cream into the lemon mixture. Then fold the mixture into the remaining whipped cream and incorporate.

※ Carefully unroll the cake, taking special care not to flatten it completely (this will keep the cake from cracking). Spread with two thirds of the lemon cream, pushing the cream under the curled side and leaving a 1-inch border at the opposite end. To re-roll the cake, lift the paper up on the side closest to you. As you lift, the cake will roll.

※ Carefully lift the cake with both hands and place it seam side down on a serving platter. Place the remaining lemon cream in a pastry bag fitted with a large star tip, such as #824. Pipe rosettes around the bottom of the cake. Alternatively (especially if you want a less dressy presentation), refrigerate the extra lemon cream and use it to dollop alongside slices of the cake as it is served. Tent the roulade loosely with aluminum foil and refrigerate for up to 24 hours.

※ To serve, let the roulade stand at room temperature for 30 to 60 minutes, then dust the top lightly with the remaining confectioners' sugar. Slice with a serrated knife and garnish with a few whole berries.

✾ FRAN'S ORIGINAL CHEESECAKE ✾

Originally, Seattle Dame Fran Bigelow worked as an accountant. Today she oversees a chocolate empire. Her chocolate confections now sell in over seven hundred retail stores across the country, including her own chocolate shops in Seattle. Yet even though her name has become synonymous with high-end chocolate, her early Seattle customers remember with raves a light-textured cheesecake they used to buy from her tiny storefront where she started business in 1982. That cheesecake was made not with chocolate (a later version adds white chocolate) but, inventively, with Brie cheese. Here's that much-coveted recipe from the lady whom chocolate lovers know as just "Fran."

Prepare Ahead

Definitely make this a day or several days ahead of serving. The cake keeps well for a week refrigerated.

10 to 12 servings

- **1 pound 10 ounces cream cheese, at room temperature**
- **12 ounces (weight without rind—purchase about 14 ounces) Brie cheese with at least 40 percent butterfat, rind removed, at room temperature**
- **1½ cups sugar**
- **5 large eggs, at room temperature**
- **Seasonal fresh fruit or a fruit sauce such as Fresh Raspberry Sauce (page 294)**

❋ Position a rack in the middle of the oven and preheat to 300°F. Lightly butter a 9-inch round cake pan. Line the bottom with a lightly buttered parchment-paper circle. In a mixer with paddle attachment, beat the cream cheese at medium-high speed until smooth, about 3 minutes. Transfer the cheese from the mixing bowl to another bowl and reserve.

❋ In the same mixing bowl with paddle attachment, beat the Brie at medium-high speed until completely smooth and elastic, about 3 minutes, scraping the bowl often with a silicone spatula. (Bigelow stresses that the trick here is to whip each cheese separately until they are of equal texture, then blend them together.)

With the machine on medium-low speed, add, in three portions, the reserved cream cheese to the Brie cheese. Blend the cheeses together until smooth, scraping down the sides of the bowl. Reduce speed to low and slowly add the sugar.

Add the eggs, one at a time, and mix at medium speed, waiting for each egg to incorporate before adding the next one. Scrape down the sides of the bowl as necessary. The mixture should be smooth and well blended. Pour into the prepared pan. Put the pan on a heavy rimmed baking sheet and place on the oven rack. Pour about ½ inch of simmering water into the baking sheet. Bake uncovered until the top is lightly golden brown and puffed, about 1¼ hours. The center should no longer jiggle when the pan is moved. Remove the pan from the baking sheet, place on a rack, and let cool for 2 to 4 hours.

Preparing Pans to Prevent Turn-Out Trauma

Spend a little extra time preparing your baking vessel, and your cake or bread will develop an attractive crust, as well as painlessly release intact from its metal mold. Pans of every shape and size require a good greasing and dusting. Those fashioned with particularly fussy nooks, divots, and slopes, however, require even more attention. Start with very soft butter and, using a pastry brush, liberally and evenly apply the butter to every inch of the pan's interior. Once it is gleaming with glossy greasiness, toss in a handful of flour and move it about, tapping and tilting the pan, until the butter has disappeared under a gossamer-like cloak of all-purpose whiteness. Invert the pan and tap out any excess flour, making sure there are no naked spots of metal. These tiny specks might seem harmless, but they are, in fact, insidious little bits that will surely wreak havoc on your attempt to release the final cake or bread. Attend to these spots by carefully spreading a little more butter over them, sprinkling some flour on top, and tapping it out. Well-prepared pans can only lead to happier cakes and bakers. At the very least, you will spare neighbors your horrific shrieks as you turn out a cake or bread with half its decorative top stuck to the pan. Ah, the joys of baking.

—Philadelphia Dame Jennifer Lindner McGlinn

✳ To remove the cake from the pan, run a thin blade around the edge to loosen. Place a piece of parchment or waxed paper over the top of the cake and invert it onto a flat surface. (Even better, a flexible cutting board is perfect for flipping the cake back into its intended pose.) Peel the parchment paper round from the bottom of the cake and invert the cake onto its serving plate. Remove the top parchment paper if used. Serve with seasonal fruits or fruit sauce.

Suggested Beverage

A Riesling Spätlese or an aged tawny port—both pair well with the Brie in this dessert.

Other Desserts

❊ FRESH BLACKBERRY COBBLER ❊

Edna Lewis was a Grande Dame by two measures—as a Dame and in the annals of American cuisine, where she is acknowledged as the "Grande Dame of Southern Cooking."

The granddaughter of an emancipated slave, she moved from her native Virginia to New York City in 1948 to work as a chef and a widely published food writer. She wrote several cookbooks, and noted Alabama chef Scott Peacock co-authored her last book when she was 87. He selected this recipe as representative of her style of simple and seasonal cooking. Here it is reprinted with permission from Alfred A. Knopf, a division of Random House, Inc., including the original headnote set in italics below.

Note that other fruits, like peaches, can be successfully substituted for the blackberries in Lewis's cobbler. Combinations of fruits and berries also make good cobbler material, says Washington, D.C., Dame Nancy Baggett—for example, rhubarb-strawberry, nectarine-raspberry, blackberry-plum, and her personal preference, raspberry-apricot.

Blackberries were always a favorite with us and fortunately the small berries ripened just about the time the wheat was harvested so that we could have a cobbler for the dinner. The berries grew abundantly along nearby streams and in wet spots in the woods and we would go out early in the morning to pick them, gathering a quart or a gallon in a very short time. Everyone looked forward to a pie or a cobbler during the season. The cobbler was baked in a large, deep baking pan with a delicious crust made from home-rendered lard and baked to a golden brown, with syrupy juice spouting through the pierced top as the berries cooked. It was served warm with the delicious juice from the berries spooned over the top.

6 to 8 servings

Pastry

2 cups sifted unbleached [all-purpose] flour

½ teaspoon salt

½ cup lard

⅓ cup cold water

1 cup crushed cube sugar

¼ cup light cream

Filling

5 cups blackberries

4 thin slices butter

¾ cup granulated sugar

2 teaspoons cornstarch

8- by 8- by 2-inch baking pan

❋ Sift the flour and salt into a large mixing bowl. Blend in the lard with a pastry blender or with your fingers. When it is well blended and fine-grained, sprinkle all the water in at once, and draw the dough together quickly, shaping it into a ball. Divide in half and let stand for a few minutes. After it has rested, roll out one piece and line the baking pan. Sprinkle 2 or 3 tablespoons of the crushed sugar over the dough, cover with waxed paper, and set it in the refrigerator (or freezer) until you are ready to fill it, along with the other piece of dough.

❋ When you are ready to assemble the cobbler, remove the dough from the refrigerator and roll out the top crust. Remove the pastry-lined pan from the refrigerator and fill it with berries, distributing the pieces of butter and sprinkling over the granulated sugar mixed with the cornstarch. Wet the rim of the dough in the pan and place the top pastry over, pressing down all around to seal and trimming away excess. With the handle of a dinner knife, make a decorative edge and then cut a few slits in the center to allow steam to escape. Brush the top with a thick brush of cream and sprinkle on the remaining crushed cube sugar. Place in a preheated 450°F oven and when the door is shut, turn down to 425°F to bake for 45 minutes. Remove from the oven and set on a rack to cool a bit before serving.

✳ BAKED BUTTERSCOTCH PUDDINGS ✳

Think brown sugar and vanilla with the cool texture of satin on the tongue. Then know that you can prepare this sweet sensation over several days before serving. All this makes the recipe truly a gift from Dallas Dame and young star chef Sharon Hage. She makes the dessert at her much-touted restaurant York Street in East Dallas. A 1984 graduate of the Culinary Institute of America, Hage spent time working in New York restaurants before returning to Dallas, where she was executive chef for Neiman Marcus. She purchased the existing York Street restaurant in 2001 and recast it in ways that have put her in the top rank of Texas chefs.

These puddings are rich, so the smaller ramekins may be most desirable.

Six 9-ounce, nine 6-ounce, or ten 4-ounce ramekins

1 vanilla bean

¼ cup (½ stick) unsalted butter

1 cup packed dark brown sugar

2½ cups heavy cream, divided

1 tablespoon pure vanilla extract

1½ cups whole milk

Pinch of salt

8 large egg yolks

Whipped cream

A favorite chocolate sauce (optional)

Fresh raspberries (optional)

Prepare Ahead

Make the custard base up to 3 days ahead of baking. The baked puddings will keep another 3 days before serving.

✳ Split the vanilla bean in half lengthwise and scrape the tiny seeds into a small saucepan. Add the bean and butter to the pan. Place over low heat until the butter has melted. Add the brown sugar and stir until melted and smooth (about 5 minutes). Stir in 1 cup of the cream and vanilla. Remove from the heat. Dispose of the vanilla bean and reserve the mixture.

✳ In a medium saucepan, whisk together the remaining cream, milk, salt, and brown sugar–cream mixture. Bring to a simmer over low heat. In the meantime, whisk the egg yolks in a small bowl. Very slowly drizzle 1 cup of the warm cream mixture into the yolks, whisking constantly to prevent the eggs from cooking. Pour the yolk mixture back into the cream mixture in a slow, steady stream, whisking constantly as you pour.

✳ Strain the pudding through a fine sieve and chill for at least 2 hours. The pudding may be made ahead to this point and stored for up to 3 days, well covered in the refrigerator.

✳ To bake the pudding, position a rack in the middle of the oven and preheat to 325°F. Bring about 4 quarts of water to a simmer in a tea kettle. Select a baking pan with sides higher than the ramekins (see box, below). Tear off a piece of foil large enough to cover the baking pan. Fold the foil into fourths and with an ice pick or a bamboo skewer, prick tiny holes in the foil. Pour the chilled pudding into the ramekins. Arrange the ramekins in the baking pan and place on the oven rack.

Safety Tips for Hot-Water Baths

Lifting pans of hot water in and out of the oven and removing baked custards can pose kitchen burn hazards. To prevent ramekins from sliding around, line the bottom of the pan with a dish towel before adding the ramekins and the water bath. To aid in lifting the ramekins safely out of the hot water, wrap both tips of kitchen tongs with rubber bands in a double crisscross fashion to hold the ramekins steady.

—*Washington, D.C., Dame Connie Hay*

Pour the simmering water into the baking pan—enough water to come two thirds of the way up the ramekins. Cover the entire pan with the prepared foil. Bake until the puddings are just set around the edges and slightly loose in the center, 60 to 90 minutes (begin checking them after 50 minutes—baking time will vary with ramekin size and water temperature). Test for doneness by inserting a knife in the center of the individual puddings; it should come out almost clean.

⁂ When the puddings are set, remove them from the baking pan and set on a rack to cool for at least 2 hours. Cover and refrigerate until ready to serve. The puddings will keep for up to 3 days in the refrigerator. To serve, top with a little whipped cream and drizzle with chocolate sauce. Hage often crowns the puddings with fresh raspberries.

⁂ BERRY PUFF TORTE ⁂

Fresh out of college with a degree in home economics and communications, San Francisco Dame Linda Lau Anusasananan found that writing jobs were scarce. So she wrote food stories for free for her local neighborhood paper. With press clippings in hand, she applied to *Sunset* magazine in 1971 and landed a job as a food writer. She stayed for thirty-four years, writing and editing recipes at the magazine. During that time she also developed a quality line of Asian sauces called Jade (featured in Williams-Sonoma stores, among many other places). Now she's enjoying a career as a freelance food writer and consultant.

In this recipe, Anusasananan exhibits her best recipe-writing talents, turning a popular and familiar item (cream puffs) into something novel and fresh: a large open-faced puff to cradle summer berries in a cloud of sweetened cream cheese and whipped cream. She says the dessert is so popular that almost everyone asks for an extra piece to eat or take home.

1 torte or 6 to 8 servings

Suggested Beverage

An aged tawny port or Australian Liqueur Muscat.

Prepare Ahead

You can make the pastry puff up to 1 day ahead. Cool and store airtight at room temperature. If it loses its crispness, bake, uncovered, on a baking sheet in a 400°F oven until crisp, 15 to 20 minutes. Cool on a rack before filling. Make the filling up to 4 hours ahead, cover, and chill. Fill the pastry with the cream mixture and berries up to 1 hour ahead, cover, and chill.

Pastry Puff

⅔ cup water

5 tablespoons unsalted butter, cut into ½-inch chunks

1 tablespoon granulated sugar

⅔ cup all-purpose flour

3 large eggs

Filling

4 ounces (½ cup) cream cheese, at room temperature

1 teaspoon grated orange zest (see box, page 75)

½ teaspoon pure vanilla extract

1 cup heavy cream

⅔ cup confectioners' sugar, sifted

1 cup raspberries

1 cup boysenberries or blackberries

1 cup blueberries

Serving

Confectioners' sugar

❋ To make the pastry puff, preheat the oven to 400°F. In a large saucepan, combine the water, butter, and sugar; bring to a boil over high heat. Add the flour all at once and stir with a wooden spoon until the mixture pulls away from the pan sides and clumps together. The dough will be stiff and hard to stir. Remove from the heat and stir until the flour is incorporated and the mixture is smooth. Let cool for about 5 minutes, stirring occasionally.

❋ Add the eggs, one at a time, to the warm mixture in the pan, beating with a spoon after each addition until the mixture is smooth and satiny. (Alternatively, scrape the warm mixture into a bowl, add the eggs one at a time, and beat with an electric mixer on high speed after each addition just until the mixture is smooth; do not overbeat.)

❧Lightly coat the bottom of a 9-inch round cake pan with nonstick cooking spray. Spoon the pastry mixture into the pan; spread evenly over the bottom and about 1 inch up the sides.

❧Bake until puffed and golden, 35 to 40 minutes. Prick the puff with a toothpick in about a dozen places, then return to the oven and bake until golden brown, dry, and crisp, 5 to 10 minutes. Cool completely in the pan on a rack. Run a knife around the pan sides to release the pastry; remove from the pan.

❧For the filling, in a medium bowl, with an electric mixer on high speed, beat the cream cheese, zest, and vanilla until smooth. Add the cream and confectioners' sugar; beat on low speed until blended, then on high speed just until the mixture forms stiff peaks (do not overbeat).

❧Spread the filling evenly over the bottom of the pastry shell. Distribute the raspberries, blackberries, and blueberries over the filling. If not serving immediately, cover and chill. Just before serving, with a sieve or a sugar shaker, top with confectioners' sugar. Cut in wedges to serve.

Suggested Beverage

A sweet version of Lambrusco from the Emilia-Romagna region of Italy.

BITTERSWEET CHOCOLATE
SOUFFLÉS WITH NIBBY CREAM

Prepare Ahead

Medrich notes, "I make the batter in advance—it takes only a few minutes—and divide it into ramekins. The unbaked soufflés can then wait for a couple of hours at room temperature or even a couple of days in the fridge, before baking. When I offer to bring dessert to a dinner party, I bring the soufflés ready to bake, and then slip them into the oven and whip the cream while the hostess is clearing the table and getting the coffee on."

One of the country's foremost authorities on chocolate, San Francisco Dame Alice Medrich likes to tell how she founded a business and a career around her Parisian landlady's recipe for homemade chocolate truffles. One thing led to another, and soon there was her famed Berkeley, California, dessert shop, Cocolat, just down the street from Alice Waters's Chez Panisse. Then came Medrich's audacious marketing of ping-pong-ball-size (some said "golf-ball-size") hand-dipped chocolate truffles that, Medrich admits, "defied all the rules of chocolatiering." And then, her three award-winning chocolate cookbooks.

Having created hundreds of chocolate recipes, she picks this one adapted from her book *Bittersweet* for its ease of preparation, its never-fail dazzle, and its simple ability to showcase chocolate. Says Medrich, "I've made this one so often, I know it by heart."

The easiest topping for these soufflés is slightly sweetened whipped cream, but if you can get roasted cacao nibs, do not miss making the Nibby Cream. Nibs are raw or roasted, hulled, and broken cocoa beans. (Roasted cacao nibs have the fullest flavor and can be obtained from Scharffen Berger online at www.scharffenberger.com or by phone at 800-930-4528.) Medrich simply infuses heavy cream with the nibs and strains them out before whipping. The result is remarkable.

8 individual soufflés

Butter and sugar to coat ramekins

8 ounces bittersweet chocolate (about 70 percent cacao/cocoa content—see box, page 321), chopped into small pieces

1 tablespoon unsalted butter

⅓ cup whole milk

3 large egg yolks

4 large egg whites

⅛ teaspoon cream of tartar*

⅓ cup granulated sugar

Confectioners' sugar

Slightly sweetened whipped cream, crème fraîche (see box, page 20), or Nibby Cream (recipe follows)

✻Preheat the oven to 375°F. Butter the bottoms and sides of eight 4- to 5-ounce ramekins and sprinkle with sugar.

✻Fill a large skillet with about 1 inch of water and bring just to a simmer. Put the chocolate, butter, and milk in a large heatproof bowl and set it in the barely simmering water. Stir until the chocolate is melted and the mixture is smooth. Off the heat, whisk in the egg yolks. Set aside.

✻In a clean, dry mixing bowl, beat the egg whites and cream of tartar until soft peaks form. Gradually sprinkle in the granulated sugar and continue to beat, at high speed, until the egg whites are stiff but not dry. Fold one quarter of the egg whites into the chocolate mixture, then fold in the remaining egg whites.

✻Divide the mixture evenly among the prepared ramekins, filling them three quarters or more full. (The soufflés may be prepared to this point, covered and refrigerated, to be baked up to 2 days later.)

✻Bake the soufflés on a baking sheet until they rise and crack on top and a wooden skewer plunged into the center tests moist but not completely gooey, 14 to 16 minutes. Remove from the oven, sieve a little confectioners' sugar over the top, and serve immediately. Pass a chilled bowl of the whipped cream, crème fraîche, or Nibby Cream to top the soufflés.

*If you don't have the cream of tartar, add a little bit of the sugar to the egg whites slightly earlier than you would normally, and be very careful not to overbeat them. All will be well.

Suggested Beverage

A Sicilian Marsala Superiore Riserva boasts roasted aromas similar to those found in the Nibby Cream.

Nibby Cream

Prepare Ahead

Be sure to infuse the cream and chill it several hours or a day ahead well before beating.

Medrich says this is "divine stuff"—the palest shade of tan with the unexpected flavor of dark chocolate. Use it to top not only chocolate soufflés, but also other indulgences like a cup of hot chocolate. Or slather it between cake layers or use in ice cream.

1 cup heavy cream

2 slightly rounded tablespoons roasted cacao nibs

Granulated sugar

Bring the cream and nibs to a gentle boil in a small saucepan. Remove from the heat and cover for 20 minutes. Strain the cream, pressing on the nibs to extract the liquid. Discard the nibs. Chill the cream until cold enough to whip. Just before serving, whip the cream to the desired consistency (as soft or stiff as you like it), adding sugar to taste.

Percentages on Chocolate Packages

If a recipe calls for semisweet or bittersweet chocolate with a specific percentage (or a range of percentages) of cacao, you will get the best results by using the suggested product. However, since most recipes do not (yet) specify cacao content for chocolate ingredients, here is a rule of thumb for semisweet and bittersweet chocolate. When a recipe simply calls for "semisweet" or "bittersweet" chocolate, it is best to use chocolate with 55 percent to 60 percent cacao. Most American brands of semisweet and bittersweet chocolates that *do not* have percentages on the label fall within this range, and these are the chocolates that most magazines and cookbook authors use for testing and recipe development, unless they tell you otherwise. You can often push to 62 percent without getting into trouble, but you may want to use 5 to 10 percent *less* chocolate to preserve the creamy texture of ganache or mousse, for example.

One might assume that using a stronger chocolate will simply make a dessert more chocolaty and thus better, but this is frequently not the case, unless other modifications are made to the recipe. As the percentage of cacao increases in a chocolate, the amount of dry cocoa goes up dramatically, with a concurrent drop in sugar. Such changes can produce devastating results: dry mousses, curdled ganache, dry overbaked cakes. Success with higher percentage chocolate often requires the use of less chocolate and may include adjustments of sugar, butter, or liquid as well. More details about adjusting recipes for high-percentage chocolates can be found in my book, *Bittersweet: Recipes and Tales from a Life in Chocolate*.

—*San Francisco Dame Alice Medrich*

❄ GINGERBREAD DESSERT WAFFLES ❄

Prepare Ahead

Well before mealtime, mix dry ingredients together. Do the same for the liquid ones. Turn on the waffle iron when you sit down to dinner. After dinner, while the dishes are being cleared, you can quickly mix together the batter and start baking waffles. Have your toppings prepared ahead as well. What a sweet surprise: hot waffles for dessert.

These rich brown waffles can be served for breakfast, topped with fresh fruit. Indeed, they'd be extra festive for a winter brunch. However, they'll reach new heights presented as a dessert, especially topped with the mixture of whipped cream and cream cheese borrowed from the Berry Puff Torte (page 315). Alternatively, top them with scoops of vanilla ice cream, warm apple butter, and a sprinkle of cinnamon sugar.

The recipe is an old family favorite from Albertson's Cooking School in Philadelphia—the oldest culinary school in the city—owned and operated by three Dames: Charlotte Ann Albertson and her two daughters, Ann-Michelle Albertson and Kristin Albertson.

6 waffles, depending on size of waffle iron

2¼ cups all-purpose flour

½ teaspoon salt

1¼ teaspoons baking soda

2 teaspoons ground ginger

½ cup milk (whole, low-fat, or skim)

1 cup molasses (any style will do, but blackstrap will produce the richest flavor)

1 large egg, separated

5 tablespoons unsalted butter, cut into small pieces, at room temperature

❄ Preheat a waffle iron. Sift the flour, salt, baking soda, and ginger into a large bowl. In a small bowl, beat together the milk, molasses, and egg yolk (reserving the white). Combine the milk mixture with the flour mixture.

Suggested Beverage

Great coffee.

❄ In another bowl, beat the reserved egg white with a whisk until stiff. With a silicone spatula, fold the egg white into the flour mixture along with the butter. This will be a very stiff batter, especially if you use blackstrap molasses. Mix well. Cook the waffles according to manufacturer's instructions for your waffle iron.

PEACH TREE COUNTRY KITCHEN'S BREAD PUDDING WITH JACK DANIEL'S CARAMEL SAUCE

San Antonio Dame Nancy Fitch gives us this classic and handsome bread pudding with a luscious trimming from her Peach Tree Country Kitchen in Boerne, Texas, just a short drive from San Antonio in the Hill Country. Should you need a dessert for a crowd, there could hardly be an easier-to-prepare choice: double the recipe, bake in a 9- by 13-inch baking dish, and you can serve at least 16. No worry that the Jack Daniel's Caramel Sauce recipe yields more than you'll ever drizzle over your bread pudding. The sauce keeps refrigerated for weeks and will be coveted as a topping for any number of desserts, starting with vanilla ice cream.

8 to 10 servings

Butter for greasing baking dish

½ pound loaf day-old coarse-textured bread

½ cup golden raisins

½ cup currants

4 large eggs

3 cups whole milk

1¼ cups sugar

½ teaspoon ground cinnamon

½ teaspoon pure vanilla extract

Jack Daniel's Caramel Sauce (recipe follows)

Butter an 8-inch-square baking dish. Cut the bread into 1-inch cubes—include the crust unless it is particularly tough (you should have about 7 cups of bread cubes)—and put in the baking dish. Fold in the raisins and currants, evenly distributing them. In a large bowl, whisk together the eggs, milk, sugar, cinnamon, and vanilla until ingredients are well

Prepare Ahead

Though the pudding reheats nicely, it's a glorious and fragrant event to lift the dessert out of the oven, all puffed up from its initial baking. It's easy to prep and assemble the pudding ahead and then place in the oven to bake while you eat dinner. The sauce can be prepared well ahead of serving.

Suggested Beverage

Break the pairing rule that the beverage must be as sweet or sweeter than the dessert—go light on the caramel sauce and bring out the sippin' whiskey. For wine, a tawny port or Malmsey Madeira.

blended. Pour the mixture over the bread cubes. Let stand for 30 minutes, allowing the bread to absorb some of the liquid.

❋ Meanwhile, preheat the oven to 350°F. Place the pudding in the oven and bake until the pudding is puffy and most of the liquid has been absorbed, about 1 hour. When the pudding is done a knife inserted into the center will come out just lightly coated with liquid. Watch carefully during baking; if the top browns too quickly, cover it with foil until done. Serve warm with Jack Daniel's Caramel Sauce.

Jack Daniel's Caramel Sauce

3 cups

2 cups sugar

½ cup water

1 cup (2 sticks) unsalted butter, cut into tablespoon-size pieces and chilled

1 cup heavy cream

¼ cup Jack Daniel's bourbon

❋ Combine the sugar and water in a heavy saucepan, stirring just until the sugar dissolves. Bring to a boil over medium heat. When the sugar has melted, increase heat to high and cook until the mixture turns a dark amber color. At this point it will begin to smoke. Swirl the mixture to even out the color; don't stir at this point. Fitch says the darker the color, the better the sauce; however, you do not want the sugar to burn, so be ready to remove it quickly from the heat and immediately begin slowly whisking in the butter until well blended. Whisk in the cream and bourbon. When cool, pour the sauce into a glass container, cool, cover, and store in the refrigerator, where it will keep for several weeks. Warm the sauce before serving it with bread pudding.

ALMOND SHORTCAKES WITH STRAWBERRY-RHUBARB SAUCE

After years of working in corporate test kitchens, Dame Ingrid Gangestad of Ontario, Canada, opened her own consulting firm, St. Croix Culinary, specializing in recipe development, nutrition, and consumer education. Her shortcake recipe is just right for late spring when rhubarb and strawberries are at the market. A plus: the layers of almond flavor from the nuts and the amaretto liqueur match equally well with later-season berries or stone fruits tossed with a little sugar and their own juices.

Eight 3-inch shortcakes

Strawberry-Rhubarb Sauce

 1 cup sugar

 1 tablespoon water

 1¼ pounds rhubarb, cut into ¾-inch slices (about 4 cups)

 2 cups sliced strawberries

 1 tablespoon amaretto liqueur *or* ½ teaspoon almond extract

Shortcakes

 2 cups all-purpose flour

 ½ cup ground almonds

 ½ cup plus 3 tablespoons granulated sugar, divided

 1 tablespoon baking powder

 ½ teaspoon salt

 ½ cup (1 stick) unsalted butter, cold and cut into about a dozen pieces

 ⅔ to ¾ cup whole milk

 1 large egg, slightly beaten

 ¼ cup sliced almonds

Prepare Ahead

The sauce can be made several days ahead. Make and form the shortcakes hours ahead of serving. Cover with plastic wrap and refrigerate; bake right before serving and serve warm. Or bake them earlier in the day and briefly reheat in a 350°F oven.

Suggested Beverage

A sparkling Moscato d'Asti or the sweeter Muscat Beaumes-de-Venise.

Amaretto Cream

1 cup heavy cream

2 tablespoons confectioners' sugar

1 tablespoon amaretto liqueur *or* **½ teaspoon almond extract**

To make the sauce, in a large, heavy-bottomed saucepan, stir together the sugar and water. Add the rhubarb, coating the fruit in the sugar mixture. Bring to a boil. Immediately reduce heat to very low. Simmer uncovered, stirring occasionally, until the rhubarb is tender, about 10 minutes. Cool the sauce. Stir in the strawberries and amaretto.

To make the shortcakes, in the bowl of a food processor fitted with a steel blade, briefly combine the flour, almonds, ½ cup of the granulated sugar, baking powder, and salt. Add the butter and pulse until the mixture resembles fine crumbs. Transfer the mixture to a large bowl and drizzle in the milk, working the dough just until the ingredients are combined and will clump together in a ball. Place the ball on a lightly floured surface. Roll or pat into a round about 1 inch thick. Cut the shortcakes with a floured 3-inch cutter. Place 1 inch apart on an ungreased baking sheet. Brush the tops with the beaten egg. Sprinkle with the almonds and remaining granulated sugar. When ready to bake, preheat the oven to 425°F. Bake until golden brown, 10 to 12 minutes.

To make the cream, put the cream, confectioners' sugar, and amaretto in a chilled bowl. Beat with an electric mixer on high speed until soft peaks form.

To serve, split the shortcakes horizontally in half. Fill with Strawberry-Rhubarb Sauce. Replace the tops. Top with more sauce and Amaretto Cream.

Little Bites

TURKISH APRICOTS STUFFED WITH CREAM AND PISTACHIOS

Washington, D.C., Dame Sheilah Kaufman became a specialist in Turkish cuisine after becoming friends with the Turkish ambassador's wife, Nur Ilkin, in Washington, D.C. Together they wrote the book *A Taste of Turkish Cuisine*. For easy entertaining, Kaufman recommends these stuffed apricots, which she learned to make from her friend Ilkin.

6 to 10 servings

Prepare Ahead

The apricots can be prepared and refrigerated up to 8 hours before serving. Note the need for 8 hours of soaking.

30 (about ½ pound) dried and pitted whole apricots, preferably Turkish

1⅓ cups sugar

1 cup heavy cream

⅓ cup finely ground raw, unsalted pistachio nuts

Soak the apricots for about 8 hours in 4 cups of cold water. Drain well. If the apricots are not already open, cut them horizontally, about three fourths of the way through, to create a pocket for the cream filling. Reserve.

In a saucepan, bring the sugar and 2 cups of water to a boil, mixing well. Reduce heat to a simmer and cook for 5 minutes. Add the apricots and simmer, covered, for about 15 minutes. Remove from the heat, uncover, and let cool. Drain the apricots and discard the liquid.

Suggested Beverage

An ice wine, a young apricot-driven Sauternes from Bordeaux, or a tangy Bual Madeira.

✳ Whip the cream until it is stiff. With a teaspoon (or a pastry bag, if you prefer), fill each apricot with a bit of the cream and close the apricot, leaving it open enough to reveal about ½ inch of cream. Dip the cream side of the apricots into the ground nuts. Place on a serving dish and chill until ready to serve.

✳ BURGUNDIAN SPICED CARAMELS ✳

Prepare Ahead

The caramels keep refrigerated for at least 1 month.

Philadelphia Dame and cookbook author Jennifer Lindner McGlinn based this recipe on the taste of some *caramels d'épices* she tasted in the French hill town of Vézelay. "Spicy, sweet, and creamy," she remembers. A working candy thermometer is essential to ensuring the caramels' luxurious texture (see box, opposite). Tired of eating caramels? Place a handful of them in a container and microwave just long enough to melt—about 15 seconds on high. You'll have an exquisite butterscotchy sauce for spooning over ice cream or fresh fruit.

45 one-inch caramels

1¼ cups heavy cream

4 tablespoons (½ stick) unsalted butter, cut into pieces

1½ cups packed light brown sugar

¼ cup light corn syrup

¾ teaspoon ground ginger

¼ to ½ teaspoon ground cinnamon

⅛ teaspoon ground allspice

⅛ teaspoon salt

1 teaspoon pure vanilla extract

✳ Lightly butter a 9- by 5-inch loaf pan. Line with parchment paper, allowing the paper to hang over the pan by several inches (this will make removing the caramel from the pan easy). Butter the paper. Combine the cream, butter, brown sugar, corn syrup, ginger, cinnamon, allspice, salt, and vanilla in a medium saucepan and cook, stirring occasionally, over medium-low heat until the butter is melted. Continue to cook to the firm-ball stage—248°F on a candy thermometer. This will take 19 to 20 minutes, but again, an accurate read on the thermometer is the only sure test.* Undercook and the caramel will not firm up; overcook and you'll miss the creamy consistency that is the essence of this confection.

✳ Immediately pour the hot caramel into the prepared pan. Caution: Be very careful handling the hot caramel! Set aside on a rack to cool completely, at least 2 hours. Lift the sheet of caramel out of the pan, cover with a double thickness of plastic wrap, and store in the refrigerator or a cool, dry area, cutting the caramel into bite-size pieces as needed. Alternatively, you can cut the caramel into squares or rectangles and wrap them individually with foil or parchment wrappers. Store in an airtight container in the refrigerator.

Suggested Beverage

A chilled Tokaji from Hungary or an Oloroso sherry from Spain at room temperature.

While McGlinn insists that an accurate candy thermometer is "the cook's best bet" for making these caramels, she does also use the "old drippy test": when the temperature reaches 248°F on the thermometer, dip a spoon into the boiling caramel and drop a few drips into a glass of cold water; scoop up the watery bits and form them into a ball; in this recipe, the ball should be soft and pliable—but firm enough to roll into a ball.

Test Your Thermometer

Whether you're using an instant-read thermometer for checking temperatures of meats or a candy thermometer for checking temperatures of confections, regularly before using, test the thermometer by submerging the sensor in boiling water. An accurate thermometer should register 212°F.

DARK CHOCOLATE FRESH GINGER TRUFFLES

Prepare Ahead

Make the truffle mixture at least the night before you plan to serve the truffles. The truffles can also be made weeks before serving and frozen. It's best to roll them in the cocoa powder when they have thawed but are still cold.

Vancouver, B.C., Dame Pam Williams shifted her career from education to chocolate making in the 1980s. By 2003 she had come full circle, founding her own professional school of chocolatiering: École Chocolat in Vancouver. This recipe clones a truffle she tasted in Paris with an easy adaptation of a French ganache recipe used by professional chocolatiers.

Williams encourages experimenting with more or less ginger but warns against allowing the ginger to overwhelm the chocolate flavor. The finer the ginger is chopped, the more flavor will be released in the cream. Do not substitute dry ground ginger—the flavor will not be the same. For the chocolate, E. Guittard semisweet at 61 percent cacao is a good choice. If you can find it in wafer form there will be no need to chop.

64 truffles

- **8 ounces semisweet chocolate, coarsely chopped**
- **1 cup heavy cream**
- **2 tablespoons chopped *unpeeled* gingerroot**
- **1 tablespoon unsalted butter, at a cool room temperature**
- **1 cup cocoa powder for decorating the truffles**

Cut parchment or waxed paper into an 8- by 16-inch rectangle. Line an 8-inch-square baking pan with the paper, letting the long ends hang over the sides of the pan. (You'll use those as handles to lift out the slab of chocolate once it is hardened. The extra paper also gives you flaps to cover the top of the chocolate slab for storing.)

Place the chocolate pieces in a medium glass measuring cup. Place in the microwave at half power until just melted, making sure to watch it carefully and stirring every 30 seconds. The chocolate should be melted in approximately 3 to 4 minutes, depending on your microwave. The chocolate burns easily, so be careful with this step.

Heat the cream and gingerroot together in another container in the microwave until heated but not boiling. Depending on your microwave, this should take about 1½ minutes at full power. Strain through a fine sieve to remove the bits of gingerroot. With a silicone spatula, beat 2 tablespoons of hot cream into the chocolate, making sure it is thoroughly absorbed. Repeat until all the cream has been incorporated.

Pour the chocolate mixture into the jar of an electric blender or the bowl of a food processor fitted with a steel blade. Blend on low speed or process for 2 minutes. With motor running, add the butter and process until it is absorbed. Process for another 2 minutes until you have a soft emulsion. Pour into the prepared pan and tap the pan on the counter to level the chocolate mixture. Allow the mixture to firm up at room temperature in a cool spot for at least 8 hours—this helps the ingredients to meld and develop flavor. Then place the chocolate in the refrigerator to firm for another hour. At this point the truffle mixture can be stored, well covered in a good-quality plastic bag, either in the refrigerator for 1 week or the freezer for up to 1 month before serving.

When ready to serve, cut the chocolate into bite-size pieces with a very sharp knife. Alternatively, you can use a 1-inch ice cream scoop to form it into balls. If the chocolate starts to soften, return it to the refrigerator to firm.

Note: When cutting the slab, store any odd trimmings you may have left in a sealed plastic bag in the freezer. Melted for just a few seconds at half power in the microwave, they turn into a silky chocolate sauce (heat too long and the sauce will curdle). Drizzle the sauce over desserts such as the Baked Butterscotch Puddings (page 313).

Decorate the cold truffles by tossing them in cocoa powder. If the truffles absorb the cocoa powder, you can re-coat them. Store refrigerated in an airtight container until ready to serve.

Suggested Beverage

A late-harvest Gewürztraminer or a VSOP Cognac served in a brandy snifter.

Pairing Seasonal Fruits with Cheese

The pairing of foods is always a matter of personal taste. Monterey Dame Lygia Chappellet, artisan goat-cheese maker and member of the Chappellet wine family, boldly suggests these fresh fruit and cheese combinations for simple desserts:

* Oranges or quinces with Manchego
* Strawberries (and other berries) or figs with fresh goat cheese
* Apricots with double-cream Brie
* Melons with Parmigiano-Reggiano or Pecorino Romano
* Pears with Stilton or other top-quality blue cheese
* Apples with Camembert or Pont l'Évêque (most delicious: bake the apples and serve them warm with either cheese)

While pondering the possibilities of cheese and fruit, consider this: Seattle Dame Julie Kramis Hearne was a guest at Marcella Hazan's 80th birthday party in Italy and recalls the most enchanting of cheese pairings. An entire room was dedicated to presenting some one hundred cheeses, all paired with different preserved fruits and honeys. Among Hearne's favorite combinations—and one she now enjoys replicating at home for guests—was the Italian Robiola (a cow's milk cheese that may also contain goat's or sheep's milk and is served either young, soft, and buttery or aged, firm, and piquant) with *mostarda di frutta*, a preserve made of mixed fruits and mustard seeds. If you can't find mostarda, settle for a chestnut honey, or make your own using Hearne's recipe.

MOSTARDA DI FRUTTA

> 2 pounds 3 ounces mixed fruit: apples, peaches, pears, apricots, cherries
>
> Grated zest and juice of 1 lemon or 1 orange
>
> 1 cup white wine
>
> 3 cups honey
>
> ½ cup whole mustard seeds

* Peel and pit or core the apples, peaches, and pears. Pit the apricots and cherries. Dice. Place in a large Dutch oven or heavy-bottomed pot, firmer fruits first. Cover with water. Add the lemon zest and juice. Cook for 30 minutes over medium heat. Remove from the heat and let cool.

* In a second pot, bring the wine and honey to a boil. Lower heat to a simmer and cook until reduced (by about a third) to a syrup, about 25 minutes. Mix in the mustard seeds. Remove from the heat and let cool. Combine the fruit mixture (do not drain) with the syrup. Mix well and refrigerate. The mostarda will keep refrigerated for about 3 weeks.

BREAD AND CHOCOLATE: A LITTLE DESSERT BRUSCHETTA

Cleveland Dame Bev Shaffer thinks part of the appeal of this recipe is its surprising combination of ingredients: bread and chocolate. The even greater appeal is the recipe's ease and simple good taste. Hot from the oven and shiny with the melted chocolate, these *bruschette* are a home-baked and easy way to close a meal. Shaffer suggests serving them with a homemade fruit conserve. Or pair them with fresh seasonal fruit (raspberries—just lightly sugared—are a good candidate) or a fruit preserve (try something lusciously tart like a gooseberry jam), or there's always a dollop of whipped cream or ice cream.

Tempted to use a food processor to grate the chocolate? Bev, who has written several cookbooks and columns, including one titled *Gadget Freak*, says not to—it's best to use a very sharp hand grater, like the Microplane coarse or medium ribbon grater.

8 to 10 servings

1 baguette, cut diagonally into at least 25 half-inch slices

4 to 6 tablespoons (½ to ¾ stick) unsalted butter, melted

¾ cup (about 3 ounces) coarsely grated bittersweet chocolate

½ cup (about 2 ounces) coarsely grated milk chocolate

¼ cup (about 1 ounce) coarsely grated semisweet chocolate

✳ Preheat the oven to 350°F. Depending on the diameter of your baguette, you may choose to cut each slice in half. You want slender fingers of bread. Brush the butter lightly on one side of the baguette slices; place the slices on foil-lined baking sheets and toast in the oven just until crispy, 5 to 7 minutes. Remove from the oven and let cool on a wire rack.

✳ Combine the chocolates in a medium bowl. Sprinkle the mixture generously atop the cooled bread slices. Return the baking sheet to the oven to soften and warm the chocolate mixture, about 12 minutes. Serve immediately.

Prepare Ahead

Keep a supply of the grated chocolate mixture ready in the pantry. Then all you need is a fresh baguette and melted butter. Bread may be buttered and toasted a few hours ahead of serving.

Suggested Beverage

An Irish whiskey, a single-malt Scotch (not too peaty), or a small-batch bourbon. Or sip a traditional café au lait.

Sauces

Chocolate sauce, raspberry sauce, caramel sauce—these and other classics pleasantly end a meal. Drizzle them over ready-mades—like ice cream or a good bakery pound cake—and no one will complain. On the other hand, more out-of-the-ordinary dessert sauces offer a nice alternative. Here are a couple from Dames who really know their sweets. An added attraction: these sauces keep for days if not weeks in the refrigerator, ready at a moment's notice.

⚡ FRESH GINGER CREAM ⚡

This cream from Charleston Dame Susan Fuller Slack is especially good with fresh berries or coconut cake. Or pour it into an ice cream machine and make fresh ginger ice cream: a fitting ending to an Asian-inspired meal.

1¾ cups

3 large egg yolks

1½ cups whole milk

3 tablespoons sugar

Pinch salt

¾ teaspoon cornstarch

**2 thin, diagonal slices peeled gingerroot (2½ inches long,
 ⅛ inch thick)**

½ teaspoon pure vanilla extract

✳ Fill the bottom of a double boiler with about 3 inches of water. Place over medium heat and bring to a simmer. Meanwhile, place the egg yolks in the top of the double boiler. Whisk in the milk, sugar, salt, and cornstarch. Add the gingerroot. Place over the simmering water. Stir constantly until the mixture thickens slightly and barely coats the back of a metal spoon, 8 to 10 minutes. Pour into a medium bowl; cool slightly. Discard the gingerroot; stir in the vanilla. Cover and chill for 1 hour or until serving.

✳ LEMON VERBENA SYRUP ✳

"If I were to grow only one herb, I would choose lemon verbena," says New York Dame Paulette Satur. In Washington, D.C., Ann-Harvey Yonkers grows lemon verbena in a pot and winters it in her greenhouse. Every fall, Yonkers makes Lemon Verbena Syrup. It keeps refrigerated in an airtight container for a month. It's exquisite over waffles, fresh fruit, or ice cream. Yonkers especially likes the syrup with poached or roasted pears. If you don't have fresh lemon verbena, substitute ¼ cup grated lemon zest and adjust the sugar to taste. The syrup also makes a marvelous base for lemonade and for cocktails, too.

2 cups sugar

2 cups water

5 small sprigs fresh lemon verbena

✳ In a small saucepan, combine the sugar and water and bring to a boil. Immediately remove from the heat, add the lemon verbena, and stir until the sugar dissolves. Cover and let steep for 10 minutes. Strain and serve warm.

Cleveland Dame Bev Shaffer has a tagline she uses on her business correspondence. Appropriately, we close with those words:

FOOD

buy it with thought
cook it with care
serve just enough
save what will keep
eat what would spoil
locally grown is best
don't waste it

METRIC CONVERSIONS

Dames in Canada not only live in a bilingual country, but they cook in both metric and U.S. customary units. When grocery shopping in Canada, weight is always listed in grams, but don't expect to see the conversion to ounces too often. Meat and produce are purchased by the gram, 100 gram, or kilogram. The charts can help you sort through the number conversions and cook with success, regardless of whether you are in the United States or north of the border.*

Units for the conversions have been rounded to simplify the process. However, if exact measurements are critical, convert between metric and U.S. measures using the formulas listed below each chart.

Note: Food formulations may vary between the United States and Canada as well. Even though a package looks the same as its U.S. counterpart, it may be formulated differently. Cheese, ketchup, breakfast cereal, and baking powder are frequent examples. Nutrition labeling also varies between the two countries. Package sizes, too, so check the label when using a U.S. recipe that calls for a certain-size can or container.

These charts offer the most common conversions for Canadian measures. Other countries may use slightly different conversion charts.

All conversion information provided by Dame Ingrid Gangestad. Gangestad spent four years living in Canada and managed her food consulting business from London, Ontario.

VOLUME

U.S. Customary Units	Canadian Metric
¼ teaspoon	1 milliliter
½ teaspoon	2 milliliters
1 teaspoon	5 milliliters
1 tablespoon	15 milliliters
¼ cup	50 milliliters
⅓ cup	75 milliliters
½ cup	125 milliliters
⅔ cup	150 milliliters
¾ cup	175 milliliters
1 cup	250 milliliters
1 quart	1 liter
1 gallon	4 liters
1 fl oz = 28.41 milliliters	
1 pint = 0.57 liter	
1 quart = 1.14 liters	
1 gallon = 4.55 liters	

WEIGHT

U.S. Customary Units	Canadian Metric
1 ounce	30 grams
2 ounces	55 grams
3 ounces	85 grams
4 ounces (¼ pound)	115 grams
8 ounces (½ pound)	225 grams
16 ounces (1 pound)	455 grams (½ kilogram)
1 ounce = 28.35 grams	
1 pound = 0.45 kilogram	

MEASUREMENT

Inches	Centimeters
1	2.5
2	5.0
3	7.5
4	10.0
5	12.5
6	15.0
7	17.5
8	20.5
9	23.0
10	25.5
11	28.0
12	30.5
13	33.0
1 inch = 2.54 centimeters	

TEMPERATURE

Fahrenheit	Celsius
32°	0°
212°	100°
250°	120°
275°	140°
300°	150°
325°	160°
350°	180°
375°	190°
400°	200°
425°	220°
450°	230°
475°	240°
500°	260°
$°C = (°F - 32) \times 5/9$	
$°F = (°C \times 9/5) + 32$	

CONTRIBUTOR WEB SITES

For more information about the organization as a whole and to visit individual city chapter sites, visit the Les Dames d'Escoffier International Web site at **www.ldei.org**.

You can also visit the contributing members' individual Web sites:

Karen Adler: www.bbqqueens.com

Charlotte Ann Albertson: www.albertsoncookingschool.com

Blanca Aldaco: www.aldacos.net

Linda Lau Anusasananan: www.jadesauce.com

Nancy Baggett: www.kitchenlane.com

Lidia Bastianich: www.lidiasitaly.com

Najmieh Batmanglij: www.najmieh.com

Susan Belsinger: www.susanbelsinger.com

Fran Bigelow: www.franschocolates.com

Carole Bloom: www.carolebloom.com

Georgeanne Brennan: www.georgeannebrennan.com

Suzanne Brown: www.browncommunications.us

Nancy Brussat Barocci: www.convitocafeandmarket.com

Lynn Buono: www.fyecatering.com

Kathy Casey: www.kathycasey.com

Carolyn Collins: www.collinscaviar.com

Ariane Daguin: www.dartagnan.com

Nongkran Daks: www.thaibasilashburn.com, www.thaibasilchantilly.com

Suzanne Dunaway: www.rome-at-home.com

Lisa Dupar: www.lisaduparcatering.com

Nathalie Dupree: www.nathaliedupree.com

Roberta Duyff: www.duyff.com

Lisa Ekus-Saffer: www.lisaekus.com

Patricia Penzey Erd: www.thespicehouse.com

Duskie Estes: www.zazurestaurant.com, www.bovolorestaurant.com

Susan Feniger: www.marysueandsusan.com

Judith Fertig: www.bbqqueens.com
Rose Ann Finkel: www.pikebrewing.com
Marianne Frantz: www.clevelandwineschool.com
Lynn Fredericks: www.familycookproductions.com
Gale Gand: www.trurestaurant.com
Ingrid Gangestad: www.ingridgangestad.com
Beverly Gannon: www.bevgannonrestaurants.com
Lucille Giovino: www.csob.org
Terry Golson: www.hencam.com
Aliza Green: www.alizagreen.com
Dorie Greenspan: www.doriegreenspan.com
Sharon Hage: www.yorkstreetdallas.com
Gina Hopkins: www.restauranteugene.com
Linda Hopkins: www.lespetitesgourmettes.com
Joyce Jue: www.joycejue.com
Zov Karamardian: www.zovs.com
Jen Karetnick: www.jenkaretnick.com
Elizabeth Karmel: www.girlsatthegrill.com
Sheilah Kaufman: www.cookingwithsheilah.com
Holly Arnold Kinney: www.thefort.com
Abigail Kirsch: www.abigailkirsch.com
Sharon Kobayashi: www.akamaifoods.com
Paula Lambert: www.mozzco.com
Anita LaRaia: www.anitalaraia.com
Harriet Lembeck: www.harrietlembeckswineprogram.com
Nancie McDermott: www.nanciemcdermott.com
Janis McLean: www.morrisonclark.com
Mary Sue Milliken: www.marysueandsusan.com
Kathy Moore: www.pluggedintocooking.com
Joan Nathan: www.joannathan.com
Marion Nestle: www.foodpolitics.com
Zola Nichols: www.executivegiftservice.com

Beatarice Ojakangas: www.beatrice-ojakangas.com

Cynthia Pedregon: www.peach-tree.com

Nora Pouillon: www.noras.com

Vickie Reh: www.macuisineva.com

Braiden Rex-Johnson: www.northwestwininganddining.com

Ida Rodriguez: www.melissas.com

Paulette Satur: www.saturfarms.com

Bev Shaffer: www.bevshaffer.com

Dolores Snyder: www.doloreswsnyder.com

Eileen Spitalny: www.brownies.com

Renie Steves: www.reniesteves.com

Marilyn Tausend: www.marilyntausend.com

Terry Thompson-Anderson: www.thetexasfoodandwinegourmet.com

Robyn Tinsley: www.wineskinny.com

Corinne Trang: www.corinnetrang.com

Carole Walter: www.carolewalter.com

Joanne Weir: www.joanneweir.com

Ann Wilder: www.purespice.com

Pam Williams: www.ecolechocolat.com

Virginia Willis: www.virginiawillis.com

Roxanne Wyss: www.pluggedintocooking.com

Ann-Harvey Yonkers: www.freshfarmmarket.org

Judy Zeidler: www.judyzeidler.com

INDEX

Q–R

S